Five Canadian Poets

Five Canadian Poets

Five Canadian Poets
Analytical Essays on

James Deahl

John B. Lee

Don Gutteridge

Glen Sorestad

A. F. Moritz

Author
MSc Miguel Ángel Olivé Iglesias

First Edition

Library and Archives Canada Cataloguing in Publication

Title: Five Canadian poets : analytical essays on James Deahl, John B. Lee, Don Gutteridge, Glen Sorestad, A.F. Moritz / editor-essayist, MSc Miguel Ángel Olivé Iglesias.
Names: Olivé Iglesias, Miguel Ángel, 1965- author, editor.
Description: First edition. | Includes bibliographical references.
Identifiers: Canadiana (print) 20210246456 |
Canadiana (ebook) 20210246766 |
ISBN 9781989786369 (softcover) |
ISBN 9781989786376 (ebook)
Subjects: LCSH: Poets, Canadian—20th century—History and criticism. |
LCSH: Canadian poetry—20th century—History and criticism.
Classification: LCC PS8155.O45 F58 2021 |
DDC C813/.5409—dc23

QuodSermo Publishing
www.HiddenBrookPress.com
QuodSermo@gmail.com

Title:
Five Canadian Poets: Analytical Essays on, James Deahl, John B. Lee, Don Gutteridge, Glen Sorestad, A. F. Moritz

Author: Miguel Ángel Olivé Iglesias
Assistant Editor: Jorge Alberto Pérez Hernández
Proofreading: Miguel Ángel Olivé Iglesias,
                  Jorge Alberto Pérez Hernández
Cover Design: Richard M. Grove
Layout and Design: Richard M. Grove

Typeset in Garamond

Printed and bound in Canada

Distributed in USA by Ingram,
                in Canada by Hidden Brook Distribution

Acknowledgements

I am deeply indebted to Richard Marvin Grove, known to friends as Tai, in the conception and making of this book. I thank him as the publisher for his bigheartedness and foresight of the book's significance. Also, for his steadfast allegiance to Canadian poetry and its promotion.

I thank all five poets whose work I received and honored these pages. Their contribution to the Canadian literary world and Canadian culture in general is gratefully acknowledged.

A special thank you to first publishers who recognized the value of their work, and who kindly allowed me to republish fragments or full poems by each author.

Thank you all for your full support to the project.

I wish to thank my wife for sacrificing many of our hours together in the name of such a worthy cause. Her only concerns were about how coherently the separate papers would harmonize into one piece, and how readers will react to the book. I hope I live up to her, the publisher's, the poets'and the readers' expectations.

Poetry

Flickering ideas
showers of emotion
needs that ache
words that heal:
poems become, take flight
breathe real.

They pulse
in the flow of time
in the melting pot of the mind
in the blissful embrace locking
poet, paper
and quill.

Miguel Ángel Olivé Iglesias

This book is dedicated
to all poets.

Your contribution
to the breadth of culture
is immeasurable.

Table of Contents

Acknowledgements – *p. vii*

Introduction – *p. xiii*

Preface – *p. 1*

    – James Deahl – *p. 9*

    – John B. Lee – *p. 61*

    – Don Gutteridge – *p. 113*

    – Glen Sorestad – *p. 165*

    – A. F. Moritz – *p. 217*

Conclusions – *p. 271*

References – *p. 275*

Poets' bios and publications – *p. 279*

About the Editor – *p. 290*

Introduction
by Antony Di Nardo

Write what you know. Write what you love, what you care about. Someone, somewhere, at one time or another, wrote these words down because they made perfectly good sense—plain, good advice written in plain, simple words. For me, nothing could be more obvious, although I suppose a post-modernist might argue that one should write to *reveal* to oneself what one may or may not know, to uncover what's buried under layers of noisy obfuscation and obscurity, peel back the curtain on the subconscious, on the unknown. I suppose. Fortunately, for this reader, Iglesias writes about what he cares—and what he cares about is Canadian poetry as revealed in the work of five poets, five gems, as he calls them, dear to his soul.

The task of many literary critics or reviewers is to serve as a guide, and in the process identify the standards against which a work is judged, evaluated and described. A review can be forensic in nature, the subject—either poem or poet—closely examined, picked apart and analyzed to determine how well its organs are functioning and whether the body of work merits being re-assembled for further attention. It can be a delicate operation, dissection always is, and bodies are often lost on the slab. But some critics are content to appreciate and admire the subject in question and let their own words serve as a conduit for presenting the work to the world. Iglesias, in these reviews, is such a critic, inclined to appreciate rather than deliver a forensic verdict on the state of the poetry. Not that he avoids the temptation to analyze and make sense of an image, or highlight the music in a line of verse, or praise a powerful insight. He revels in that sort of thing, but he does it with complete admiration at the wonder of poetry produced by these "five gems" of the Canadian canon.

Iglesias is gaga over these gems. It is obvious from this book and his many other pieces on Canadian poets and poetry, that he is passionate about poems crafted north of the 49th, poems about the boreal wilds of Canada and its broad, uninterrupted landscapes; poems forged in busy, bustling cities and in quiet, sleepy rooms where even there nature seeps in and controls the metaphor. He reads closely, reads with an eye to engage and embrace, make sense of a country that as a Cuban he has never visited, a people he has only ever met face to face on his own island, away from their homes. It is a testament to his courage as a reader and critic that he can delve so deeply into these foreign poems and celebrate them with such vigour, determination and clarity.

If you are unfamiliar with these five poets, be prepared to be introduced to work as diverse and as varied as the country is wide. Iglesias takes the time to carefully polish several individual poems by each of these poets and coax from them that inner gleam and subtle brilliance that he deems gem-like. The image may be over-stated. But you will find that Iglesias' patience and precision with each of these poets is not far from that of a gemologist with a loupe in one hand and a pencil in the other making careful notations of every facet, admiring how the light within is refracted into a spectrum of possibilities.

James Deahl, John B. Lee, Don Gutteridge, Glen Sorestad, and Al Moritz, five gems of Canadian poetry that Iglesias values and appraises, five gems that merit being praised, if nothing else, for a lifetime of devotion to poetry. Iglesias, however, does more than that. He recognizes the uniqueness of their voices, the way they work and ply the broken line, the themes that surface and re-surface to give their poetry a patina in which Iglesias sees himself reflected. In the end, you will notice that there is a sixth gem in this collection, that of the critic who is, although self-effacing and non-intrusive, prominent as a beacon for the reader heading for the shores of Canadian poetry.

Antony Di Nardo
Poet, Critic, and Teacher

Preface

by MSc Miguel Ángel Olivé Iglesias

My clearest awareness of poetry and my relating to it dates back to my Senior High School years: I discovered Pablo Neruda and other greats in my Lit classes. I was young and falling in and out of love, so his love poems captivated me, but as I grew up his entire contribution to poetics defined my life. When I entered college for a major in English, I had to study English and American poets. It would be futile to try to list who my favorites were. I was already caught in a web of imagery and passion, of beauty and truths being penned in as many styles as there were poets: Buffon's "*Style is the man himself,*" and Oscar Wilde's "*… one's style is one's signature always,*" are two convincing arguments to confirm my assertion.

I still wonder, appreciatively, why poetry attracted me so much. One reason lies in the fact that my mother loved it and my father would profit from it by saying poems to her. I was a lucky witness to those moments even before my more cognizant encounter with poetry in school. My home was filled with books of all genres yet poetry beckoned to me alluringly. Cuban, Latin-American and universal poems overflowed our bookshelves; therefore, it was almost impossible to escape from picking them at least out of curiosity.

Another plausible reason I can think of are Lit teachers I had in High school. I remember some of them (a name comes to me, Raisa) were enthusiastic, knew their craft well and shone in class talking about Neruda, Homer, Tagore, Shakespeare, Byron, Victor Hugo, Poe, etc. They led me through the poets' works and planted what I see now as the seeds of literary analysis by explaining, quoting, opening a world of words arranged in an appealing structure. In college, another knowledgeable and passionate Lit professor I recall is María Teresa.

It was in 2016 that I added a new geography to the poetry pages. Canada entered my life in the person of Richard Marvin Grove, Canada Cuba Literary Alliance (CCLA) President, poet, prose writer, publisher, friend. His commitment to his country's poetry made me look at it with hungry eyes. That is how I started to "devour" from milestone pioneer authors to contemporary ones.

My journey has been fortunate and rewarding: sowing the seeds planted in me back in school, I started reading Canadian poetry and writing reviews and essays about it. I have authored two books with my critique, *In a Fragile Moment: A Landscape of Canadian Poetry* (Hidden Brook Press, 2020) and *A Shower of Warm Light Upon this Land and Us. Reviews and Essays on Canadian Poetry* (work-in-progress), edited four others with other critics' and/or my reviews and essays included, *The Light Candling the Mind: Critic and Author in Harmony. Essays and Reviews on Canadian Literature* (work-in-progress), *Flying on the Wings of Poetry* (Hidden Brook Press, 2020), *The Divinity of Blue* (Hidden Brook Press, 2020), and the Bridges Series V bilingual collection, *The Heart Upon the Sleeve* (SandCrab Books, 2020).

I have published my essays in other formats as well, *Canadian Stories* magazine (2019 and 2020), the CCLA official magazine *The Ambassador* (2019 and 2020) and the CCLA official newsletter *The Envoy* (2019, 2020 and 2021).

The book we are presenting to you maintains this "love affair" I have with Canadian literature. My previous publications laid the foundation of what we offer here. Large in scope and intent, big in the names chosen to be on these pages, *Five Canadian Poets*, allows me to showcase five authors who can be comfortably counted amongst the very best in Canada's huge literary foundry.

Such distinction is vastly justified. Once we walk through these pages, it will become abundantly evident why the choice of these five authors is valid and unquestionable. Two clear-cut characteristics in our five poets – which heighten their value – are their unanimous surrendering to and belief in the magnetism of poetry, and that theirs is but a modest contribution to the realm of words.

This is how James Deahl sees himself in reference to his writing: *"Being merely human, I fail more often than I succeed."* However, James' prolific career as a poet has extended from the 70s brilliantly into 2021. James bowed to poetry years ago, *"I needed poetry in my life… If I could find a way to speak to people…"* He sought full expression of his self through it not to selfishly gloat but to speak to others. He has impressively reached and surpassed his potential as a writer. His *failures* have given him a life-long career.

John B. Lee reveals his modesty the best way he can, in a poem. He says it is *"… the beautiful irony of my predicament as a wordsmith"* and leaves us his "One Reason I Write Poems": *"Because until now / I have been writing the wrong poem"*. John has successfully been writing "wrong poems" and been thereupon repeatedly "punished" with worldwide recognition, awards and titles for a significantly sustained period.

Let's recall his own words: *"Although John B. Lee, the 'I' of this sweet incarnation, became an enthusiastic practitioner of the writing of poetry, he has never chased the idea of being identified as a poet. When a hockey-playing friend of his asked, "Do you call yourself a poet?" Without hesitation he replied, "No. I'd far rather be referred to as someone who writes poetry than be called a poet."*

Don Gutteridge's attitude towards life and poetry is evidenced in his poem "Defy," *"poetry is both bliss and consolation, a way of speaking to the world that subsumes both shy and defy."* Notice how Don, like the other poets, beholds poetry as communication. Every poet understands that poems do speak to people, they state something, they grant happiness in the realization of the self, and bring comfort to the poet's soul.

Glen Sorestad recognizes the bewitching power of poetry. He is one with it and feels grateful for having the gift of writing: *"I like the state I'm in when a poem takes hold and won't let go."* Glen feels poetry as a reified being conquering him. He appreciates that it won't let go of him. Such "bondage" has made Glen one of the most fertile writers of his generation.

Proof of his modesty is A. F. Moritz's "Author's Note and Acknowledgements" in *The Sparrow* (House of Anansi Press, 2018). He says, *"I long to acknowledge all the people who have helped me by welcoming my poetry over the years since 1966, when I first sent some of it into the world…"* and finishes the note, *"I'm eternally grateful."* It is in Moritz's DNA to turn thankfully to those who read him. He feels indebted to their generosity and loyalty all these years. We are talking about a multi-awarded poet concerned with the role of poetry from a moral and socio-linguistic standpoint: *"… is duty, belonging to a community… poetry's role is as the guardian and developer of language."*

Thus, *Five Canadian Poets* offers readers a voyage into five quintessential poets' lives and work. In "buying the ticket," we travel towards knowing the man's origins; we are introduced to the poet, who he is underneath, to an understanding of his concerns and motivations. We find helpful clarification on his craft and edifying feedback illustrations from the poems under analysis. Finally, I hope you arrive at the necessary revelation of why editor and publisher decided to appraise these jewels of Canadian poetry.

Readers must be prepared to go deep into each poet's core, frown, open eyes wide, laugh, cry, interpret, learn, grow, sigh, lean back, lean closer and, upon returning from the book and the poets' lives and work, see the world differently. Readers will feel their hearts beat synchronically with a cosmos where time, space and movement flow from and into legitimate imagery and true passion glowing from five polished Canadian gems.

The poets appear in the book in the same order they entered my life and my first attempts at treading on the poetic paths they have woven. As editor and essayist – an outsider who admires Canada and Canadian literature – I present these five world-class poets viewed from my perspective, sifted in my own terms and with my modest tools. The task has been edifying, an act of learning and treading on sacred land.

Glen Sorestad kindly encouraged me by saying he has always believed that when writers finish a poem and send it out into the world, their job stops there. From then, it is the literary critic's moment to illuminate for the readers what the poem has to offer.

John B. Lee recognizes the critic's job too: "... *The luminous writer and the illuminating reader join hands with the third reader, the one who returns to the original work carrying the light candling the mind... we shine, however briefly, with understanding and communion in service of deep need. We are all the more human for the rarity of those complimentary voices. The original voice, and its radiant echoing when the critic and the poet sing in harmony, we hear perhaps the voice of angels as we join the choir." (Taken from his introductory words to my review book, In a Fragile Moment: A Landscape of Canadian Poetry. Hidden Brook Press, 2020)*

The five Canadian gems' worth always known, now reexamined through my eyes and evidenced in their self-standing craft, opens a chapter with this book that the publisher and I aspire to continue with other equally outstanding names from the maple leaf nation, which has been cradle, shelter and muse for a multi-colored line of great poets.

MSc Miguel Ángel Olivé Iglesias
Associate Professor. Holguín University, Cuba
CCLA Cuban President
Author, Poet, Writer, Reviser, Editor, Essayist

Question:

Could you just irreversibly stop writing poetry?

Answers:

"No. This is what the Creator wants me to do. This is why I was "sent" here when I was born. Poetry is my destiny."
  James Deahl

"Death! A coma. Serious debilitation. Mental destruction. Otherwise, I breathe, I write."
  John B. Lee

"Nothing short of a stroke could stop me from writing poetry... I seem to dream poems and wake up writing them... I am very fortunate that the Muse has never let me down."
  Don Gutteridge

"I absolutely must write poems; it is what a poet does because he must... I cannot conceive of ceasing writing poems, so long as I have my faculties and my senses intact. Only death silences the poet."
  Glen Sorestad

"Maybe. I don't know. I don't think so, but I don't want to be closed to any transformation, no matter how immense it seems... I think I "am a poet", that is my mode of existence..."
  A.F. Moritz

JAMES DEAHL

Only the Owl

A late night in early spring,
far too early in the season
for insects, so silence falls
complete. The blackness

is so intense the world
cannot be seen—perhaps
beyond the lamplight
it no longer exists.

And the poem is moved
by this darkness, moves
ever through darkness,
coming into focus beyond

this lighted room, out
where the garden lies
cloaked in mystery,
where grass continues to grow

with no one watching.
Only the owl hunts this night.
Some of her darkness remains
in the dew as a new dawn breaks.

James Deahl
To nudge a poem along toward its beauty—
—Robert Bly

A look at James Deahl's fruitful career as a poet, guest lecturer in universities, critic, editor, and as a man, ought to begin, in my understanding of his achievements, with his words about himself, as I pointed out in my introduction: "*I needed poetry in my life… If I could find a way to speak to people…*" In his book *Under the Watchful Eye* (Broken Jaw Press, 1995), Deahl tells us he was resolved about his life: "*In January of 1964 I decided to become a poet.*"

He had been indelibly marked by Allen Ginsberg and Lesley Irish: "*Both of those poets spoke to me in a way that allowed me to see that poetry was something that could not only speak to the issues and concerns of one's own life, but could operate as a tool to allow the poet to discover an organizing principle outside the day-to-day human life. That is, poetry could support one in the efforts of living one's own life.*"

It was in the middle of his high-school final year that he had a turning-point revelation: "*… I needed poetry in my life; I needed to read it and I needed to write it.*" So he did. Besides Ginsberg, Deahl was influenced by Swedish-American poet Carl Sandburg. He refers to Sandburg as the poet who "*taught me what poetry could be.*" Other poets followed, Carl Sandburg, Robert Bly, W.S. Merwin, Patrick Lane, Denise Levertov, Shinkichi Takahashi, Milton Acorn, Seamus Heaney, and Michael Wurster. When I asked him what other influences he may have had, he replied: "*My friends within the poetic community.*"

Deahl has also acknowledged Spanish-written poetry influencing his work: "*One thing you should note… in my poetry is the influence of poets like Federico García Lorca, Pablo Neruda, and Antonio Machado especially, and also César Vallejo, Juan Ramón Jiménez, Octavio Paz, and Blas de Otero to a somewhat lesser degree.*"

The year 1970 brought another decision in his life, which he admits was positively ground-shaking in terms of poetry writing and reading: "*I wrote poems* (before 1970) *that were highly derivative; there is no other way to learn the craft. I never developed my own voice, my own vision, until I moved to Canada in 1970.*" He acknowledges that "*No poet learns the craft without help and sage advice from those who have already achieved a higher level of writing."* (*Taken from Under the Mulberry Tree: Poems for & about Raymond Souster. Quattro Books Inc. 2014. Edited by James Deahl*)

Logically, Deahl recognizes the strong effect surging in when he moved to Canada: *"Although I had been writing and publishing poetry for a few years prior to my move north, I managed to write only three worthwhile pieces during the 1960s... Thus, one must take Canada and the experience of immigration into consideration when evaluating my work."* (*Taken from Under the Watchful Eye, Broken Jaw Press, 1995*)

Deahl was born in the U.S.A. in 1945. Initially impressed in his younger years by the Pittsburgh and Appalachian contexts, as he grew up among the rivers and hills of Pennsylvania and West Virginia, he wrote poems describing those experiences plus his legacy – and *in situ* learning as he was a miner and a steelworker – of mining and steel plant jobs, inter-mingled with detailed, heartfelt depictions of his backgrounds.

He loved his West Virginia-Pittsburgh trips with his parents and reminisces in *Under the Watchful Eye*: *"I loved them as I loved the steel mills, especially Bessemer converters and open-hearths... When I was employed at the Edgar Thomson Works of United States Steel it was almost a century old..."* Along the process of absorbing nature during those trips, he also saw hard work and social change, describing reality with forceful vividness and surgical precision, pouring out fine tropes emerging from his *"non-conscious mind,"* as he puts it. Here three poems that address those themes:

"Husk" (*excerpts*)
After the first hard frost
farmers enter upon their frozen land
to bring in the year's feed corn.
Along rough county roads...

All autumn the men go
silent among the ragged trees that
mark off field from hand-worked field.
Stiff with sleep they dream of corn,

dream of that bullet of frost
lodged in the heart of every kernel,
of the dead weight of each iron
ear in the shucking hands.

"Possum Hollow" (*excerpts*)
Thirty years ago the family on the town side
kept the cleanest garden
now the apple tree grows large,
unpruned.

Coal mines shut,
no work but for logging and that not steady.
Young people drift

leave for Morgantown,
Clarksburg,
                or the tired mill towns of Pennsylvania.

Possum Hollow beneath a late spring sky
that first hint of dryness at the back of the wind...

The following lines, taken from his "Hiorra Summer," speak not only of
a poet recalling his boyhood and family attachments but also the poet laying
foundation as well as original leitmotifs (landscapes) and motivations to
write, which would become a lifetime career:

Every boyhood summer
we'd visit the old home Ulysses built
on the high slopes of Chestnut Ridge.
When thunder invaded the night
I would listen to the mountains,
try to catch their words
when they thought no one could hear...

Poetry took deeper hold of the poet. This is how he remembers his
beginnings: "... *my devotion to poetry started over half a century ago during the*

winter of 1963-'64, and my early heroes were Carl Sandburg (Honey and salt) and Allen Ginsberg (Howl and Other Poems). They remain major heroes, but I have absorbed many other influences, initially from English-language literature, and a bit later from world literature. In terms of Canadian poetry, I quickly gravitated toward the work of Milton Acorn, Dorothy Livesay, and Raymond Souster. Acorn, Livesay, Souster, Al Purdy, and Sam Simchovitch soon became lasting friends, as have many of the poets whose work is to be found in the present volume, such as John B. Lee, Ronnie R. Brown, and Bruce Meyer. Thus, my roots are in Populist/People's Poetry, but I have never been limited to that or any other school. Indeed, my admiration for the poetry of Robert Lowell and Richard Wilbur has never been more passionate." (Taken from Tamaracks. Canadian Poetry for the 21st Century. Lummox Press, 2018)

Such thematic broad-spectrum reading and writing in Deahl has granted him a special place within literature. His variety, also in technique, is clearly stated by his answer to my questions, *What are your key motifs when you write poetry?* and *What guides you in terms of poem structure/format?* He replied that "*I don't know that I have any (motifs) that could be considered "key". I use too many different motifs... Some of my poems are free verse poems and others are formalist. It all depends on how the poem presents itself. The initial lines that come to me determine this.*"

Deahl's signature is distinctly sealed by his discernment of direction, location, human imprint and genuine, passionate experience. In recreating these, he pastes reality upon reality – no prevalence, no lopsided favoritism – where greatness, simplicity and suggestion merge pleasantly. James Deahl is a painter whose words, gentle dabs and deep strokes disclose sensual images of both nature's and intimate moments with keen detail. It is people, history, geography, society – that "*collective subjectivity of the race*" Terry Barker sees in Deahl.

As is commented on the back cover of his book *No Cold Ash* (Sono Nis Press, 1984), in Deahl's work "*is found an unusual breadth of subject matter.*" What ensues applies, in my opinion, to his entire production: "*These poems... begin and end in the metaphor of the natural world; minutely observed recordings of the poet's physical senses, which are made through subtle conjunctions beyond mere logic, to speak of a self which might be all of us.*" These quotations sustain Deahl's vision of what poetry is all about, posed at the beginning of this essay.

From this book, one of his favorite pieces, "Midsummer," a passionate piece written yet felt like a movie scene, abundant in excellent imagery played out in storyline form, showing the poet's universal culture in allusions made in-text and his own grasp of events (*excerpts*):

… We were passing through a village
where women were carrying crates of dried fish.

Not a word was spoken, yet the odour
of salt and the singing blood moved us on…
Beyond this light the village lay in darkness…

Despair comes easy. In the opening fields
we remembered Goya. The murder of the patriots
could have happened here, the blood of
innocent and wise forever contained
	in this earth.

We recover our history…
the moon is a long black finger.
On either side is the muscular night.

Deahl's adherence to nature, landscapes and love, rooted in his U.S.A.-Canadian leitmotifs, goes on in *Even This Land Was Born Of Light* (Moonstone Press, 1993). About the book, Hilda Thomas says that *"Deahl combines a strong feeling for place with a sense of history. Lyric descriptions of landscape or season are linked to moments of human insight." (Taken from back cover comment about his poems)*

Together with his grasp of all that surrounds him, one recurring element in his poetry is the necessary, invigorating physical nourishment that he infuses so well into his pieces. The poet describes with steady, gratifying hand what surrounds him, the exquisiteness of environment and the woman beside him. It is a harmony of sights before him, next to him.

Deahl knows Pittsburgh; Pennsylvania; Canada's biggest city: *"fine-arts,"* *"suave-café-bars"* *(Taken from Canada. Eyewitness Travel Guides. 2002. Dorley Kindersley Limited, London Penguin Company),* Toronto; Niagara Falls; countryside Ontario, and many other places and countries. Deahl knows the Potomac, the Appalachian Mountains, and falls under their charms as I explained before.

Let's read fragments from "Pittsburgh," a long ode to his origins, pain knifing him for what he sees:

1

The Monongahela is brown muscle
pulling its thick waters steadily past
the National Works. A single switcher
shunts empties where four tracks had been a flow
of coke and steaming pigs. One blast furnace
lies dismantled in sepia haze.

August, and only the cold mill works this
week; a hollow clang of rollers across
Steel Valley. My city is dying...

Deahl treasures in his mind Spadina House, a landmark of Toronto's cultural mosaic. Deahl knows outdoor life – and he knows a woman who fills his stirring indoor journeys and his poetry. He carries these experiences running in his poet blood. Deahl is a privileged comer touched by Canada's wand, and he fortunately writes about it. There is pride in what he exposes in his poetry. No wonder Terry Barker comments that Deahl explores in this book "... *the reality of the Canadian spirit." (Taken from Terry Barker's Beyond Bethune, Synaxis Press, 2006)*

A man who has fallen in love with land and a woman surely has motivation enough to come up with such a book. An illustrative piece is "Arrival." The "we" warms the narrative. The author's camera joyfully pans the incredible geography, regaling us fine imagery: *"Snow like the frozen*

sea," "*we becoming a ship,*" "*out of the sun come voices.*" Earth, snow, sea, hill, water, people, inhabit the lines. Poet and woman arrive and, overwhelmed by the sight, enter themselves,
We rode in silence.
On an eastern slope
jack pines cut green fire among buckled maples.
The snow was brighter now and
    we were entering ourselves;
    becoming warm with life…

    becoming the ship
    at the mouth of the harbor.

In constructive and clarifying exchanges the poet and I had while I was drafting this paper, he said to me that "*I also believe the transcendent can be seen in human relationships, especially within a marriage. This is to say that the Creator is on occasion revealed in both nature and the love between man and woman.*" Such positive belief seeps through his poems, both nature and love-related ones.

"Archipelago of farms," connotes peace too and brings people in. Peacefulness is reinforced by the pause the poet enters: "*we stand at the gate.*" They are reveling in the setting and the now. Singing vibrates, playing a substantial part in the poet's recollections. Evidently, nature and people are central to Deahl's poetic formula.

"January" is a short, eloquent piece we read, anticipation throbbing at every word. Here the poet's constants, personification ("*dead snow*") and nature-people blend in a sensuousness that is typical in Deahl *(excerpts)*:

Sun through an east window
and the wind
shaking dead snow off the roof

From roots
and deep frozen water
insects return…

… return
with your face
bright

with your mouth
open

If we talk about blending in with surroundings, we have to mention "Setting the Charm." Here the poet records for posterity geography at his fingertips. Besides, poet and woman fuse with it as they *"begin to inhabit our bodies,"* and *"open the door to the lake"* to breathe in the aroma and take splendid delight *(excerpts)*:

Mountains emerge with feathers
and the flight of feldspar.
The prairie is a long green cloth.
This is where we are:
       rock-shield, field and forest.
It will not go away.

Deahl's rich imagery comes from his thought-out notions on how it works: *"Images and metaphors that arise from my non-conscious mind are usually better than images and metaphors that I consciously "work" to develop. They are truer. Poems that I try to force tend to be weaker, less true to the matter under examination. I am always thinking. I think in a conscious, directed manner. And I think in a non-conscious, spontaneous manner. In my conscious mode, I think about topics and issues that are important to me. My non-conscious thinking is completely undirected. It simply happens. I often go to bed and, as I fall asleep, focus on a literary problem. I usually wake up with a solution. When I start writing a poem, I usually think I know where it is headed. But sometimes it goes in a different direction altogether. And that is OK."*

For James Deahl the idea of a good poem lies in the axiom that *"a poet has a vision and articulates that vision well… What makes a great poet ultimately is the ability to think and write well."* *(Taken from Under the Watchful Eye, Broken Jaw Press, 1995)*

And he adds, *"Poems, as Keats noted, concern truth and beauty. To the degree that a poem expresses truth and beauty to its readers, it is a success. Bad poetry contains neither truth nor beauty; it is not even poetry. Transcendent poetry speaks its truth clearly to many different kinds of readers. Most poetry is neither bad nor transcendent. This has nothing to do with how long or short a poem might be. Nor does it have anything to do with how complex or simple a poem is. The more truth and beauty, the better the poem."* *(ibidem)*

Deahl had the harrowing experience of war close to him when he lived in the U.S.A. *"We learned that our generation must put an end to war… We children were shown what an actual war was like, and I grew into manhood hating war, racism and violence."* *(ibidem)* Unfinished Monument Press published in 1999 his *Blackbirds*, a vigorous poetic claim against war, penned, as Terry Barker tells us on the book's back cover, *"… not with reference to political platforms and slogans, but by means of spiritual/philosophical reflection."*

Deahl wields his themes on steelworks including a poem titled "Steel-workers" where job and war collide quite graphically, a piece with a shocking texture flowing on slow-moving structure, displaying with realistic, critical spin the underbelly of scourges like poverty, war, bereavement. We are in the presence of a committed poet, one horrified by destruction.

An advocate of one of the key roles of poetry – wisely set forth by Sainte-Marie, *"The job of a poet is to get information across in a way that's effective in making change."* *(Taken from Tamaracks: Canadian Poetry for the 21st Century, Lummox Press, 2018. Introduction by the Editor. The editor, James Deahl, refers the reader to Reader's Digest Volume 191 Number 1,144 (November 2017). Page 38. Print)* – Deahl informs poetically, willing to effect necessary change, pained in the fact, as Canadian poet Antony Di Nardo says, that *"I write write write and nothing happens."* *(Taken from Antony Di Nardo's Skylight, Ronsdale Press, 2018)* This is a heart-rending poem.

"Steelworkers" (*excerpts*)
The men leaving the mill are tired.
Some are middle-aged with the heaviness
of their years of work, a few are young,
lean with the hunger for homes and families.
All are soiled, black streaks marking pants,
salt stains on shirts and undershirts…

And, like love, the surrounding hills make holy
this valley, its homes and churches.
In the marriage bed his wife touches
the sensitive triangle between his shoulders
and all the tension and all the anger of the day
passes and is gone in the long cool hours.

It is as if there were no war. No death
from clear skies, no rattle of gunfire
in far-off villages, no blood in the rivers…

And when the flashing shrapnel pierces
that spot between his shoulder blades,
the bright metal dragging him down
into his tender blood, what drowning words
escape his flooding throat as he sees
the surrounding hills the final time?

One of Deahl's preferred poets, and dearest friend, iconic Milton Acorn, whom he recognized as being valuable for his own writing, addressed the miners' subject too. "The Miner's Wife," for example, is Acorn's superb chant to the sacrifices made by both miners and miners' wives. Acorn exposes the harsh living and working conditions of the miners (this is later reinforced in his poem "Pit Accident"). In "Steelworkers," Deahl sings to the miner while abhorring the calamities of warfare.

In 2001 the poet appears again with *When Rivers Speak* (UnMon America). Critics praise his previous books: "*In his precise articulation of landscape, we get a highly charged evocation of place... he allows the natural world to form the most eloquent syllables of human experience. Deahl is organic, earthly, erotic." (Taken from the book's back-cover comment by Sandra Nicholls)*

Notable themes in Deahl's oeuvre harmonize in *When Rivers Speak*, nature and landscapes taking the leading role through the poet's voice, with a golden addition, the poet's choice and translation of poems by Spanish classic, García Lorca.

Amidst nature's gift limned by the poet with *"an imagist's care" (ibidem)*, he dabs onto the poetic palette another of his top themes, love and his beloved, blissfully colored with the close advent of a new life in the poem "October":

We awaken to autumn's
first scattering of snow
and feel our baby move.

With your great round belly
you lean into the cold
to gather our last green tomatoes.

They fill the window sill,
ripen slowly
turning the light to water.

Dawn, holder of expectation, hope and beauty for the poet, is suggestively photographed in "First Light," alongside the concert of nature heralding a new day:

Aspens appear from autumn mists
their boughs yellowing
under northern clouds.

The sound of a creek
still hidden in darkness
comes through the open window.

We lie quietly in bed
enwrapped by the coolness
of early dawn.

A Lyricalmyrical 2009 jewel by James Deahl reached my hands a few years ago, his handmade book *No Star is Lost*. In his poem-prologue, Deahl outlines his philosophical approach in what will be the book's general tone:

Time thus
    mirrors the span
    of a human life –

one start, one finish

with mystery at either end.

It is this mystery,
        not life,
that lives eternal...

... Consider then
that the hills of London
are not
      gloomy

cannot reject their part
in a luminous creation.

One cannot elude in this time-pondering poem the pleasing Shakespearean sonnet air: "*And nothing 'gainst Time's scythe can make defence...*" (Sonnet XII); "*Devouring Time, blunt thou the lion's paws...*" (Sonnet XIX). But then Deahl raises his bouquet of meditative poems, honoring Shakespeare's "*And yet to times in hope, my verse shall stand*" (Sonnet LX). The opening piece, "Hamilton," reads (*excerpts*):

What prayer would help
lessen the grief time brings?

Or should grief
be lessened?...

The beauty of the sumac
is in the dying...

... The beauty of the harvest
is in the work...

The years run on
          bringing a lifetime's end ever closer,
and, like rivers rushing to their sea,
          we count down our lives to mystery,
which,
          unlike the sea,
is eternal.

And of course "Hiorra," one of the poet's favorite poems. In it, he pokes
at the enigmas of life. *(excerpts)*:

For at that point
                    light and night
balance at mystery's gate,
          the world's breath

held in wonder, held
                    for that spun instant
when turning returns
          with new life.
November, and the hunter's hounds
          run the brown woods,
smokehouses curing the season's kill;

                    for only the oaks
          retain their leaves...

Concerned with life's riddles, Deahl elaborates on this not only in his poetry. He remarked in *Under the Watchful Eye* that *"… this life passes away and that the things of this life pass away… The thing I'm struck by now is how brief — how fleeting life is, and how long eternity is. There's an order in the universe… that we might become aware of if we are thoughtful and reflective."*

As I commented before, Deahl has vast travelling experience. Out of it has emerged an enormous potential for poems. Motivated by impressive realities before his keen eyes, the poet engages in memorializing moments spent everywhere, either as a young boy with his parents or as an adult visiting other countries.

The book *Opening the Stone Heart* (Aeolus House, 2010) is the result of such immersion in another nation's culture. In his introduction to this book, Deahl says: *"During twenty-two days of crisscrossing Britain, I had the good fortune to see regions that impressed me greatly in terms of landscape, architecture, and history… As a result twenty-two poems were written after I returned to Canada."*

Poetically haunted by his memories of mills, steelworks and poverty, Deahl writes a poem titled "Men Worked Here." He is able to sense the past, as critics have noted, and walks the places he describes with *"… the full amplitude of the Romantic sensibility." (Terry Barker's words on the book's back cover).* We feel his amplitude and sensibility in this poem (*excerpts*):

On a rail line north through Midland's chill
we rocket past the derelict corpses
of industries abandoned, long forgotten.

Forgotten, too, are their workmen
who laboured decades for wife and children
but now sit tired, bypassed, in used-up pubs.

Those men could be our fathers…

Now massive hollows of brickwork and corroded pipes,
the factories ring each town, rise lonely
as our train rocks into darkness, night.

The poet's heart leaps out to the memory in sad homage, especially poignant in the line *"Those men could be our fathers,"* to which Deahl relates personally. He skillfully handles metaphors and epithets, emotions and images: *"derelict corpses of industries," "our train rocks into darkness."*

Deahl pulses as he writes three-line pieces – a constant technique in his wide-range style – "Five Poems Written While Looking West Toward Ireland" (number III), superb in image knitted in the last line, evocative of sound and light:

III
Sometimes a sadness comes
over the face of the water at that hour
when birds summon the dawn.

IV
There are other darknesses:
the salt-tang of the west wind at night,
the cry of the moon in her mossy gown.

A solemn poem leaves the poet's hand to render a photo-like thought. "The silence" is by all means an eloquent narrative *(excerpts)*:

At Rannoch the moor
reaches to all directions…

and my heart is cut
by the land's raw edge.

I stand on the very spine
of Scotland…

There is nothing,
nothing at all except

this hard stone silence,
this granite wind.

Even in the few lines chosen here, the reader is moved by the wording and its semantic-stylistic implications. The word *moor* in itself is ominous, the feeling reinforced by the next lines, *"my heart is cut by the land's raw edge."* Repetition and opportune epithets heighten the poem's gravitas, *"nothing, nothing,"* buttressed by implied heaviness in *"this hard stone silence"* and even coldness in *"this granite wind."*

James Deahl and Richard Grove joined hands and talents to produce *North of Belleville* (Haiku and Photography), Hidden Brook Press, 2011. Photography was contributed by Grove (also a poet), haiku by Deahl, in a splendidly conceived book where Deahl shows his honed grace at writing haiku. The book is a celebration of color and motion, of nature and life.

He praises nature but returns to one of his pet themes, steelwork. Two haiku from the book are:

"Steel Valley"
The steeltown —
   smoke from blast furnaces
first time in years.

   Charging red furnaces —
the steel mill surrounded
   by spring willows.

Nature calls the poet, a call he would never avoid. Let's read three more haiku from "Red Hill Valley" where he plays magically with color, sound, hints of snow, image, perfectly dovetailing with Grove's photos:

   October valley —
one spruce set green against
   frost-red maples.

   Almost like rain
the sound of leaves falling
   in autumn wind.

Two brooks join –
maples raise flaming hands
    to an empty sky.

In the piece "Wellington County Autumn," we feel the photographic aura attained by Deahl, elegantly buttressed by Grove's photos, reinforced by the sense complements the poet intentionally sprinkles (hearing, touch) among nature's elements:

The hawk's feathers
    ruffled by the first wind
        of autumn.

  Low to the east
Orion obscured
    by black maples.

False dawn –
a rooster's sudden call
pierces the rain.

As a reader, motion (spatially and acoustically) waves in my mind propped by words like *ruffled, wind, rain, sudden call*; as well as onomatopoeic hints (*feather, ruffled, first*). Moreover, motion is visually implied by stanza arrangement. None of the three haiku in this piece are structurally presented in the same way: the poet seems to have calculatedly pressed spacebar or backspace key to that effect. This happens in all his haiku, mirroring, perhaps, nature's inherent endless-movement qualities.

The book's last haiku (From "The Pinery") is quite expressive:

  Fourth week of August,
a single goldenrod in tall glass –
    the whole world yellow.

In 2012, Deahl closes a cycle of four books he had started in 1984 with *No Cold Ash*. Parts of this series were *Even This Land Was Born Of Light*, and *When Rivers Speak*. His new title is *Rooms the Wind Makes* (Guernica Editions). While Deahl himself claims that many of the poems in the book are about *"the brevity of life and the universal fact of suffering and death" (Taken from the book's back-cover comment by the author)*, we encounter many refreshing pieces too.

We find beauty and truth, as the poet defends, evident in:

"Midsummer Poems" (number I)
Before they bloomed
we thought them weeds –

evening-primrose
by the side of our house.

"Gift" (*excerpts*)
And suddenly the season
        changed
 and a chill
        crept into the night
and stayed…
The sky opens and clears;
        seemingly life
could go on
        forever.
A gift.

We see hope and optimism in them born from coldness, cracks, weeds. And the poet relies on nature's – time's – healing powers to salvage the place or at least sprinkle life back to it. Notice the interplay of explicit-implicit colors (red, orange, winter's and lilies' whiteness, the explosion of hues in spring, fire, black):

"Abandoned Brickworks"
The great kilns are cold,
their roofs so cracked the sky breaks through.

Scattered red-orange bricks
lie in weeds. The doors stand open.

Let the snows of winter
purify this place of toil;

let spring rains raise lilies
where fires burned the daytime black.

"Dark Honey," however, does give us the nostalgic poet trapped in meditations that visit his mind. Here we come across those themes he says are present in the book, the futility of life, death. Nevertheless, beauty remains untouched, as truth and sensuality, unfolding in the soft melancholy of the poem (*excerpts*):

Old age is better than death
I was told. But every year
more of the great shade trees die...

Let the river move instead,
pulling steadily on the roots of willows,
sucking away the soft clay banks.

It is my contention that the poet likens a river to life (and death). It flows and takes life away, "*sucking away*" the freshness of youth depriving us of "*the soft clay banks.*" But from here, the poet seeks refuge in his beloved, giving the poem a sweet twist, capitalized in the oxymoronic noun phrase extended "*beautiful sorrow,*" that reminds us of Shakespeare's "*sweet sorrow*":

And let your nightgown fall open
that I may bury my face,
your breasts already swollen
by the dark honey
accumulating year after year —
that beautiful sorrow few men know.

Also in 2012, Deahl publishes a Lyricalmyrical handmade book, *North Point.* In my essay "Ars Longa, Poetry Eternal. Comments on John Di Leonardo's *Conditions of Desire* (Poetry) (2018) Hidden Brook Press. Canada," I praise the poet's capacity to turn the impressions paintings and sculptures left on him into poetry. James Deahl proves to be equally capable. It gives us a very sentient poet, moved by Tom Thomson's paintings. His sensitivity led him to write the fourteen pieces included in *North Point.*

In Di Leonardo's *Conditions of Desire,* he writes inspired by images, he turns into poetics what was already poetry, as he lets us know opening his book with a quotation from Simonides of Ceos: *"Painting is silent poetry; poetry is painting that speaks."* Deahl reaches that moment of "transference of format" as well, delighting the reader with elegant pieces.

James Deahl infuses himself with the poetry subsiding in the painting; from there, he paints his own words, speaking for the images that spurred him in the first place. James is a poet who sees through the webs of life, capable of shaping and reshaping them poetically.

In my paper "A Shower of Warm Light Upon this Land and Us. A review of James Deahl's *Even This Land Was Born Of Light* (Poetry) (1993) Moonstone Press. Canada," I state: *"I am positive this book was visited by the Group of Seven. They mysteriously conferred it with that forerunning contribution bequeathed on their canvases. Thomson, a pioneer, regales us with "brightly coloured, impressionistic sketches of the wilderness." (Taken from Canada. Eyewitness Travel Guides. 2002. Dorley Kindersley Limited, London. Penguin Company)*

And here we are, reading Deahl's introduction to his *North Point*: *"… the reader might expect my favorite Canadian painter to be Tom Thomson, and in this the reader will not be disappointed… Thomson… did not merely paint the surface features of the Shield; he painted the spirit of Canada… no other painter went as deeply into the very nature of our country. In fact, Thomson showed Canadians who they were… and what Canada was… My 14 meditations on Canada were sparked by his (Thomson) retrospective and by my quest to experience the real Canada."*

The first poem, "The Jack Pine," takes us by the hand into the original images (*excerpts*):

Always a lake.
Always the rock
bare and severe.
Always a renegade pine
shaped to wind and storm.
This, then, is our station,
our emblem
and point of pilgrimage.
Here on this jut of earth
we begin and end,
like any year, its cycle
starting and finishing
on that shortest day of all.

The jack pine, fireborn
years ago when lightning
flashed a forest...
waits at the border
of water and stone —
a pioneer rising where
little else survives...

We perceive a Purdian urge in Deahl when he faces painting and image in this poem. Purdy's "Home Thoughts" ("*And our mountains... // Moving from east to west the land / rises... like prairie billiard tables / where players of sufficient stature / can't be found in the immediate vicinity...*") has points of coincidence with Deahl's piece. *(Purdy's fragment taken from Beyond Remembering. The Collected Poems of Al Purdy, 2000. Harbour Publishing. Cross-references with Al Purdy's interest in the land, the primitive stone as well as places of today can be found in Al Purdy. Essays on his Works, edited by Linda Rogers (Guernica Editions, 2002), especially Stan Dragland's "Al Purdy's Poetry: Openings.")*

Sandra Nicholls has defined Deahl's poetry as a "*precise articulation of land-scapes... as if the reader were the first person to stand there... he compresses considerable emotional resonance into a single detail.*" *(Taken from back-cover comments by Nicholls)*. I like this resonance element Nicholls cleverly pinpoints about him. Every Deahl book I have read verbalizes a medley of realities laid out before his eyes, be it landscapes, seascapes, skies, birds, abrupt geographies or the alluring anatomy of the woman he loves.

The resulting emotional quality so transparent in his poems bursts and falls in perfect place near the reader: we are transported into the specifics so vividly that we feel we are *"the first person to stand there." (ibidem, Nicholls)* Let's walk through stanza one of another poem in this collection, "Red Sumac," where we become first-hand witnesses of his X-ray depictions highlighting color in a simile:

Like flames cast to the sunset wind
the leaves of fate dance crimson
among the purple and yellow-green woods.
Here and there an occasional paper birch
breaks this meditation of bright colours.

The end lines fly on the wings of metaphorical beauties brightening and expanding our sensations. Hearing is built into the poetic sonata:

... we seek footholds
in the turning season as ears awaken
to a quiver of music gathered, dispersed,
and re-gathered with the slightest shift
of wind...

Then, the man in the poet surges closing the poem with sensual, ground-shaking, mind-provoking metaphors. The last line is precious and evocative of color and voluptuousness:

... The sumac blazes the way lust
and love twist together into their
incandescent filigree of desire.

Deahl dexterously handles images, tropes, emotions throbbing in this poem. These regularities in his style are noticeable in most of his production; we saw them in the handmade book previously analyzed and welcome them in his 2014 Cyclamens and Swords Publishing *Two Paths Through The Seasons*, a breathtaking joint collaboration between James Deahl and his wife, Norma West Linder.

We relive the involving narrative of "Midsummer." It invites us to enter the poem from its beginning, *"We begin in darkness, / in error and in not knowing,"* and won't let go of us as it reaches its enigmatic final lines, *"We find the word "Forgiveness" carved in a wall."*

Enigmatic is the closing poem, "Old Crow At Sunset." A pensive Deahl muses, puzzled by the circumstances of life, nonetheless clinging to the pleasures of living (*excerpts*),

Seasons arrive and pass;
old friends drift away, leave no
forwarding addresses.
Valerie and Gwen die,
Chris and Dieter go mad,
bewildered by a world
they no longer understand...

I've become fat and old...
... How is it then

you enter my bed...

I ask, expecting no answer,
but merely to express wonder
at this inexplicable life.

Deahl's previous books, *When Rivers Speak* and *Rooms the Wind Makes*, featured preludes of a poetic prose he has been working with for some time. In 2015 Lummox Press publishes his *"definitive book of prose-poems, destined to be a classic of the genre..." (Words by Katherine L. Gordon on the book's back cover), Unbroken Lines.*

In her foreword, Gordon explains: *"James Deahl's prose-poem form allows the freedom of disparate experiences to be gathered with meaningful connection into the paragraphs poetically linked. The form is not limited to a single insight, but has the sweeping vibrancy to allow geography, time, season, and circumstance to flow together…"* And she proceeds, *"Unbroken Lines heralds a welcome new experience in poetic expression, leaves you hungry for more…"*

Deahl steps into a challenging path and he does it gracefully. The prose lines flow as freely as his poetry. He comments: *"I came to be interested in prose-poetry/poetic prose after I read Robert Bly's The Man in the Black Coat Turns in 1983. I consider his "The Ship's Captain Looking over the Rail" to be among the finest examples of Bly's work in the short prose form."* *(Taken from his preface)*

Location and precision go hand in hand with sentiment and description in his prose-poems, once more the surgical, detailed rendition in words of physical scenery that made Michael Wurster state that Deahl reminded him *"very much of Andrew Wyeth… (Deahl) does in poems what he does in paint."* *(Taken from the book's back cover)* *(excerpts)*:

"Sunrise"
The stone arches of Glasgow Bridge stride across the Clyde
from darkness to light. Its pillars stand rock solid in the residue
of night as they pull their river into the dawn. A crow's hoarse
croak comes out of a line of poplars, and the great city awakens,
grey as flint…

Cloudbanks separate and bright sun streams over slate rooftops
to catch Saint Andrew as he stands one rung below Heaven's
gates. He, too, pulls the silent river, pulls it toward that first
light into which the children dive.

"Concert At Port Eliot"
I sit on the grass and watch the sun going white into the
glowing west. Cattle and sheep dot distant pastures where the
mists of evening already overspread the richest parts. In this
landscape I don't know whether I should walk down to the port
or sit quietly among the fringes of night…

I look north as if expecting the moon to rise from a clump
of pines. Shadows move in the dark pools, a footstep on dry

gravel, a rustling among the reeds. Surely we are relieved of our sins and failures. Surely we discover the mound at the heart of the maze, return to the long house of night.

"Spring Rain"
Morning brings a dampness into the orchard. Throughout the woodlot, branches of northern hardwoods shine in their black skins. Early spring — faint green begins to outline the crowns of wild cherry and aspen. Maple blossoms, brought down last night, speckle the path.

The rain starts again, drifting in sheets across yard and pasture. I go down by the lake where silence has soaked into the beds where reeds sleep…

Lummox Press publishes Deahl again in 2016. *To Be With A Woman* is a book of high poetic flight, built on utter despair. He explains his deep grief in the introduction: "… *there is a genuine break between the poetry I wrote from 1964 until 2007 and the poetry contained in this volume. My wife, Gilda Mekler, died on February 7, 2007. Four months later (on June 5th of that year) I wrote the first poem collected here. When Gilda died very shortly after her fifty-third birthday, I thought I would also die. Readers will note that this feeling informs several of the poems that follow. A few months later, my grief entered its second phase. When it appeared that I was not going to die, I passionately wanted to die, I longed for my days of sorrow to end…*"

Particularly illustrative is "Dark Water" where the mourning poet questions his being still alive (*excerpts*):

Morning offers its bleak wall
to my window,
and I awaken, still alive
without thought,
without understanding.

Unbelievable!
My heart pumps blood,

my guts process food,
my beard grows longer,
all without my help.

Beyond the harbour
and its dishevelled steel town
a black sun rises
bringing with it
a wind of departure.

He resumes his inquiries and doubts about life in "Our Travail." Here Deahl reflects on and examines the way things are, pessimism still racking his thoughts (*excerpts*):
So much of our journey occurs
between two great silences.
We must either walk the path
of the blood-red moon
or go down to the river
and welcome whatever rises
from its black depths.

As the book comes to an end, Deahl finds hope. About it he says: "*The present volume closes with a handful of love poems written during the latter half of 2010 to an outstanding novelist and poet, Norma West Linder, who has, perhaps rashly, consented to join her life to mine. Between the Gilda poems of 2007 and the Norma poems of late 2010 lie several meditations on mortality.*"

"Autumn Cellos" and the "Cardinal's Dawn Song" are two fine examples of positive expectation, a new turn for the poet,

"Autumn Cellos"
The sweetgum's red
        casts a deeper tone
so far north of its native
        Appalachian soil.

It's an American exile
        seeking refuge

where summers grow short,
          winters long.

A dark sonata
          fills the October wood
as if our earth
          would release its tears.

In the gathering dusk
          music penetrates the heart
like the voice of God
          calling the unbelievers.

"The Cardinal's Dawn Song"
In the midst of a world of snow
a cardinal sings in the cold light
creeping from the east before dawn.

All the joy of Heaven fills his heart:
a red spot in the black and white
woods of a grieving land.

His song instantly transforms
the visible world; all the colours
of spring bathe winter's frozen realm.

Finally, faith restored, the poet is given a "second chance." He meets
Norma West Linder. One of the poems in this section (This Inexplicable
Life) was quoted, fragments, when I talked about *Two Paths Through The
Seasons*, "Old Crow At Sunset." Here, the clarifying hope element, end lines:

… How is it then

you enter my bed at this late hour
all firm breasts, supple skin,
and welcoming thighs?

How can spring rain cast her veil
over a barren November
where no leaf clings
except on a few gnarled oaks?

I ask, expecting no answer,
but merely to express wonder
at this inexplicable life.

In 2016 Cyclamens and Swords publishes his book *Landscapes* with fine poet Katherine L. Gordon, whom I wrote about in my review book *In a Fragile Moment: A Landscape of Canadian Poetry* (Hidden Brook Press, 2020). About the book Ronnie R. Brown said, *"To read Landscapes is to experience Canada from the comfort of your armchair." (Taken from the book's back cover)*

Deahl focuses on describing the landscape, one he is familiar with and has previously shown great sensitivity for and ability to take in and transform into words. His poems are "... *an overview of Canada few have seen." (Taken from the book's back cover)*

"North of the Great Lakes" is an apparently rhetorical query the poet poses to us. The closing line gives us the answer *(excerpts)*.

Who can love this land
shackled by stone and winter?...

Who can love the silence
of black lakes imprisoned by pines?

Too far north for gardens,
too little summer for corn,
each warm day hoarded shamelessly...

Frozen streams embrace
the land's bare ribs,
blue shadows bruise the snow.

So far north of summer,
only love can save this land.

As we move down the spectacle of Canadian geography turned poetry by Deahl's magic wand, we read "Winter Moonrise Over Kennebec Lake" to re-savor those Purdian echoes I mentioned in my comments about *North Point*'s "The Jack Pine," a piece republished here in *Landscapes*. Let's read fragments from "Winter Moonrise Over Kennebec Lake":

Just east of Peterborough
        acres of wind-bleached corn
remained unharvested in fields
        shadowed blue with snow.

But no farms exist this deep
        in the Precambrian Shield;
the few cabins have been secured
        against this harsh season.

Cloaked in mist and cloud-smoke,
        a vast orange moon
rose quietly from the passages
        of Kennebec's frozen heart.

No dog barks. This is the pure joy
        of advanced age:
the unblemished beauty of winter,
        a silence which is music.

We find prose-poems in this collection. "Algonquin Highlands" stands on short-story-like structure recreating inspiring views (*excerpts*):

Thunderheads tower over the rock-cuts of these
northern lands presaging rough doings, the ragged skyline
pierced by the occasional sentinel pine. Early summer, the
creeks still up, beaver ponds a bounty of fresh, green plants:

arrowhead and pickerelweed, all new growth. Away from
the roads these highlands remain unchanged from the era
when only Native hunting parties roamed these forested
hills, this spreading muskeg…
As dusk draws down, thunder rolls in
from the west, a few lightning strikes bring on a heavy rain.
And the muskeg will continue to spread across the lowlands
with all this water falling without pause, falling from the
dark mansions of Heaven and so few remaining to bear
witness.

"Winter Hawks" is an ode to nature, a feat Deahl is very good at. From
the description of vista and bird, the poet sings to all natural things, bird,
landscape, the passage of seasons (*excerpts*),

Blackbirds fill the Wawanosh reeds.
They are rarely seen, yet their chatter
drifts over the wetlands. If not for
their migration, the silence
would be complete as autumn closes.

Identified with what surrounds him, allured and brooding, the poet closes
the poem with fitting expressive means, simile and oxymoron, a tinge of
confidence and the resolution we know already that led him in the direction
of poetry:

Sometimes I think the body
lives like these northern lands,
its seasons passing year by year. Soon
November's moon will bring its cold fire.
I, too, can stand the winter one more time.

Guernica Editions, Essential Poets, issued in 2017 James Deahl's *Red Haws
to Light the Field*. About the poetry included in this volume, Kevin Higgins
said, "*James Deahl is capable of writing very good poems; there's ample evidence of
that here.*" *(Taken from the book's back cover)*

The poems in this book are vast in theme, profound in approach. Deahl remains loyal to his style. Narration of places and facts, genuine imagery, which he has claimed comes out much better if not too elaborated upon. We read poetry prompted by a painting, as in previous books (*excerpts*):

"Wychwood Park"
>   *after a painting by Mary Hiester Reid*
Near dusk a November sky
dips its hands into the pond.
Nightbirds hide among pale reeds;
the first parlour lights switch on.

The silence of the world surrounds you
as your shadow stands in water.
Ripples move, spread, relapse.
Night is the only philosopher –

your living blood the only warmth
as air and earth embrace.

A cosmopolitan Deahl, a cultivated author, reverberates in "Flame Tower":

The fire through the trees
is a Moorish window
hung on the wall of the night.

Inside the flame, lust flows
and is consumed
by its own burning, its own desire.

I think of Mingus playing in
the south of France,
sailing free on a hot breeze of summer.

An airless wind comes out of Africa,

a desert where the soul is lost
and found again in its blue sirocco.

As I mentioned at the beginning of this work, James Deahl is a poet, critic, lecturer, editor. To study his oeuvre it is unavoidable to look at his work as editor, starting with his contribution to the Canada Cuba Literary Alliance publishing formats, *The Envoy* (newsletter) and *The Ambassador* (official magazine).

He has also edited landmark books. One of them is his *In a Springtime Instant. Selected Poems* (2012) Mosaic Press. Canada, about top Canadian poet Milton Acorn. Another fundamental addition to his editing work is, undoubtedly, *Tamaracks: Canadian Poetry for the 21st Century*, a poetry anthology published in 2018 by Lummox Press. U.S.A.

I call it exceptional and transcendental comfortably shielded in central arguments. The first one is based on the opinion voiced by one of Canada's most qualified and prolific scholars, Terry Barker, who stated:

"Tamaracks: Canadian poetry for the 21st Century serves a similar function in today's political milieu as the Canadian Poets anthology did just over one hundred years ago in 1916. While I am not qualified to comment on the literary merit of the poetry in Tamaracks, it seems to me that it fulfills its two chief goals, as set out clearly by its editor at the beginning of his "Introduction": (1) "to present readers with some fine poetry" and (2) "to show where Canadian poetry stands about one fifth of the way into the 21st century." (Taken from "Tracking the True North," by Terry Barker) Barker places the anthology in a position of privilege and impressively – deservedly – ranks it among the most representative works of this type in the last hundred years.

The second argument reflects what Bruce Meyer, a well-known Canadian poet, said about it: *"This is the most solid, broad, astute, and engaging selection of poetry yet published in the US or outside Canada. It doesn't make its selection based on sneering favoritism: these are all tremendously readable, beautifully written, and entirely expansive poems that speak to the complexities and breadth of Canada.*

Deahl has presented us with a selection that shows the greatness of Canadian poetry from coast to coast. He is judicious in his choices, yet he is entirely open to the great range of expression that this country has to offer. This is not a dot on the map of a generation, but a geography of words and ideas unique and enlightening unto itself. If you want to experience Canadian poetry, start with Tamaracks. You won't be disappointed. It is a brilliant collection!" I need not explain this passionate, established, respected criterion.

The third argument is a more personal, modest one, mine. As a reader, I am entitled to have opinions about what I read. *Tamaracks* educated me in very much the same terms and grounds as Meyer expounds in his heartening words or Barker considers it enjoys in its role as a comprehensive anthology, even if some fine poets did not submit their poetry for a variety of reasons.

Meyer and Barker defined from their angles the significance of a book that was needed. On the book's back-cover comments, we read *"It's the first book of its kind in decades."* Above, Michael Wurster and Judith Robinson had posited *"It is about time a contemporary anthology of Canadian poetry was published... and James Deahl... is the perfect choice as Editor,"* and William Oxley opened the comments by saying: *"... is a valuable and much-needed collection... the anthology is both a delightful and intelligent survey of contemporary poetry in the Canada of today."*

James Deahl has played his poet (he is in the book) and editorial roles flawlessly. He has been called *"A champion of poetry and poets"* by friends, and is considered one of the most knowledgeable scholars when it comes to Canadian poetry. His fervor in bringing this anthology to fruition made him a personal "overseer." I have read poets and poems in *Tamaracks* and felt as happy and optimistic as Meyer on the solidity, broadness, scope and beauty of the poems, as well as the editor's judiciousness.

Tamaracks is a jewel as a book, and a success as a literary endeavor, thanks to James Deahl in the first place. He has done a professional's job showing his true genesis and projection as a literary figure. He may make plans to send a second round of invitations to new poets, especially inclusive of those who did not appear in this first edition, with his mind specially set on a probable second edition of the anthology. The job he has done deserves to transcend.

As editor-poet, Deahl included some of his own favorite pieces in *Tamaracks*. True to the spirit of my book, I quote one of the poems he wrote:

"Confronting The Idea Of The Good On A Rainy Night In Early May"

We should have known
during those dark years of Vietnam
America's democracy had ended,
that all our used-up ghosts
were leaving the vacant mills along the Mon.
Tonight, freight cars lurch
where a rail line used to run;
the old marsh returns
making a place a heron might walk
if only in dream.

The rains won't relent.
I will see my parents' graves
and the home where they raised me
never again.
And they were good Presbyterians.
They voted Republican
every other November,
never once failed to keep the Sabbath,
tried to make me into the man
I should have been.

What can we do with the rain?
Looking back half a century
I still can't tell
what I could have done.
Despite this cold Canadian spring
our mulberry finds the strength

to put forth fresh leaves, our lilac prepares
to bloom. I know
beauty to be good; my wife, a good woman.
Across the river: the dead nation of my birth.

Deahl has been published by publishers of renown. Guernica Editions, Essential Poets, presented his *Travelling The Lost Highway* in 2019. It is an outstanding compilation of poems, written from 2011 to 2018, which presents us a mature poet who is always growing, whose acumen in observing, noticing, decoding realities and souls and penning all those experiences with fresh imagery and level-headed layout, ranks him among the most representative Canadian poet-chroniclers of love, life, society and nature.

The book is a man's story told in poetic form. He offers his vision of things, his insights based not on supposition or instinct but on his determination to gain knowledge of his themes while traveling. In his words: "*One got to know the nation... one got to know the people.*" He is primordially interested in finding ways that "*might recapture the values that once animated the American and Canadian people.*" *(Both quotations taken from the book's introductory words by Deahl)* You get a taste of all that in the book.

About it, David Haskins said: "*There are meditations, eulogies and laments contained here, passionate love poems, poems that call upon national and generational history...*" *(Taken from the book's back-cover comments by Haskins)*

With these assertions in mind we read Deahl's opening poem, "A Music Innocent Of Time And Sound." A somber pun comes in the first line, where Deahl seriously plays with the overlapping meanings of "dead": "*No Jews visit their dead during the dead / of winter.*" Solemnity in wording and intention envelops this piece, with a full-grown visualization of death. The last two lines struck a biblical passage in me, my hypothesis leaping back to Jesus' lesson about a first stone being cast only by those without sin. In a way, Deahl's variation,
We, the living, are never so innocent
as to fearlessly watch that casket down,

is evocative of teachings and truth in that scene. In the poem, innocence and fearlessness of the living must bow while they *"watch that casket down."* In my view, "casket" does not mean only the coffin. Contextually, it develops into extended metonymical shades referring to death or even final judgment of our acts in life.

A hymn to death and life – natural, human and societal – is heard in "Woodlot." The poet has no choice but to seek refuge in nature, elicit hope from eager line-wishes: *"buds proclaim / spring might be near at hand,"* where spring is hope and buds are the slowly blooming evidence that hope will eventually crystallize.

Even when *"All is born anew in this woodlot,"* the second stanza pierces hope with a crude reality:

… last month the remains
of the young teacher were dumped,
whatever life remained
leaking from her forty wounds.

If in the first stanza we read of *"plague-struck elms,"* the second bares another kind of plague, a sadly social one. The closing lines are ominously vibrant (*excerpts*):

her blood,
as if to claim this land her own,
tried, but failed, to penetrate
this frozen soil

It sends a message of posthumous symbolic will to claim a life that was prematurely stolen from her.
Another poem I want to comment briefly is "Bells That Beat Against The Heart." Metaphors surprise us in this piece, like the one emerging from the title and retaken in the lines (*excerpts*):

trees stand frozen where
water will pool in spring;

they are bells beating
against a fragile heart.

The way the poem is structured, the poet returns *"through darkness"* from nature, depicted in stanzas one and two. Then his *"fragile heart"* leads him to refuge in his salvation, *"the woman I love."* He had previously emphasized her relevance in the line *"This is my only life,"* where "only" does not cage the man; it voices a choice, a preference of being within nature and with his woman.

That was stanza three and line one in the next. Stanza four goes back to nature, and metaphors (*"dawn summons heavy clouds"*), as if he felt safe between stanzas and right in the middle with his beloved.

"A Book Of Snow" is actually a poem filled with warmth, beauty, passion and high-style imagery. Feel the benignity of a shock in *"the sudden shock of your beauty,"* or the tender metaphor *"your embrace is the song of bells in the night"* which overwhelmingly escalates to (your embrace) *"the force of an ocean at full tide."* We rejoice in Deahl's (*excerpts*)

… miles of buried fields awaiting spring's touch.
The sky's a cathedral of light, a place
where only the impossible happens.
The poet speaks in wonder of nature's might:
What strength do we have before implacable
nature? Even the green thought of April
grows ever more distant, exiled by
winter's fierce grip, by snow's vast solitude.

Yet, every time we make love it's like our
first time: the sudden shock of your beauty,
of pleasure beyond all expectation.
Your embrace is the song of bells in the night
or the force of an ocean at full tide.

He runs to his lover's arms and shivers at "… *pleasure beyond all expectation.*"
He knits a grand finale, breathtaking and unforgettable,

Waking beside you after our night of love,
I want to give you the gift of my life
and February's book of snow.

The poem "Sarnia By Starlight" *(Published in The Envoy 93, November 2019, taken from Travelling the Lost Highway, Guernica Editions, 2019)* is a harmony of cityscape and natural scenery, superbly, sensually blended by James to sing to his beloved Sarnia:

Sarnia's adorned
by a skein of lights
strung between sky
and night's river.

The city is suspended in a symphony of blue pulses, evening falling, a girl's open blouse, a skein of lights, sky, night's river and starlight giving us a cozy feeling of home, sweet home:

Must every object
that summons desire
be beautiful?
An ashplant?
That girl's open blouse?

Nature is a diva in his poetry:
A slow, blue pulse
from cold water.
Call and response
of smoke and wind
as evening falls

He magically bestows it with human traits in a first-class combination of simile, metaphor and personification:

Starlight enters
with ancient airs
like a bride,
the music dancing
on her shy lips.

The second poem, "Quince-bush In Winter," is the poet's sharp eye capturing beauty in winter and trees. Still connected to the human reference in the poem, James grants the leading role to the quinces' warmth that "spreads through January's cold." He portrays the bright side of things with metaphorical expressions:

My neighbour's quinces have all put on white caps.
She never harvests her quinces
so they hang all winter, orange globes
lighting my mornings as the sun begins to rise.

(The reader may go to my essay "Architects and Epitomes. A Word about Three Canadian Poets: Richard Marvin Grove (Tai), John B. Lee and James Deahl. Comments on poetry they have published in The Envoy, the CCLA newsletter (Poetry) (2019)" in my review book A Shower of Warm Light Upon this Land and Us. Reviews and Essays on Canadian Poetry (Hidden Brook Press, 2021)

A poet charmed by Canadian beauty, he feels mesmerized, what is reflected in "After Coming to the North":

For miles around: only rock,
trees, these cold spring lakes.
And our tiny lives.
Ovid never saw this, nor
the Elizabethans, for all
their brilliance. Already night
has started to draw heat
from the day, its deep sky
searching, reaching ever deeper.

The impression left on him is obvious, and straightforwardly expressed in his midlines:

Ovid never saw this, nor
the Elizabethans, for all
their brilliance.

To the poet, there is nothing that compares to the Canadian scenes before him. Yet, his most eloquent "love affair" with Canada, as I have commented, is the fact that he moved in 1970 never to move back to the United States. *(The reader may consult my essay "My College Canada; My Sentimental Canada. A Brief Reflection on Canada and its Influence on Canadians and Cubans," also in my second review book)*

The year 2020 came with Hidden Brook Press publishing an anthology edited by Don Gutteridge, *Hearthbeat*, where poems by James Deahl were included.

We quote, full, the poem he submitted. As I explained before, this is a foundational poem for Deahl in many senses. In it transpires a budding poet, who reminisces his past life and anchors the roots of what would eventually become his unending passion, his long-standing career.

Let's read the whole-hearted things he has to say about this poem and its significance to him: *"I do want to thank you for mentioning "Hiorra Summer". To me it is a seminal poem. My father was born there, and it was at Hiorra that I wrote No Star Is Lost. In many ways it is my spiritual home."*

"Hiorra Summer"
Every boyhood summer
we'd visit the old home Ulysses built
on the high slopes of Chestnut Ridge.
When thunder invaded the night
I would listen to the mountains,
try to catch their words
when they thought no one could hear.

August's lightning would come by stealth,
the way death might strike a young man
with a bad heart, he never knowing
how beautiful his last breath could be.
In the night the long-dead miners
were released from their mausoleum
of sulphur and coal, from their dreamless sleep.

Within the storm's aura their lives
were more than lives, their goodness
retained in family legend,
all else cleansed by nature's violence.
This is what the mountains whispered
when darkness came down the ridge
to silence all our clocks.

The Canada Cuba Literary Alliance, founded in 2004 by Richard Marvin Grove, has had the unwavering support of James Deahl as a contributing poet and as an editor. An alliance created to promote friendship, culture, literature and art, it opened formats to publicize the work of Canadian and Cuban writers and artists. One of these is the official magazine, *The Ambassador.* Well-known poets from both countries have been systematically presented in its pages, some of which are dedicated to a Guest Poets section (Milton Acorn, Al Purdy, John B. Lee, José Martí, Fina García, Carilda Oliver, etc.). The magazine's 16th volume, 2020, featured Norma West Linder and James Deahl as Guest Poets.

Both poets have a many-petal link of love of nature. This is a truth that applies unfailingly to Canadian poets. In James Deahl, the bond is signed by sheer, detailed descriptions of the animate and inanimate world, seasons and occurrences; not in an isolated or detached way but in a personal involvement, an intimate commitment. He does not separate the outside world from his experiences, joyful or painful, hopeful or in despair, connected with God and creation in many aspects.

Let's read some of Deahl's the poems included in *The Ambassador*'s 16th volume *(Taken from: To Be With A Woman (2016) Lummox Press. Library of Congress. United States of America: "The Hawthorn In Spring," "The Cardinal's Dawn Song." Red Haws to Light the Field (2017) Guernica Editions. Canada: "Edge," "In Praise Of The Autumn Rose," "Reaching The Ocean." Landscapes (2016) (with Katherine L. Gordon) Cyclamens and Swords Publishing. Israel: "Hidden Moon.")*

"The Hawthorn In Spring"
The new season is marked

by the return of our starlings.
As they forage in my yard
I read of Mary Magdalene,
the lover of Jesus, humbled
in her sorrow.

The hawthorn tree carries
crystals of light
on the tips of its spikes.
Even this brilliant spring
cannot relieve the darkness
of the human heart.

"Edge"
Dune grasses, milkweed,
poplar seedlings,
and wild grape
        torn by wind

have colonized
this ragged edge of sand.

World of hot sun
and drought in summer

ice storms and
gales
        all winter

yet a few plants
survive
each year.

How like love,
these roots
that
        bind

shifting land

to hold it
      whole.

"In Praise Of The Autumn Rose"
Dark sounds linger
      in the autumn rose
            before dawn opens
                  its petals.
The heart knows best
      — always the heart —
            in shimmering waters
                  every end a beginning.

So our winter becomes
      a fresh year
            under each greening leaf
                a thorn of beauty.

"Hidden Moon"
What can we know of November's moon
      hiding among bare trees?

Rabbit tracks in snow are a dark bruise
      on earth's sensitive skin.

An impervious hawk looks down
      with the eyes of a killer.

Midnight: every farmhouse stands silent
      among these fields of death.

"Reaching The Ocean"
Travelling south all morning
I finally reach the ocean
and suddenly the land looks small.

Beyond a stone jetty — only sky,
water, and the tang of brine;
only this endless azure
effortlessly filling the world.

It's like the second day of Creation—
God separating the blue of the sea
from the purer blue of Heaven;
or perhaps the generous, blue heart
of God making paradise actual.
Such a day arrives as a gift
like a south wind in January,
or forgiveness.

About this latter piece, Deahl explains to me: "… *my poetry, like "Reaching The Ocean", often seeks the transcendent. I believe that the transcendent can be discovered in nature; the eternal can be perceived in the temporal.*"

In November 2020, James sent me his fresh Aeolus House 2020 book, *Earth's Signature*. The back cover comment says, "*Both the natural world and the decaying industrial landscape are also vividly imaged. With phenomenal virtuosity, the author utilizes the Jackpine form as a means of searchingly evoking and evaluating both bygone times — what lasts from them and what is lost — and the contemporary scene they led up to, even including the era of Donald Trump and the arrival of COVID.*"

The front cover is a gift to the eye. A fitting choice of picture, an elegant jack pine against a solid blue of hill ridges and greenery, its roots copiously distinguishable, firmly anchored to a welcoming earth.

About the sonnets, James explains in detail: "*One thing I like about Earth's Signature is that it displays how my sonnets have evolved over 40+ years. I can see three phases:*

1. The Jackpine Sonnets I wrote from the late 1970s until about 1990 were influenced chiefly by Milton Acorn. These are at the beginning of my book.

2. The influence of Robert Lowell grew and this, perhaps, can be seen in my sonnets from 1990 until the current century. These Jackpine Sonnets are a bit less rigid.
3. The present. Over the last two decades the Lowell-inspired sonnets of Seamus Heaney have really caught my attention. Of course, the Heaney sonnets date from 1979, but it took twenty years for me to really see their value...
My contribution — if we want to call it that — is the nature poem."

We notice modesty again in James' words, a virtue I referred to in my Introduction about him, which transpires in his own opening words for the book:

"I believe my poems found herein will speak for themselves. I have no desire to defend them." Truly, these Jackpine sonnets rise their limpid voice to stand for Deahl. He confronts reality. He goes back to his backgrounds and original themes (I have reviewed them in this paper) *(all excerpts)*:

"Pittsburgh"

I
The Monongahela is brown muscle
pulling its thick waters steadily past
the National Works... a flow
of coke and steaming pigs. One blast furnace
lies dismantled in sepia haze...

He indulges in a streak of pleasure describing nature and scenes with naturalness I can almost touch:
Dawn calls a clean white note from an English
sparrow, but by noon everything's gone grey,
fine soot falling ridge to ridge. Now a bitch
ploughs snow, her muzzle hot on a graveyard
squirrel, jumping cold half-buried stones. Below
this hill a shortened freight stutters on its
high iron trestle, swings black across the Mon.

We walk with a solemn, reverent poet in "In A Place Such As This":

MSc Miguel Ángel Olivé Iglesias

Dedicated to the faithful who have kept, and still keep,
 The Cathedral Church of the Holy and Undivided Trinity.
 God is design, even our ugliness
 is the goodness of his will.
 — Robert Lowell

I
There lives a silence in the stones themselves
dressed and set by Norman hands into stout
round pillars that bear the tower's weight and
eight centuries. The air's massive, too,
with towering quiet as if we lived
before the Word; walked through a world intimate
and direct. Grey light slants across the nave.

Our mouths water, our senses perk up with "Tasting The Winter Grapes":
All morning a heavy mist off the bay
washed the mountain's foot; by late afternoon
the sky's blown clear, our whitened sun skims low.
I walk out on my birthday — December fifth,
nineteen hundred and ninety-four — to taste
winter grapes picked fresh from their frosted vine
along the old rail line where the shadow

of a Chicago and North Western car
turns the bright track black. Such freakish warmth!
Some miracle holds winter's steel at bay...

His poems have a "... *feeling for place with a sense of history...*" Hilda Thomas
says on the book's back cover. Both places and personal history blend in
his "Jasper Newton Deahl" *(excerpt)*:

I was a country boy from Barbour County.
Real coal country. Following Harvard
and Columbia, Phi Beta Kappa,
my doctorate, and all that, I returned
to my Mountain State to teach, and rose to
Dean of the College of Education
of West Virginia University.

Morgantown was my Heaven and Mary
my angel; our children arrived as gifts…

Nature poems cannot be left out in this formidable volume *(excerpts)*:

… Deep in the valley, the scent of woodfires
lingers. Black ash shadow moist bottomlands:
wood for barrel staves and farmers' baskets, the
dark heartwood singing through our moonless nights.
Even at this peak of autumn, winter
rises — each cold spring hungering for snow.

James Deahl strums the strings of feeling and stirs diverse emotions. He has been doing that in the fifteen books to his name I have in my bookshelf. I have tried to condense in these pages the life and work of one of the most representative writers in contemporary Canadian literature. Whether I succeed or not in summarizing is irrelevant, as long as I was able to provoke the reader, to plant tidbits of interest and curiosity for James Deahl's contribution to Canadian poetry.

See how Deahl views the idea of success: "I… *do not believe in success in terms of this world. I write to please my Creator and to celebrate the beauty and goodness of the world in which we live. But I know the world of the flesh to be brief, the realm of the spirit to be eternal. When my first publication — In The Lost Horn's Call — rolled out I was almost totally unknown.*

That was in 1982. In less than four decades, I became nationally prominent as a poet and critic. I can go to any city or university in Canada to present a public reading and many people in my audience will have read one or more of my books. And that is nice. But it does not confer a halo. And it does not make writing easier. The fact that my books might be widely read does not matter. I still face a blank piece of paper. And using language, a flawed tool, I have to explore the truth and beauty of Creation."

These are amazing thoughts, marked by humility as a human being and as a poet. They are charged, evidently, with deep spiritual conviction and *joie de vivre.* They have inspired Deahl to leave us a formidable oeuvre. As impressive is Deahl's expertise on Canadian literature (besides his encyclopedic knowledge of universal literature), especially when it comes to his love for poetry, a zeal he has frequently shown by ending his emails to me with *"Long live poetry."*

His literary prowess does not come by unconscious assimilation; it is the accumulation of years devoted to it, during which he has arduously combined natural talent, contexts, influences, passion and conscientious study. These are but key ingredients towards a solid competence few chosen ones enjoy. Deahl is categorically one of them.

John B. Lee gave us a vital discernment of Deahl: *"If there is anyone anywhere more dedicated to the craft of poetry than James Deahl, then I can honestly say I have not met them. ... He is a Canadian poet to be cherished and revered."* *(Taken from the back cover of Deahl's Earth's Signature, Aeolus House, 2020)*

A truly insightful criterion is Michael Wurster's. I conclude my paper with it. It speaks for itself and is justly praiseful. The number of authors writing in English is staggering, so this opinion places Deahl among the best of the best: *"James Deahl is one of the ten or twenty finest poets writing in the English language today."*

JOHN B. LEE

Kissing the Darkness
When the Pages Close

my poem is there
kissing the darkness
when the pages are closed
and silent
as a dreamer's mind
the quiet sleep of fragrant ink
locked within the verso and
the recto
like seed life in the frozen earth
that longs
for warm release
in stranger's light
to feel the fertile germination
of a sentient breath
transforming
tight-packed syllables
of interlocking words
between the speaking and
the hearing
lies the soul that moves the hand

John B. Lee

The best start – certainly the most provocative – to write this paper is by quoting George Whipple's opinion about John B. Lee: *"The greatest living poet in English."* It can be easily followed by hundreds of similar viewpoints but it is a peak opening. Uninformed readers might frown or smile, the statement is quite categorical, yet when we delve into Lee's career and numerous publications, we will inevitably tend to side with Whipple.

However, a poet's career and his published material are not enough. We would have to read the poet, decode his gift, his "vessel" condition, as he calls it, read him time and again until foundations and motifs, motivations and urges, words and message, intent and depth, surface from a charming alchemy of transcendent imagery and substantial puissance: we are spellbound, irreversibly.

This is how Marilyn Gear Pilling sees Lee: *"The boy was born to write. Before he started school, he was opening his grandfather's books and scribbling the pages with pencil. He sat with extended family and hired man at a table rich with story. This boy, the fifth John Lee, would develop a lyric voice that sings with a pure and supple flow that has not been heard before in this country. While Lee's melody soars and praises, the tenor line is often wistful, poignant, or gently melancholic; there is often a pervasive nostalgia for lost worlds..." (Taken from The Ambassador, volume 004, 2006)*

Gear draws our attention towards a key revelation of Lee's covenant with the muses, *"a pure and supple flow that has not been heard before in this country."* When I asked Lee where his motifs came from, his answer was poetry too, his words coincidental with Gear's position: *"In that I am a fifth generation shepherd who abandoned his heritage as master of the flock, and in that I have taken up the mantle of writing poetry, in no small part because of the impression made on my younger self by the poet Dylan Thomas, and in that I too aspire to write for the love of man and in praise of God, I'd happily say that every poem drawn from the deep wells of the self partakes in that aspiration."*

Poetry in Lee is native to his heart. His earliest recollections take us back to poems that would spring up from every-day events. Below, one that he wrote right after a hair-cutting issue with his parents *(excerpts)*:

"The Day My Mother Cut My Hair"
All my life til then
I'd been
An obedient boy
My hair kept short
As was my father's wish …

As Lee notes, it's the closing lines that were a revelation:

… it was my mother's hands
and her sweet surmise
in that snip and silence
with the sharp skill
of the heart
when in the red quiet
of a woman's breast
she embraces her son
and carries him forward
like the rib shadow
of a great tree loosening its shade in gloaming

In his introduction to *This is How We See the World* (Hidden Brook Press, 2017), the poet said, "*I had the good fortune of knowing exactly what I wanted to do with my life after first reading Dylan Thomas's poem "Fern Hill." I discovered my own particular avocation having fallen deeply in love with reading poetry and with the craft of writing poetry.*" Therefrom sprouted the first fundamental seed in Lee, which would chart for him his ulterior bearings as a writer. He named one of his sons Dylan.

In this respect, Gear posits, "*Lee's poetry comes from the deepest well of the self, a place of rare depth and beauty fed by omnivorous reading and open-hearted living. As well as writing the work he has formally researched and re-imagined, he pours his daily life into poetry every morning, creating a skein that contains the natural and the human worlds, the public as well as the private.*" (*ibidem from Gear*)

Lee's major influences and preferences are from top five Classic Canadian poets: Irving Layton, Margaret Avison, Al Purdy, Raymond Knister,

Archibald Lampman. As he pointed out, his all-time favorite poem is "Fern Hill" by Dylan Thomas, and he likes very much "Julia's Clothes," by Robert Herrick. Obviously, as he remarks, *the list is too long*." His choice of living Canadian poets goes to Marty Gervais, Roger Bell, Marilyn Gear Pilling, Don Gutteridge. By Marty Gervais, he likes the poem "Sweet Hope." By Marilyn Gear Pilling, "My Mother's Legs."

All his readings, early influences and learning have bestowed John B. Lee with the rare touch of turning anything into a poem. One of his books, *Never hand me anything if I'm walking or standing* (Black Moss Press, 1997), precisely stems from a friend's suggestion to the poet to use a chance remark by Lee as a title. The book opens with such poem *(excerpts)*:

"Never hand me anything if I'm walking or standing"
Never hand me anything
if I'm walking or standing
or I will lose it surely
as a sleeper loses time
though the moon comes rapping
at his window like a pearl...
Never hand me anything
if I'm walking or standing
even the sweet gift of
your absence left behind
in scribbled notes...

We are carried away by the poet's lyrical flow of words, moonstruck perhaps, as he neatly, softly unravels the riddle of sentences. There is *"lyrical rhythm playing throughout the book." (Taken from the book's back cover)*

In my analyses on James Deahl, I approached some of his mine-related poems. Lee continues this theme in the book with "The Coal Miners." As arresting as Deahl's, Lee's lines call a spade a spade in his unique style, heightened by expressive means like similes and metaphors *(excerpts)*:

The one coal miner says
he loved his work
says, he knelt
like a priest at prayer
all day
and played his banjo spade so hard
his hands bled black
to keep the coke clear...
You knew by the look of him
he'd dig a chimney to the sky
and breathe the moon.

When I asked Lee if his parents read poetry or prose to him as a child, he replied, "*Yes. Dad was a sentimental man who loved doggerel and Mom read me Mother Goose nursery rhymes.*" One of the poems in the book is "My Mother, Reading At Night." It is both a sweet piece seeping from Lee's inexhaustible fountain and homage to his mother, who went to great lengths to read. Maybe that reading fever was passed on to Lee years later as a peculiar DNA legacy. There is an underlying mystique in the words the poet conjures to write the poem. It finds welcoming port to dock in our own childhood experiences *(excerpts)*:

She says she ruined her eyes
reading late at night
as a girl
being furtive in bed
under the blankets
with a book and a dim light...
to follow the unlocked and heavy door of the plot
the print...
transformed by the beauty of thinking
into the colour play of dreams and memory...

Cranberry Tree Press published Lee's *An Almost Silent Drumming* in 2001. In the introduction by the author, he describes South Africa as both "*a beautiful and terrifying country.*" His impressions, obviously well-rutted, are reflected in the book. One of my favorite poems is "Taken," a fine piece where the protagonist role goes to a lion, the awe of predation within the food chain, the shudder at the thought of being attacked, deprived of life *(excerpts)*:

In the mind of the lion
the entire floor of available earth
is a banquet.
It matters not
whether we are poets
or pious strangers.
She will take as a huntress
at our prayers...
She'll humble all her hungers
to one belief of beggars
under a glorious insouciance of stars.

The last poem, from which the title was taken, "An Afterness," is tremulously meditative. It involves the reader with "*an almost silent drumming*" of Lee's "*human heart.*" While the first stanza, of only five lines, slowly invites us to the possibly lullful rhythm of drumming, the second-last stanza, twenty-lines long, is a dreamy slide, nonstop, nearly an esoteric confession from the soul. Structurally, the poem takes no punctuation marks, what adds to the sensations arising as we read it *(excerpts)*:

... I'm lost
between
the fearing of the known
and unknown ecstasies of life
so at the end of every measuring
the stilling pulse
will seek and find and soothe so lovingly
the long lacunae of an afterness.

They say Africa has hidden charms unclosed only for the alert, sentient seeker, charms that will never leave him/her. Lee was a fortunate, "charmed," recipient, graced by the endless wilderness before his poet eyes. It helped him see through the skein of different cultures and realities.

As Pérez, Velázquez and González tell us, *"From all corners of the world he has brought poems. With a keen eye for cultural jewels, he has seen the entrails of "the others" with love and compassion, linking their fortunes and tragedies with those close to him at home, in Canada."* (Taken from the paper *"Cuba and Canada: Chosen Places in John B. Lee's Work"* by PhD Adonay Bárbara Pérez Luengo; PhD Manuel de Jesús Velázquez León and MSc Alison González Cuba)

In 2004, Passion Among the Cacti Press published *Through Their Joined Hearts Drummed Like Larks*. In his back-cover comments, taken from his words as Judge for the 1999 Poet's Corner Award, Eric Miller says, *"This collection is tremendously evocative—a feat all the more impressive because it relies so heavily on research."*

Lee embarks on a voyage across history, rendering direct, descriptive pieces. I chose one piece, last in the book, "Walking on an Ocean Beach at Dawn," which presents us the beauty of nature. It is persuasively expressive, filled with sustained metaphorical exploits and fresh similes, interspersed with actual physical experiences that retain, too, the enrapturing poetic aura the poet's hand can render.

Transparent, like the ocean it depicts; pristine, like the views it frames, the poem attracts for the power of its imagery, its imaginative vigor, and the surging afterglow that lingers once we finish reading it *(excerpts):*

The sun is at the rim of the world
where the blue
comes bannering free both water and sky
like the run of a knife in a bolt of silk.
I walk among
the backward dash of crabs...
There in that grand eternal
clock of water and weather
I hear ships and the wheel of stars...

As was the case with James Deahl in *The Ambassador* 016, 2020, John B. Lee was Guest Poet too fourteen years before. *The Ambassador* 004, 2006, had him deploying his enthralling poetry. Gear shares her views with the readers in her introductory words to the poet's chosen poems: *"Enter the work of John B. Lee at any door. The grand and lovely osmosis of the universe is what you will find, sung into being by language played as if by the hand of the divine."*

The divine is obvious in "How Beautiful We Are," an elegy to beauty and truth, which, as we discussed earlier with Deahl, are two essential pillars of poetry. We read an eager poet singing to life, voicing his dreams, his urges to cross dimensional frontiers and fuse with nature. Two recurrent elements we perceive in this poem are *sky* and *water*.

Despite the ending, objectively set in by the poet as a warning – a truth – we optimistically choose to be the ocean, the river; we choose to fly *"when the sky looks down and sees how beautiful we are"*: there is beauty in our existence and *"we believe in flying because we've been dreaming the dew,"* a treasured possession, that of dreaming. Enjoy:

I say to you
I want to be the water
the way the lake waves
love our bodies to the very heavening
even old men stand
their loud red shoulders
shining in the sun as if scrubbing away a difficulty
their bellies puckered
like gathered rubber
and women
with legs like thin ink
a wet bluing on white
and the trickling off of secret longing
like roses after the rain
if I watch
wet weather greening
a burned brown lawn

how then
the drought drowsed
Fuchsia lifts itself
like someone waking in the heat
some shy dancer
rising to take my hand
as we leap
beyond the window
we're that sad about
the gravity of clouds
but we believe in flying
because we've been dreaming
the dew
that clings to the filigree
of web and weed
I want to be
both tide pool
and the ocean
I want to be
the river rising
like expensive stockings
drawn on slow
as you walk deeper
and deeper
into love
I want to be
what happens
when the sky looks down
and sees
how beautiful we are
but there's war at the edge of the sea
where nothing is true
but dying

Let Light Try All the Doors is a Rubicon Press book from 2009 where the poet opens his gift of writing to the full-streamed light that grants him further clarity, more limpid appropriation of his craft.

The notion of overcoming darkness and the themes of light is present in many poets, Canadian and universal. In "Echo's Revenge (i)," for example (only excerpts are picked), Lee trespasses the realm of our dimension, pushing into a surrealist proposal, subconsciously constructed to have Dali, or Magritte, watch:

Sit very still
and walk within your body
like a house of many rooms
let light try all the doors
and craft a slowness
where you dream the walls away…

In Echo's Revenge, piece ii, Lee comes up with a phantasmagory of images even if they represent an actual object or phenomenon:

what shadows there were
were but
the uninvolving shades
that catch
the artifice of indoor light
the lux
that's cast from bulbs
like the stains
old paintings leave
upon a paper wall…

Lee's visits to Cuba brought about the conception of an ambitious project masterminded by Manuel Velázquez (Canada Cuba Literary Alliance – CCLA – former VP, author and editor), John and Richard Grove, in which Lee shone as a translator. The initial idea ended up in a book entitled *Sweet Cuba. The Building of a Poetic Tradition: 1608-1958* (Hidden Brook Press, 2010). That foundational day is described by Lee as follows: "*It was a momentous day because it was the day we decided upon my taking on the mantle of translation as proposed by Manuel for what would become Sweet Cuba. The three of us had a lively discussion about what the book would be, and I reluctantly agreed to work up two poems as examples to see if I was capable of the task.*"

The book joined Manuel and John in compiling, editing and translating representative poetry from early 17th Century up to the end of the 1950s, in an original format in which history and poetry filled the pages, with José Martí, our Apostle, setting up, as Manuel explains in the book's Foreword, *"the internal structure of this compilation and becomes the moment in which all the tones sketched during the protracted configuration of the national poetic consciousness take shape in a coherent and harmonic voice..."* Lee adds, *"... I find an apotheosis in Martí. And so, we have chosen to honour the work by weaving the poems of Martí into the fabric of the entire body of work into one unified whole..."*

Sweet Cuba is, in my opinion, an unequalled volume born within CCLA history yet its meaningfulness and aesthetic proposal resound far beyond. It significantly draws a line at the frontier between before and after in poetic anthologization regarding scope, combined synergy towards its completion, and outcome. It was also a deep personal involvement, as Lee remarks, *"As a poet I come to this work humbled by the task at hand... a poet visited by Martí at my desk... overlooking my beloved Lake Erie, haunted by the spirit of Cuba."*

The book was widely presented in Canada and Cuba, in book fairs, universities, literary meetings, etc. On the book's back cover, Linda Rogers commented about the editing and compilation work done: *"These poems... are the poignant story of Cuba, and nothing is lost in translation."* Rosemary Sullivan stated, *"Cuban poetry is a mystery to us. To have it so brilliantly translated by John... and Manuel... is indeed a gift... They translate... with a master's hand."*

One of Lee's most formidable collections of poetry is *This is How We See the World*, published in 2017 by Hidden Brook Press. It compiles many of his previous publications in separate sections.

For someone who would *"... far rather be referred to as someone who writes poetry than be called a poet"* *(Taken from John B. Lee's book This is How We See the World, Hidden Brook Press, 2017. His introductory words)*, Lee has an irresistibly mysterious way with words and images few ever acquire, much less develop in a lifetime. Bernice Lever says Lee is a *"master craftsman... (his) ... lines flow smoothly from one fresh new metaphor to the next."* *(Taken from back-cover comments on This is How We See the World, Hidden Brook Press, 2017)*

If we assume poetry as a remarkably creative, lettered crystallization of outer and inner realities, we will discern the poet's identification with his lines (poem "… how to read this poem:"): "*Imagine yourself as one / or all of these lines.*" The poet is one with his creation; he is part of that reality he cups in his hand and magic-wand-touches in his mind. The poet identifies with the reader, and sees himself as a reader too.

By using a simile, "*Imagine the poem closing you in / like a cell…*" Lee proposes a micro-instant of experiencing a physical-mental solitude in encasement; to then oppose the idea with a thesis of unbound freedom writing/reading provides: "*read this poem / to set yourself free.*" Let's enjoy the whole piece:

"… how to read this poem:"

This poem
is a dance
a ritual
imagine each line
hammering on the floor
like a spoiled child
or spinning an insane dervish.
Imagine yourself as one
or all of these lines.
Imagine the poem closing you in
like a cell
read this poem
to set yourself free

I asked Lee, *What guides you in terms of poem structure/format?* and he replied, "*Instinct, learning, practice of craft, and lifelong reading of the masters who have gone before inform the hand to follow what the mind intends. If a poem wants to be a haiku, or an imagist poem, or a narrative poem, or if it yearns to cage itself within the beauty of an inherited form, it will inform the writer and resist all efforts to make it behave otherwise.*"

Implicated in the act of crafting poetry and extolling it, the poet never forgets the woman his books are consistently dedicated to, Cathy, his wife.

Shakespeare would have blushed in his secret wish to have forged "I Wake to Breathe Your Beauty In." *(Shakespeare's Sonnet XLI reads: "Thy beauty, and thy years full well befits, / For still temptation follows where thou art. / Gentle thou art, and therefore to be won, / Beauteous thou art..." Taken from Complete Works of William Shakespeare, Volume XVIII, Philadelphia David McKay Publisher, no year)*

Neruda would applaud this poem and cite his Sonnet XXVII, "... *tienes líneas de luna, caminos de manzana, // Desnuda eres azul como la noche en Cuba...*" *(Taken from En el corazón de un poeta. Instituto Cubano del Libro. Editorial de Ediciones Especiales, 2006, Biblioteca Familiar) ("You have moonlines, apple roads // Nude you are blue like the night in Cuba")*

Lee sets this piece in the after-waking moment, a soft, dream-like atmosphere nudging his hand to pen:

I wake to breathe your beauty in
your soft pink sex...

Bare sensuality, as the woman's, throbs in the lines. The phrase

... your shape procures
a note so faintly played
upon the felts
it leaves no mark...

suggests not that her shape is unsubstantial. It rather highlights in stunning poetic dissertation its delicacy, how it gently sits on the textile, kindling in the poet's eye a proud notion that her shape is worthy of posing for an artist.

Surmising she is asleep while he watches her, I could not refrain myself from recalling Margaret Atwood's loving ""Variation on the Word Sleep," a poem I commented in my first review book. *(In a Fragile Moment: A Landscape of Canadian Poetry. Hidden Brook Press, 2020)* I said then that poets – artists and singers as well – "*find a source of inspiration in watching their beloved ones sleep. Atwood has created a lyrically sweet poem, a peaceful contemplation of her lover.*"

So has Lee, singing to his wife, finding beauty in her, as much as Edgar Allan Poe expressed in his classic "To Helen" *("Helen, thy beauty is to me / Like those Nicean barks of yore, / That / gently, o'er a perfumed sea... // Thy hyacinth hair, thy classic face, / Thy Naiad airs..." Quoted from memory).* We tremble in the physicality of Lee's poem, how it fuses with "... *the interior journey, the progress of the soul...*" Roger Bell refers to in his Foreword to John B. Lee's book *This is How We See the World.* (Hidden Brook Press, 2017)

The poet achieves a crest where an illumination of spirituality communes with the physical element. One complements the other, eroticism handled with artistry:

… and I with sad melodies unsung
with wordless names and voiceless calling
dream the mild narcotic
of your gently moving breast.

If you were pleased with the previous poem, "Lovely Woman in the Lake, My Wife, My Love" is as delightful. Aphrodisia unfolds slowly, as the letters the poet gracefully molds, one by one, in his inspired ode to Cathy.

This is a poem that sensually drips water – remember Songs of Solomon: "*I arose to open for my beloved, and my hands dripped with myrrh, my fingers with flowing myrrh, on the handles of the bolt. I opened for my beloved...*" *(Also known as "Song of Songs" (The Holy Bible) www.biblegateway.com/passage/?search=Song...Songs)* – where the poet skillfully exploits the element:

… a kind of liquid everywhereness
fluxed within contours
inner motion and the softened fulcrums of your sex

The lake and the "Lovely Woman" unite: "*Where you move / water is desire – desire water.*" The poet is caught up in the sight he rejoices in and carves unstoppable imagery out of like magic *(excerpts):*

all flag and wind
is man
caught up

his architecture aping strength
until the instant of forgetting...

The last three lines are immortal, as much as the poet makes explicit what
he feels, what he aspires:

... reside within the incredible dominion of your flesh
thinking about being alive
and nothing else.

What we expect to find in a poem, an explanation of beauty, life – death,
a philosophy of the soul unfurling in tropes of genuine birth; what has
been said and written so many times now re-worded and re-engraved in
floating, streaming poetic lines, which finally perch upon our trembling
realization – an enlightenment – and construal of veiled things and feelings,
and sit upon our sentient, vulnerable hearts, is explored by the poet in
"By the Shore's Collapsing Waters I am Bound."

Lee finds it all and exposes it resorting to an inspiring source, the sea,
which he acknowledges in his closing simile, "... *like the surface of the sea.*"
He enters meditative, inquisitive realms only chosen ones tread on, leaving
behind his revelatory penning *(excerpts)*:

Something you notice
in memory
some half-forgotten pain
some darkening flaw of love...

The line "*The long shadow you cast / standing in your lifelight,*" invites to an
inward reflection of our lives, to a revision of that shadow we cast,
understood as influence, mark, legacy; that he puts in perspective for us
to see and ponder.

I leapt again in reading this poem and remembering mine, "The First
Day," a contemplative piece I sent to him and he generously praised and
offered advice for improvement – that other gift he has of helping others,

honoring James Deahl's words: "*No poet learns the craft without help and sage advice from those who have already achieved a higher level of writing.*" *(Taken from Under the Mulberry Tree: Poems for & about Raymond Souster. Quattro Books Inc. 2014. Edited by James Deahl)* I have been helped by many poet friends of "a higher level of writing."

In my piece I say, humbly, "*… awake at this hour in the sleepy waterside / I calibrate my existence as I surf / with the tide / weigh my crests and shallows / skin-deep essences retained / substantial unrepeated // this is where I stand, / before the primordial source. // my eyes receive awakening / this pulse of life refreshed / to embrace me / like the first day of all creation.*" *(Published In The Envoy 92, Newsletter of the Canada Cuba Literary Alliance. October, 2019, and republished in my second poetry book, This Pulse of Life, These Words I Found. Hidden Brook Press, 2021)*

Lee confers dreams a special significance in his poem, as we lie down and rise every day from our transit phase of sleeping and dreaming. Such phase is biologically mandatory in human and natural cycles, and is lyrically drafted by Lee in his poem's final lines:

The Kama sutra of many sleeps
where you curl and change
like the surface of the sea.

Dialectical in its underlying sinews, the poem claims for change – over sleep; change that must be channeled positively – in awakening, in our reflection of living, colored by the manifold interpretations sparkled in the readers through this allusion to Kama sutra. The whole poem below:

"By the Shore's Collapsing Waters"
I am Bound
There are certain ways of making brevity seem brief.
Something you notice
in memory
some half-forgotten pain
some darkening flaw of love
like a gnat in the gloaming.

The long shadow you cast
standing in your lifelight.
The Kama sutra of many sleeps
where you curl and change
like the surface of the sea.

One of my reviews of Lee's oeuvre led me to say that "*I had to force myself to commenting on only seven poems, tempted by scores of them!*" *(Read Lucky Seven: Monumental Architecture. A review of seven poems from John B. Lee's Bread, Water, Love (Poetry), in These Are the Words, by George Elliott Clarke and John B. Lee. In a Fragile Moment: A Landscape of Canadian Poetry. Hidden Brook Press, 2020)* Therefore, I will have to stop my analyses here briefly referring to the poem "Starless and Blue at Midnight."

Universe and nature are described and related in seven lines – a biblical-seven allusion? – where the poet uses attractive images like "*the moon has lost her clock*," poetically giving a personification symbolism to the satellite. The poet himself pauses to contemplate what he has been able to hold in his poet hand and sigh into a poem: "*... the water colder for that hour / where the bunting flutters / and goes quiet.*"

He charmingly bonds in one scene the "Baffin skies," "midnight," "the moon," "the mountains," "the water," even "that hour" and the fluttering "bunting." It is an observant, all-inclusive apprehension by the poet of what surrounds him at midnight: scenarios, phenomena, nature (fauna and landscape), time, open spaces ("skies") and references to absent objects ("starless"). The poet pans around the vista, from upper-layer observation through more earthward, far sights, to closer land "companion": "*the water colder...,*" and *in-mid-air creature that complies to the hour and "flutters and goes quiet*" – in the seventh line... Peace soars in place and time. Let's enjoy it fully:

"Starless and Blue at Midnight"
Baffin skies
starless and blue at midnight

the moon has lost her clock
hiding among the mountains
the water colder for that hour
where the bunting flutters
and goes quiet

In his Foreword to Richard Grove's *A Small Payback, Ode to Victoria Lake* (Hidden Brook Press, 2016), Lee said: "*In this book… you have the spirit of the place… A glimpse of grace. Rare and precious.*" I dare state Lee's "Starless and Blue at Midnight" captures that essence too, that spirit of the place flitting about in the tranquility provided after the bird "*goes quiet.*"

A further – and final – observation I do not want to obviate. Reading Lee's poems, especially "By the Shore's Collapsing Waters I am Bound" and "Starless and Blue at Midnight," I felt flashes of Al Purdy's poems "Pause," and "Red Leaves." *(For in-depth comparison you will have to read The Canadian Titan of Land and Time. A review of some of Al Purdy's poems in Beyond Remembering: The Collected Poems of Al Purdy (Poetry) (2000) Harbour Publishing. Canada; and of course these two poems in Beyond Remembering: The Collected Poems of Al Purdy)*

Purdy's "Pause" "*presents a moment when poet and reader sit together and watch. Dimensional layers are peeled off and a conundrum floats up for Al and for the reader, one combination where frontiers are blurred…*" *(Taken from the aforementioned review)* Admiringly, Lee journeys on this path of enigmas he poses to the reader (which he has posed to himself before), this earnest questioning and search for answers in "By the Shore's Collapsing Waters I am Bound."

On the other hand, the Purdy poem "Red Leaves" is, in Dennis Lee's statement, Purdy's "*broad movement in space-time.*" *(Taken from Al Purdy. Essays on his Works, Guernica Editions Inc., 2002, edited by Linda Rogers. Denis Lee's words in his essay "The Poetry of Al Purdy." He thoroughly analyzes this concept in Purdy's "Love at Roblin Lake")* Matters connected to the universe "*… and higher questions… and finally back to Purdy's line "this tranquil season," (ibidem)* reflect John B. Lee's own serious scrutiny of these subjects, as is skillfully evoked in "Starless and Blue at Midnight" and most of his poetry.

As I said at the beginning of this paper, George Whipple calls John B. Lee "*The greatest living poet in English.*" He adds that Lee "*… sows everyday experiences with a timeless gravity and awe.*" *(Both quotations on John B. Lee's back cover of This is How We See the World, Hidden Brook Press, 2017)* I have little to add – and keep my promise to stop – except that I am more than honored for having read, understood, learned from and e-met this transcending "*someone who writes poetry.*"

Allow me to quote, fully (with permission from Publisher and poet), two of Lee's poems in the book. I picked them to illustrate my previous analyses:

"Prologue:"
I retrieved this poem
from the rubble of my notes
as a child
would pluck a dead cat
from a demolition site.
I hold it swinging in air
like the scales of Athena
over my last conquest.
This poem
like the only moving part
in a Swiss timepiece
divines itself.

"I Wake to Breathe Your Beauty In"
I wake to breathe your beauty in
your soft pink sex
mummed like a secret-keeper's mouth
the stone imprisoned by its fall
could no more hang upon the wind
that I hold back this love
your shape procures
a note so faintly played
upon the felts
it leaves no mark

like a dustless butler's glove
and I with sad melodies unsung
with wordless names and voiceless calling
dream the mild narcotic
of your gently moving breast.

I close this section with "The Day Jane Fonda Came to Guelph." What interested me mostly about the poem is what I have stated before and will be stating on: the poets' gift to turn things around and give them that luster which makes them look, sound, feel, even smell differently.

The impact of a celebrity visit to the city is exquisitely described by Lee. It goes beyond logical human reaction: it affects things, nature, objects. In the halo of the visitor, magic falls upon the city. John B. Lee records the experience for posterity in his unique mastery to convey thoughts, images. Here, the poem, full:

When Jane Fonda came to Guelph
factory smoke
twisted in the air like half-naked catalogue models
and the river
lay in its bed all day
pretending its name was Marilyn.
All rearview mirrors
played their best angles like yesterday's rushes
and birds fluttered in their nests
like nervous hatcheck girls
under a whiskey sun
that poured itself out in dark corners
where the wind was a breathy Hollywood blonde
looking to get laid for a cameo.
Every storefront lothario preened and posed
while outside of the city dogs sang in the far hills until dark.
Yes, when Jane Fonda came to Guelph
even under the loose and tumbling
shook-down hair of willowy late-autumn rain

everything sashayed
and grew important for a while.

Two Thousand Seventeen (2018) Sanbun Publishers. New Delhi. India, was a two-poet collaboration between Lee and Richard Grove. As I quoted before, Lee has been able to craft poetry in his travels or as a result of those experiences, *"From all corners of the world he has brought poems"* (Pérez, Velázquez and González). This new book is proof.

The two poets' poetry sings of the every-day things that pulse in the lives and minds above culture, language or creed: family, friends, love, respect, places and memories. These motifs are served to the reader with delicate, humorous, intimate and honoring tidbits of nostalgia. Mr. Grove's and Mr. Lee's masterly and generously mold their distinctive styles.

Universal themes and subjects are recreated in their lines, bringing their lives to us, their remembrances of special locations that are special because their next of kin, their ancestors and their offspring, colored them with their presence through the years. Homeland is at the center of their writing, so are their families and many others whom they have met in their friendship-packed, ever-blessed journeys towards the timeless slumber.

Lee opens his section with a splendid, soul-caressing piece, "Living at the Monk Motel," that starts:

I wake in the morning
to the crimson hallelujah
of divine sunrise.

From there, a rainbow of depictions, narrations, colors, experiences carrying the reader elsewhere and everywhere *(excerpts)*:

brilliant-winged tropical hallucination
something from the forests of Sri Lanka
something from the treetops

of Costa Rica
the lost green song of a canopy
ringing the bells
and climbing up the Lilliputian ladders
of their farmhouse kitchen...

Lee also pays tribute to family, especially his mother, in "Blue Sorrow"
(excerpts):

Marilyn Monroe
and my mother
were born the same year
and my mother
born in the little house
on the hardscrabble farm near Mull Crossing
was also a great beauty
my mother
in
the apple orchard
wearing a ragged straw hat
her hair
still
long to her shoulders
captured in a late-summer photograph

In "Alive Enough," Lee reminisces and philosophizes most probably due to
the ancient winds surrounding him, trying to find answers to his questions
and doubts:

and I wondered for a moment
am I alive enough
to listen like
an infant-unborn
swimming
through water sounds
towards a second darkness
lost as I am in the first.

We will feel the romantic poet in Lee too, roaming physically and mentally, giving the readers an idyllic vision harmonized with a mature view of his own life in "Oh Silo My Columbarium":

for me
the ghost on the
hill of the family farm
comes shaded
in the white-shadow-shape
of the silo by the barns
for it has lost its all
from the
fragrant seasons
of my youth
when the air seemed sorghum
sweet
in the early fall
and the silage line
came greening up
the inner walls
like the harvest as a water line
in a handsome well.

These poems blend faith, tradition, time, death, and much more with outstanding expressive means and stylistic devices that never repeat themselves. The fountain of imagery expressed by both writers and the freshness in their style do not cease to amaze me.

As we move on through the poet's poetic legacy, we come to Lee's section "Bread, Water, Love" in *These Are the Words* by George Elliott Clarke and John B. Lee, also a 2018 Hidden Brook Press publication. In his Introduction to John B. Lee's "Bread, Water, Love" ("The elemental Is Monumental: A Contemplation of John B. Lee's Bread, Water, Love"), George Elliott Clarke stresses the poet's gift to make what's elemental a constituent of the monumental.

Like a journalist who covers the news, Lee presents the facts of outdoor life, mingles them with "the news" of indoor and "inside-the-head" life. He tells, as journalists do, what is true and what is real, harmonizing the objective and the subjective into a single piece of art. His brilliance lies in his original, indelible, sweeping signature, his "architectural" approach to language and reality.

"Bread, Water, Love" is an epic poem – obviously not in length, but in puissance – an ode to three elemental fulcra of humankind: sustenance in bread (our "daily bread"), bread that stands as nourishment. Water – one of the elements (natural environment, weather conditions, forces of nature; BUT also bread and wine that are used in Holy Communion) – so powerful, so overwhelming, so decisive in the making of life the way we know it, in designing the world we live in, so vital for existence. Then Love, spiritual sustenance, savior of it all.

Lee is aware that language is alive, that it can embrace us: *"in the living arms of language."* Lee keeps it very much alive and holds it in his genius poet hands to pour out excellent products. His coda for the poem is second to none, humans are lifted from *"our common sleep of dust"* to the *"gift of breath"* through the three pillars of life which echo across the poem in a repetition that gives strength to their role in the text.

Something I was drawn to was the use of phrases that replace words like death (*"common sleep of dust"*), and life (*"gift of breath"*). Lee celebrates life and makes a statement, *"what better words than these"*, in favor of bread, water, love.

Read these excerpts:

bread, water, love
if I lie
in the living arms
of language
what better words
than those–

bread, water, love
to give our common sleep
of dust
a gift of breath

Lee has been endowed with the magic of language. He sculpts language into another dimension. Asked about what processes cross his mind when he is in "creative mode," he said: "*I want to vanish into the work, so I have engaged in strategies for getting out of the way. One involves internalizing through learning, reading, practice, engagement, and distraction of the conscious mind, tricking it out of the room, so that the poem flows through the body onto the page with as little interference as possible.*"

In "Unmistakable Strangers" we think about a life that is hard socially speaking, but it is also hard for wildlife. Shortages, especially in harsh winters, knock on every door, house or forest. Lee talks about a human-animal connection, admires his wife for what she does, and recreates nature presenting, one by one, a procession of graceful, grateful creatures:

squirrels, exotic red-capped woodpecker, blue jays, common starlings…
finch… a plentitude of squirrels…
One particularly fat princely squirrel comes… in the morning
along with the early light.

Being the squirrel "*no longer anonymous,*" the poet suggests a new scenario of co-habitation between "*the nameless throng of the dog-worried neighborhood*" and the "*unmistakable stranger.*" The last stanza is sui generis, metaphors and similes deftly handled by the poet:
cold-nosed snow shrank to a blink,
… to a blink like wet paper gone water-grey in the gravel drive.

Lee moves from the natural to the human/social, he compares primeval nature with our "second nature." our built world. In the last four lines, as Elliott states, "*There is so much undiluted, unembarrassed, just frank and obvious excellence in such imagery.*" There is naked truth/reality. The "elemental" made "monumental" poetry.

A piece of joy for me is "ii" where the poet plays, like a sentient artist, with color, light, sound, illusions, where the last line deals a stab of mortality to the day. A wonderful simile is *"like the ghost bride of lost sailors"*:

... fog-in-the-morning
come in veils trailing over the lake
like the ghost bride of lost sailors.

He is captivated by what he sees – takes in:

how my pulse quickens
in this newly lonesome cold
and I am become the robin
wanting to be someone else's last thought
before sleeping
when the sky draws down
on aging daylight

"Beyond the last sandbar" is a poem for rest and contemplation. Poet imbued, focused on and lured by the majesty of the scenes before him. From the quiet "fresco" of the first stanza, *"gulls float at rest,"* *"circle of windless motion,"* *"rhythms of a sleepy measure in calm dreaming,"* *"lassitude of blue silk settling,"* to the lively ripples of *"Canadian geese... blinking their webbed feet coming in and going thence;"* to the ominous presence of *"a sudden hawk."*

I see humane aching – curiosity? – in the poet for knowing, *"I wonder,"* living *"in the wind,"* *"to be born in the rough nest of the aerie."*

The last stanza is as "sweet" as the poet's remembrance and as "lovely" as his knowing how *"the forest forgets and the forest recalls..."*: Mystic personification of the forest, a metaphor which carries also alliteration – an instinctive ingredient of all-time poetry, and of the English language – closes this precious piece.

As I have been trying to argue in this paper, Lee is a milestone in the rich mosaic of Canadian poetry, literature, culture, broadly viewed as human input and shaping of a heritage that is handed over from the past to us and will outlive this generation, next generations.

Lee's contribution and adherence to the long-standing tradition of celebrating nature – awesome, edifying, unavoidably present, whether we see it or not, whether we want to see it or not, is transcendental. Canada's formidable scenery owes to poets as much as they owe to its being so glorious. That is culture, whole, the natural one Canada generously exhibits, plus the created one these awesome poets beget enraptured by their nation and what it makes them feel: the objective-subjective all-embracing foundry of beauty and spiritual growth. Lee also celebrates life and turns his language and his style into forging tools leaving for us such poems.

No better insight into Lee than this quotation: "… *a true idiosyncrasy of style is the result of an author's success in compelling language to conform to his… experience.*" *(Taken from I.R. Galperin. Stylistics. Moscow Vyssaja Skola. 1981)* Lee's style has notably achieved that. It is monumental architecture.

One of the longest, yet most captivating journeys is about us. It includes a time ride to our ancestors and to lands beyond our borders and imag-ination. John B. Lee makes me look back at that thought with his book *Into a Land of Strangers* (2019) Mosaic Press.

He does it with an impressive journey to a millenary nation we look at with feelings of intrigue, distance, curiosity and respect for its greatness and its contribution to culture. Into the prevailing Chinese contextual vortex, Lee pulls other occurrences, characters, settings and situations.

Lee's writing gift has made him a recipient of as many awards as it is humanly possible. He has tirelessly crafted piece after piece in his long, prolific career. He has written nearly about everything with unique perspective and penmanship. He has memorialized his travelling exper-iences in books about his own and other countries as I have illustrated here.

Lee's own words are explanatory enough of his aspirations as a writer: *"I want, in poems… the soul to thrill to a commingling of temporal and extra-temporal things… I want the past alive, the present reified and the future remembered in words so perfect they sing alone and in chorus the name of names." (Taken from John B. Lee's essay "Even at the Worst of Times" in And Left a Place to Stand On, Hidden Brook Press, 2009)*

Into a Land of Strangers is about "temporal and extra-temporal things." It sings to family roots, life, sacrifice and honor. Lee takes words, touches them and – like King Midas turning things into gold – waxes them into indelible witnesses, and erects them as mementoes of events and lives past.

Lee tells us he was *"born into a family of bibliophiles."* It planted on him an unquenchable thirst for the poetic, and led him to his wondrous encounter with muses, who have never since then abandoned him. The poet embarks on a discovery epic *"into a land of strangers."* Even though it remains true that place, people and events are foreign to many, what is depicted in Lee's own early experiences (*"Chinese characters displaying the exotic logograms of the realm of the Han"*) is now masterfully decoded for us from the very outset and through both prose and poetry.

As he accurately expands on the idea, I quote Roger Bell in reference to Lee's manifold abilities: *"Wherever John Lee takes us… be it China, Thailand, Korea, Baffin Island… or the shores of our great lakes, readers must be aware of the archetype of his journey. Yes, the physical voyage has weight, but it is really the interior journey, the progress of the soul, that counts. While he so fluently details the world around him, Lee is more deeply in search of the ch'i, the vital force… something just beyond the circle of light." (Taken from Roger Bell's Foreword to John B. Lee's book This is How We See the World, Hidden Brook Press, 2017)*

The book is a stunning chronicle, as overwhelming as the nation being portrayed, of Lee's great-aunt, a missionary in China. It took him time, *"It would involve another fifteen years of maturing as a writer before it occurred to me to return to that fertile ground and to tell the story of grandma's aunt Ida,"* to finally give shape to the book. As a reader, I could not avoid being involved in the historic and bibliographical facts Lee exposes with a magnifying glass that crosses time and territories.

In a previous review about James Deahl I stated: *"Poets have a gift: they provide light, a different one. They craft words and images in ways no one else can and lay them down for us to marvel at a world that had been there but we hadn't noticed."*

This is what John B. Lee does over and over again unfalteringly, magically. He has uncovered a strangers' land; but when you finish "visiting" it through Lee's genuine vision and artistry, you realize the land is no longer that far, nor is it just strangers what you have in mind.

Lee's is essentially a poetry book – and more – conceived in love and serious research. It is a tribute that highlights, in polished harmony with himself and the universe, the meticulous researcher, the caring nephew, the formidable prose writer and poet. He has emphasized that *"I want, in poems… the spirit to surround and be surrounded by an interplay between the deep wells of the self and the stars beyond the farthest stars we might dream…" (Taken from John B. Lee's essay "Even at the Worst of Times" in And Left a Place to Stand On, Hidden Brook Press, 2009)*

To me it is an in-depth poetic treatise of Chinese lifestyles and epochs, one that flows with textual merging yet grants each part its self-standing worth. It surpasses Chinese frontiers connecting allusions to the rest of the world, to conflicts, misfortunes, etc.

Suffice it to read Lee's initial words on how much he studied to give birth to this work: *"In doing research for this book, in addition to reading and gleaning important details from my cousin Dorothy's genealogical records, I read dozens of books on China including revisiting Chinese poetry in translation through several anthologies…"*

The poetry section presents facts, carved by Lee with the hand of a master. He is able to narrate history ánd fate, beginnings and ramifications, sorrows and consolation, catalyst tragedies and sequels, marked by gender-signed, individual plights framed in the unreceptive end-of-19th-century *"interesting times"*:

when your papa died
after an accident in the forest
your mother widowed
you and your sister
suddenly
fatherless
as you lived there then sorrowing on the cusp
of
first menses
three women
in a manless house
you
mourned the loss
though the consolation
of faith
gave
sorrow meaning.

Lee stands philosophical amidst all this unfurling of lives and happenings. He holds invisible threads that poetry weaves and surrenders to him, thus he becomes a traveler who explains:

the past must disappear
as warmth through mist
becomes
a clarifying blur
of cooling light...
the present
burns like
sunlit chrome
a brilliant
blindness flashing
in the mind
too bright to see
or seen as fire
sees its fuel in flame...

the
future's
like a water moon
where light lies
twice removed
in mysteries of deep
refraction
tilted by a shaded stone
transfixed in motion
like white-washed granite in the sky.

In a feat of conceptual consistency, Lee has posited this before: *"… I want the past alive, the present reified and the future remembered in words so perfect they sing alone and in chorus the name of names." (Taken from John B. Lee's essay "Even at the Worst of Times" in And Left a Place to Stand On, Hidden Brook Press, 2009)*

From its factual-experiential basis, Lee's poetry is aware of the dynamics of times and the role of motion; but it also regales us with – as in all his books – superb literary expertise in exceptional similes:

the
future's
like a water moon…
like white-washed granite in the
sky.

A feature I appreciate is that Lee addresses his aunt, there is a conversation between nephew and aunt. He creates a bond with the past, not an empty or impersonal or futile one, but a significant, transcendent, face-to-face tale-telling. Somewhere in mid storytelling Lee does shift to third-person narrative, still honoring his genealogy, Chinese culture and history, and he solidly sets his poetry foundation on quotes by great Chinese men and the Bible.

At the center of it all stays Lee's aunt. His constant returns to her life, the impressions she left on him, either by stories he heard, material he read,

or a picture, tell us of how relevant she is to him and to the book. His
poem "At Least for Now" gives us a woman in all her particulars, physique
and costume,

a lean woman
her long-boned body
draped in a black silk
dress
she is seated
in a stiff-spined rocker
her well-shod
feet crossed
at the ankles
adorned in high-top shoes
laced
almost to the knee
like greaves,

along with existential, mental, even theological attitudes and projections:

she grips
the arms of the chair
as though at any moment she means to
rise
or rather resist
the weightless phantom
that floats her
spectral complexion
from the white collar
of this pale-fleshed visage
she, with the self-assured
physiognomy of the righteous
certain of the purity of her Christian soul
with
the rectitude
of a widowed woman
bearing the carriage and
posture of
her place in time.

A complete delineation of her fortitude and endurance is skillfully revealed by the poet in the closing lines:

she poses
in her parlour in China
and she
means
to be herself forever
at least for now.

Well-informed, tender, natural, historical, biographical, direct, cultivated, freshly lyrical are some of the adjectives I can use to talk about John B. Lee's homage book. I can safely say as well that I felt it is slightly different from Lee's other works I have read: a mixture of biographical work, poetry types, prose and verse coexisting in finely distributed order and pertinence.

Picking from my comments in the previous book Lee shared with Elliot Clarke, I can state that elemental and monumental fit in this new book's theme and scope. If you want to plunge into a rapid's broad turmoil of love, calamity, personal and world history, hopes and sketches of human/social/universal significance told with scrutinizing solemnity, come to Lee's *Into a Land of Strangers*.

Roger Bell validates my invitation in saying: "*I encountered a writer of greater scope, and poetry even more profound and wide-ranging, than I was accustomed to… John Lee's wide and deep observations of this wondrous life… the gravitas he brings to his visions of this world.*" *(Taken from Roger Bell's Foreword to John B. Lee's book This is How We See the World, Hidden Brook Press, 2017)*

If you are willing to know of China's splendid cultural mosaic, I strongly suggest you start with this book before you venture into further readings about a land and a family tree that are by now more familiar to me. Enter Lee's travels, thorough findings, dreams and poetics flooding this book:

when I see
the moon
over China

I cannot help
but recall… how
lonesome the light
without us
how dark
those brilliant
beams.

Do rejoice in those *"brilliant beams"* and glow with anticipation: there will be more, as Lee told me that "… *my favourite poem of my own is the one I have not written yet.*"

I have alluded to Pablo Neruda in my paper. John B. Lee's 2020 Hidden Brook Press book, *Darling, may I touch your pinkletink*, opens its pages with various quotations. One of them is from Neruda, "*I want to do with you what spring does with the cherry tree.*" *(Taken from Twenty Love Poems, Pablo Neruda)*

Both hilarious and revelatory, the book is divided in four general sections (Childhood, Adolescence, Youth, Old Age) preceded by many quotations illustrating aspects of sex, and short personal stories about the sex theme in his family told by Lee with carefree fluency. Such organization allows the reader to transit with the poet through the stages of his discovery of sex. Lee does not relinquish his conjurer's touch to craft imagery and story into a poem. In "Anatomy Lesson" (Childhood) he writes *(excerpts)*:

your coral-coloured female body
fascinating to behold in lamp-lit soft relief
like the morbidezza
of a work of art
I confess
I was filled with awe
to glimpse a flash
of the incomparable beauty
of the fold of flesh

Curiosity holds the learner's hand in any field. This Lee speaks about it in

"Seeking the Words for the Body" (Childhood) *(excerpts)*:

we were there together
in the two-gendered upstairs hallway
on the farm
out of earshot
of the adult world
when we were young
and body-wonderful children
curious to know
the most perfect word
for those private places
we dare not touch
even by saying aloud
forbidden words
we were tasting the sinful lexicon
of that devil's dictionary

The last two lines are sensuously yet innocently provocative, a fact supported by defining sexual parts as beauty:

look down and tell me
about beauty then ...

The way in which the poet addresses these topics shows how well-educated he was, especially by his mother, who inculcated a shame-free approach to sexuality. He fondly recalls her in the initial prose part of the book: "... *And my mother took me aside and said, "No shame. It's only natural to be curious. You must always remember to respect your body." And though I blushed to be schooled, I cherished her kindness forever. And I tell you this story in love and remembrance.*"

In "Oh, how very, very sweet! How lovely!" (Childhood) the poet holds the mystery of night and nature and blends it with sex allusions, well-balanced, hintful in an interplay of meanings to describe a budding awakening to sex *(excerpts)*:

did you dream of me
as I once dreamed of you
in the fragrant darkness
of a farmhouse night
tasting the fruit
of the knowing tree
where it lingered in wait
of the sentient hand
like the heart responding in the breast
of evening
oh to wind the fragile stem
to the breaking point
to feel it leap within the branch
that learns the loss in the shivering leaf
like the lifting away
of a bird in flight
that fluttering of absent wings
where the body
hosts all sleep
eventual and perfect sleep
> *and oh, how very, very sweet!*
> *how lovely!*
the bountiful and fertile beauty come alive
in the secret garden of our youth...

The section Adolescence starts with "Origin." Lee does not forget God is
the ultimate Creator *(excerpts)*:

imagine God's great finger
sculpting Eve
shaping her there
in the malleable mud
of her beautiful body
tracing her breasts and
forming the labial petals
and pink throat

of her flower
setting the pearl of pleasure
at the choral-coloured threshold...

A full-fledged awakening is strongly felt now in "And there was this."
With metaphorical feats, Lee depicts sex:

... I longed to know
with my tongue, my eyes
my nose, my hand, to taste
to see to scent to feel
to savour the fragrance
like a scent of a mollusk rolling in from the sea
the colour of flesh, the flavour of musk
like cider and salt the texture of watered clay
and human heat and satiny damp
of that enclosure and depth
for all possible explorations of intimate flesh
in the pleasure petals of her inner sex
surrendering all as one might a flower
and she opened her thighs
to the centre of divine desire
as though in the book of the world
she flexed her ruffled pages
and I read

From section Youth, I propose the readers "... and this." We are in the presence of an erotic poem, carved meticulously by the poet, where biblical allusions overlap with rich imagery. The phrase "and this" is highly suggestive; it leaves in the readers' minds only the cue, the rest is to be imagined, anticipated by them at the burning threshold of innuendo, sensations and cravings. Lee's metaphorical sleight-of-hand does not cease to amaze us,

remove the leaf my love
where knowledge makes you shy

and I will
be the shade beneath
the restless shadow
of a walking eye
to call it sin
improves on darkness
darker still within
the moon-fold
of a silent kiss
the hurry-hearted sigh
one silver tear to cry
and this …

As we have commented before, many poets include light in their poetic musings, oftentimes as opposed to darkness. Lee is one of them. In the section Old Age, he holds it in his hand coupling it with sex in the poem "The Light that Sees Us." *(excerpts)*:

I am not alone
in the multi-mirrored room…
flexing my limbs in straight-arm flight
like the wing beats
of a human bird
my body unwillingly reflected in silver
flashes of artificial light
meanwhile
in the strange intimacy
of the gymnatorium
a young woman
lying on the floor
engages in a rapid series
of pelvic thrusts
breathing harder with each
subsequent exertion as though
she were responding to the illusory
movements of a phantom lover

and I am not the last bad angel
betrayed by the beautiful energy of a blue sky
I am not Icarus
my wet feathers gummed in warm wax
falling to the floor
through the dark melt of a sun-drenched sea, no
I'm simply an old man
standing with
the marionette of my will
strung to the muscled machinery
of my bones
and so I carry on
until…
I make my exit
doing my very best
to seem like the silent departure
of a careful father
to the young woman
breathing heavily, her eyes closed in concentration
as it is with each of us
when we hold
our individual and otherwise invisible darkness
as though it were enough
to make the light that sees us disappear

John B. Lee is a world-class writer transcending place and time. It was place, timing – and friends – that led him to write one of the poems he likes best, "So, this is a place of places." I wish to finish my journey besides him blending two pieces he has published in previous books but he includes now in his new book as editor *The Beauty of Being Elsewhere* (Hidden Brook Press, 2021).

In my introductory words for the Hidden Brook Press book *Flying on the Wings of Poetry*, 2020 (a publication I will refer to later), I said, "*… I must say this book we are presenting tells us dreams are also possible in other places that feel like home. At least this is what the four fine poets visiting these pages prove to* *us. Their way to write about themes showing their involvement at an affective-creative level with geographies far from their homes reveals a connection that we appreciate as readers. They cannot elude — nor do I think they have tried — the charm, the magnetic force pulling them in, prompting them to craft fact-depicting, mostly experiential, strings-attached poetry."*

This is so extraordinarily true about *The Beauty of Being Elsewhere*, another 2021 publication by hard-working, prolific Hidden Brook Press and edited by Canadian gem John B. Lee. His summoning power groups more than a hundred poets in an anthology that continues the wonderful work done by James Deahl with *Tamaracks: Canadian Poetry for the 21st Century* (Lummox Press, 2018).

This time, *The Beauty* features Canadians and non-Canadians. If *Tamaracks* exhibited a momentous spectrum of exclusively Canadian poetry for readerships everywhere with themes proposed by the poets, *The Beauty* unfolds with an attractive, I'd say "exotic," leitmotif, traveling. Emily Dickinson (a Lee favorite) speaks to us in the book's opening quotations, *"Go travelling with us!... By routes of ecstasy."* The quotations page finishes with an excerpt from one of Lee's poems, *"… a Cuban evening feeling the lovely melancholia of being elsewhere …"*

Reverence and flashback reflection are felt in the pieces included in the book, outlined in the editor's Preface, lines wherefrom the title was born: *"… inspired by the journey or the sojourn these poems were written and have been gathered here to honour the beauty of being elsewhere."* Every poet offers his/her experience, the wide-open hues of each pair of eyes enticed by what they perceive and breathe in. It is an entire anthology singing the marvels of learning, seeing, touching and safeguarding in the mind's niche *"things of beauty"* dazzling like a rainbow, heart-touching as if an angel's invisible soaring reached there.

John B. Lee's editing is magnificent but he also turns into an agile stair-climbing tour guide roller-coastering us from sweet little Cuba in the poem I wish to comment on, "So, this is a place of places," *"we climb the four hundred steps / to the Cross of Holguin / and Manuel says / "So, this is a place of places ...*" / *and we stand* / *above the city...*" to cyclopean China in "Climbing the Great Wall of China": "*I climb the stairs* / *to where the great wall* / *breaks its spine* / *along the grey-green ridge* / *of smoke and fog above the Yanshan mountains...*"

Readers will appreciate this new book's "journey." I found familiar names brought to this feast of poetry by Lee – some I have written reviews about or recognized from *Tamaracks* – and ran into new ones. Mostly, I have shared the stirred nostalgia of traveling I have enjoyed too, limited but experiential; short but indelible. As to *The Beauty*, it is unlimited in scope, widely experience-based, warmly long, and absolutely indelible for poets, editor and readers. Let's see Lee's own elucidation of what traveling may mean, an excerpt from his poem "I Too Can Show the Way":

Where would you lead me friend?
into what future
and from what past
and by what light guide
and for what purpose go
and to what end
and with what faith ...

In traveling we meet with the past, savor it; we envision tomorrows, lean hopefully on them pedestaled on our present. In traveling we grow and become informed humans, we are invested with the gift of constructive comparison and contrast, we forge purpose, seek end and stand trustfully on faith. In traveling our individuality waxes as universality that we lacked as "locals," and we learn to appreciate "thereness" and otherness in geographies we had at our fingertips and encounters we embraced. And after our Ulysses ventures, we value more our *home sweet home*, where we sit before a desk and thank Calliope, Erato and Terpsichore for the blessing of poetics. We must thank John B. Lee for this new chapter of fine poetry, sceneries, people and beauty.

He wrote "So, this is..." inspired by Cuba – Holguín, The Hill of the Cross – above all inspired by a mixture of beauty, stark realities and friendship, both right before him in a moment of special significance. This is how Lee remembers the moment when Manuel's phrase stayed with him: *"The phrase "so this is a place of places," was purely conversational… my Cuban companion Manuel said to me "so this is a place of places." He simply said it in casual acknowledgement of the importance of that particular locale. I immediately stored it away in my mind bank for future reference…"* The fragment describing that experience is the following:

we climb the four hundred steps
to the Cross of Holguin
and Manuel says
"So, this is a place of places …"
and we stand
above the city
looking east where the sun
is laving the neighbourhood…

There was beauty in the friend's words, *"So, this is a place of places …"* setting it as a landmark, as there was beauty in *"the sun is laving the neighborhood."* The poet builds distinctive experience upon experience as they move beyond, pushing into the kiln of poetry images apparently disparate yet melted in Lee's foundry:

…   another day
we descend to the west
follow a crumbled trail
down the green stone
pathway knobbed
with bone and broken glass
and ancient coral from the sea…

To complete this aesthetic fabric, the poet backstitches into the end of the poem a reality of social implications entrenched in the Cuban stained-glass, where joy – a typically colorful Cuban trait – closes the piece. In "Apotheosis" – a piece he emailed to me – Lee recalls what he saw and later became the poem, *"The boy moving through the street with a heart in his hand is an image based upon a boy we saw that day happily carrying his purchase, which was clearly a heart..."* Let's read this in poem form now:

and I hear
a sudden laughing in the street
where a shirtless boy
with a heart in his hand
a heart which is
hand sized—a goat's heart
I think, or perhaps a sheep's—
comes chasing the joy of his own way home.

A comment John B. Lee made to me in an email reads, *"I am grateful to have had the opportunity to write the poems that visit my desk and flow through my pen. I am simply a vessel, and I am thankful when the muses visit."* Read "So, this is a place of places," dedicated to Manuel Velázquez and Richard Grove (Tai), two of his dearest friends standing next to him. You will notice the muses fluttering, you will see the human vessel hold words that flow through his pen and pause to delight us, as always. So, this is a poem of poems.

(For Manuel and Tai)
we climb the four hundred steps
to the Cross of Holguin
and Manuel says
"So, this is a place of places ..."
and we stand
above the city
looking east where the sun
is laving the neighbourhood
and staining the squares
like the light
lacquering of old wood
for the restoration of a much-loved dollhouse village
another day
we descend to the west

follow a crumbled trail
down the green stone
pathway knobbed
with bone and broken glass
and ancient coral from the sea
we are coming down
through the nuisance ground
with its frail rust
and tin aromas
its pungent swill of vegetative rot
and paper scuttle sounds
when I see
the gyre of ravens
hovering and circling
over the blackened body
of a bent-ribbed dog
disarticulated by maggot work
and the carrion hunger
of those scavenging shadows
as I pass
I look and take in
the final sneer of canus lupus
many days dead
and I think of the night
with its tongue of stars
and the sorrowful solitude
of that morbid moment
of his passing
that full exhale of his
final lying down
and am sad
not to have been there
to give comfort
as my companion says
"see there"
pointing to the green valley

dividing the urban boroughs
"to the left of that bottleneck
is where the poorest of the poor live
you will know them
by their naked children"
and I hear
a sudden laughing in the street
where a shirtless boy
with a heart in his hand
a heart which is
hand sized—a goat's heart
I think, or perhaps a sheep's—
comes chasing the joy of his own way home.

The poet explains the realities and by-images to bring up this excellent poem: "*I maybe conflated two visits to Holguín, but one of them involved either climbing the steps or descending by way of the steps, one involved driving to the top, and that same day, Tai, Cathy and I descending by way of the back trail through the nuisance ground. Everything in the poem is based upon that experience.*"

The poet wrote our next poem when "*… my wife and I had the privilege of traveling to China. While we were there, along with about thirty fellow travelers we visited the Great Wall and I wrote this poem about that experience. "Climbing the Great Wall of China" won the 2017 Literary Encyclopedia Award.*" Let's read the whole poem:

I climb the stairs
to where the great wall
breaks its spine
along the grey-green ridge
of smoke and fog above the Yanshan mountains
and as I rise
I carry nothing more
than a shadow's weight of daily cares
and as I glance
I am amazed to see
how worn away by walking

are the stones
beneath my feet
how smoothed as though
by water over time
and leather trod
eroded by the come and go
of hordes of trekking solitudes
and as I touch
a single shape of chiseled rock
I feel the slave's fardel
the spirit burden of a broken life
the fragment of an empirical fear
the horse's heavy heartbeat
on the warring earth
the blackened hoof
that thunders on the steppe
with arrows singing
in a mind of troubled dreams

I pause
to let a lucky tourist
take a photograph
his friend
leans smiling as she breathes
to catch her breath
her bosom heaves *alive alive* and lets it go

I'm warm enough to wait a while
my quickened pulse
is like my father
at my morning door
it knocks to wake
an answer from my over-weary bones

and if he's there, or not
I rise
and seek the purchase
of a greater height than this

The year 2020 was very fertile for John. As I said, I would comment on more publications with Hidden Brook Press. One of them is *Flying on the Wings of Poetry*. I was given the honor of being the editor. The book, in Spanish and English, invited four Canadian poets (John B. Lee, Antony Di Nardo, Laurence Hutchman and Richard Grove).

In my Introduction I explained that the poets' poems travel with their exploring lines. In Lee's case, he sent me poems that reflected his Cuba memories: *"I've sojourned on that beautiful island in the company of family, friends, fellow poets, and Cuban writers, and though I am destined to remain a tourist I long to return a traveler, stronger in broken places, knitting the us-and-them into one community of one people."*

Thus we read exploration lines from "Stronger in Broken Places": *"out there just beyond the edge of ice where the blue beauty of moving water begins to shoulder over the white line."* We see Lee glide, rise, plummet with facts and feelings in a phantasmagoria of metaphors in "One Morning in Mayabe": *"a lone vulture soars, kiting the thermals the black flag of his dropshadow drifting echo-darkness over the mango groves caressing the orchards by the lake as though with the sorrowful breath of a widow's veil,"* and we feel his rejoicing or suffering in "Forgetful": *"here within this sand-white arc of bent bones long-lost in the disinterment of a deep grave at the sad moment when the heart drops through as on some archeological grey-water gloaming when heaven refuses the light loss."* Finally, we ease into a poem we have approached before:

"On the Beauty of Being Elsewhere"
I look out through
window glaze freshly frosted in last-night's snow
like the clinging there of new-washed linen
and beyond that glimpse
the sublimation of bushes
those fine-boned creatures
purified by winter
even where wind song
seems at this white hour
in the burning cold

overfull with sunlight calcified
like chalkstone—oh my Ontario morning
I am saying farewell
as I'm rising in the belly of this silver bird
emerging into a post-prandial blue
walking the humid torpor
of a Cuban evening
feeling the lovely melancholia
of being elsewhere

like a rose of ice
I water away
una rosa blanca
dying in the crystalline wave
Irish linen grown old
a snowflake on the tongue
of a child reciting Martí
amused by a poem he knows
as he knows in a moment
of ice and water
and water and sky's blue aspic
concealing the invisible flavour of light

SandCrab Books published in 2018 the fourth volume of the Bridges Series Books, *Where the Heart Lies*, with two Canadian and two Cuban poets. The poems' core significance had to do with writing from the heart about places it has been touched by, topics emerging from a sentient identification with them. *Flying on the Wings of Poetry* follows that chord leading beyond the poets' frontiers.

The book makes it evident that poetry nurtures and uplifts; that poets are everywhere. It is their duty and pleasure to discern the many realities offered to us with different eyes and present them to people. This is what Lee and the other three poets have achieved, outstandingly, with their *hearts upon their sleeves*, as reads the title of the fifth Bridges Series Books volume (I am commenting this book here too). I cannot call this "heart-related" aspect of poetry publishing by Hidden Brook Press or its imprint, SandCrab Books, a mere coincidence. The bond between poets and context, between their gift and their product at the service of life, is significantly appreciated in this new book and flaps like a proud banner for the publisher, who always aims at the best, at the most representative, heartfelt literature. Lee has certainly contributed to this golden representation of Canadian poetry.

The CCLA Bridges Series Books (a two-Canadian, two-Cuban bilingual SandCrab Books production), volume V, was privileged to have four high-caliber poets (John B. Lee, Roberto Manzano, Lourdes González and Richard Grove). In my Foreword as editor, I said that we would be reading *"poets whose achievements impressively precede and present them to the readers as prophets in and outside their own lands."* In *The Heart Upon the Sleeve*, we are in the presence of fine representatives of contemporary poetry in Canada and Cuba.

In reading the two Canadian poets, I can list salient features: deep connection to the land; identification with nature and wild life; a rooted sense of belonging to Canadian geography; a feeling of proud nationality /nationhood; freshness and versatility in the use of expressive means and images; etc. Other traits are particularly salient and heart-warming: their commitment to family and values and the poets' constant reminiscences of childhood and their recollection of friends and friendship.

John B. Lee's writing gift has made him a recipient of numerous awards, as I have said. Lee's contribution and adherence to the long-standing tradition of celebrating nature – awesome, edifying, unavoidably present, whether we see it or not, whether we want to see it or not – is rock-solid. Read these lines from "How Deep the Water Goes":

... the ducks are sleeping
on the silver surface
of the lake
six or seven
mallard drakes

their heads turned
tailward
their bills
tucked in their feathered wings…

Lee revels in life turning his language and style into forging tools leaving us with such poems. Lee's elegance has notably achieved that: he eases us into the natural world, the coupling of rain and soil, for example, and the chain of unfolding events, revealing the magic of what otherwise might seem like ordinary (from "What Drew Us All Out"):

… there at the wintering
edge of a
glazier's dream
what stilled their motion
like the wet tip
of a painter's brush or
the nib of a pen at the moment of pausing
with unwritten words yet to come

A final thought to conclude this paper is that John B. Lee is both an implicated beholder of life around him and a seer of the human soul: he elaborates on these universal themes with word-codes I have been able to construe on my learning path across his work. Lee is, undoubtedly, a favorite of the muses, an architect of form, content and feeling.

Lee has been given the extraordinary genius of word and language not just to use it the way we mortals do: he is a chosen one – our five gems are – who knows the ins and outs, ups and downs and left and right of sculpting word and language into poetry. Once we put down one of his books, we will be experiencing an after-reading sensation lingering inexhaustible, wondrous – and monumental, as George Elliot Clarke has termed Lee's poetry.

DON
GUTTERIDGE

Ruthless

And me composing poems:
inklings I tease
towards some sense
in words whetted upon
the wheel of memory
and swerving askance
upon the page where they lean
upright, enlinked,
ready to be swallowed whole,
raw and ruthless
in rhythmic pursuit
of the truth.

Don Gutteridge

Life closes and opens doors for us in ways we hardly ever expect or even hope or want to. Don Gutteridge's extraordinary career as an acclaimed writer had its origins early in his childhood. In an email he commented to me:

"I wrote my first story ate age 8 and my first poem at age 12, and I've been writing almost daily ever since. When a poem "comes right" I am happy with it. I give it a day and a second look and that's it."

This is what he tells us in his bio: *"In October 1944 I contracted rheumatic fever and was hospitalized for a week. The high fever opened the valves of my heart… Dr. Christie… ordered complete bed rest for seven months. I was a precocious reader and spent my bedridden hours reading whatever I could find. I never left the bed once until May of 1945."*

1945 marks then the auspicious beginnings of this outstanding Canadian author. School contexts and his teachers also influenced him: *"I returned to school to finish grade two with the support of my wonderful teacher, Mrs. Young, who brought me homework to keep me up to date. I wrote my first story for Miss McDonald, my grade three teacher, (and a poem about it in God's Geography). From that time on I found a group of fast friends in the village whom I have put into poems and novels. It was a great life (as the books show)."* Eventually, during the 1960s, he became a teacher; teaching became a passion for him: *"I instantly fell in love with teaching."*

Gutteridge has intensely and extensively recreated his *"great life"* in his books. His poetry and novels have brought to us years of his life. We wonder as we read him if there was any event or character he has left out. In his answers to a survey I sent him, Don explains: *"I write on many themes over a long life, but more recently I have concentrated on memories of childhood experiences, friends, romantic crushes and sexual awakening, on elegies for my beloved wife and grandson who've passed away recently, tributes to friends and poems about the process of writing poems."*

When we read his work, we cannot fail in finding all his experiences outlined, elaborated on, colored in the excellent penmanship we enjoy across his oeuvre. Names of people, places (Point Edward being an unavoidable one), schools, locations, flash through the hundreds of pages we could bind together in all his books.

As I mentioned above, Gutteridge had an almost unisonous start at writing poetry and prose. In his bio he recalls this gift always stayed with him:

"I thought that if I were to become a novelist I had better learn to write dialogue. (I learned later in the decade by taking the advice of Alice Munro: that dialogue comes naturally from the creation of strong characters put in the same room.) Meanwhile I had had my first poem published in a real magazine: "This Maple in my Fallen Yard" in the Fiddlehead (1961 or 1962 and republished in The Village Within). Encouraged I started to write both short lyrics about Point Edward and several long poems about the Jesuits in Huronia, Champlain and LaSalle."

By this time, Gutteridge was collecting what he had planted. Novels, poems, and substantial advice given by Munro started to chart his course. The pieces of advice and influences he had were obvious and durable:

"Favourite authors are Hopkins, Dickinson, Hardy Alice Munro and many others. I am from a working-class family and there were few books in the house. I was encouraged to write by my aunt." (Taken from his answers to my survey)

A key "icebreaker" in the literary world was *God's Geography*, about which Michael O Nowlan said, *"Don Gutteridge, who has established himself as an authentic voice for Canadian literature, has produced an unusual text in God's Geography. It may be classified as a book of poetry, which it is; but it goes far beyond that dimension. It is really an album of memories… God's Geography is a stirring piece of work that provokes memory. It is the kind of word-experience one would obtain by translating the family album into verse. There is much here for many readings. Like his memories, Gutteridge's work strengthens with time."*

He started to write short lyrics about Point Edward and long poems about the Jesuits in Huronia, Champlain and LaSalle. In 1967 he read *Strange Empire* by John Kinsey Howard and began work on a series of poems about Louis Riel. This is how he reminisces it: *"… eventually* (I finished it) *as Riel: A Poem for Voices. I sent it off to Fred Cogswell at Fiddlehead and he agreed to publish 500 copies if I would subsidize the printing. Somehow, with a growing family and a new apartment in Inglewood Park, I squeezed out $200 and my first of more than 65 books was published in 1968. I was an author."*

Riel: A Poem for Voices, a historical narrative poem published in 1972 by Van Nostrand Reinhold Ltd., came after an "accidental" occurrence while Don was watching TV: "*… I remember being fascinated by the play, the story, and the man." (Taken from the book's Afterword by Gutteridge).* The book was a result of both passion and meticulous study. Upon reading G. F. Stanley's biography of Riel and John Kinsey Howard's *Strange Empire: The Story of Louis Riel*, he furthered on the topic. As he stated in his Afterword, he was "*making poetry out of history." (ibidem)*

I wish to quote a small fragment from this formidable book just as a brief example of how spiritual and influential it is. The fragment speaks of the Métis connection with earth, the rooted conceptions they had, a bond that accompanied Riel all his life:

They were walking: as a Métis always walked
Because a man could feel the Mother Earth through the palms
Of his feet, and know the firmness of her flesh
And the great unturning heart at the centre of her...

Readers will relish in the spirituality of Don's words, the deep-seated recognition of the earth's significance, acknowledging it as an animate being.

Oberon Press published in 1973 his *Coppermine*. It is a narrative book whose center can be initially elucidated in the fragment below. There is transcendence, history and fine imagery in these few lines:

Matonabbee speaking
"Where the mouth of the grand river opens
To swallow the sea, lies the Copper-mine:
And they say the metal sits there in chunks
As big as a bison's flank...

Borderlands, Oberon Press (1975), is a story based on facts. John Jewitt was a prisoner of the Nootkas during three years until he was rescued. Gutteridge took that and turned it into the poem we have. On the book's back cover we read: *"His* (Jewitt's) *remarkable story is the point of departure for the moving poem."*

Borderlands is indeed a touching poem. Rich imagery outstands in it. How it ends, Maquina's (Chief of the Nootkas) words, stays with us linguistically – for its expressive means – and culturally – for its impact, vision, wisdom and resolved hortation:

We are the people
of the coast, we
make an edge
against the sea

My body is a beginning,
a coast of skin
for the sea-dream
of my race

Let us inhabit
all borderlands

let us sing our morning-songs
before the sea rises
to claim her coast

Oberon Press continues publishing Gutteridge. In 1976 the public is offered *Tecumseh*. On the book's back cover we read: *"Gutteridge is the kind of poet who can make poetry that is at once public and passionate, at once true to the actual human event and epic in scale, solemn, prophetic."*

Passionate, human, somber and visionary is the entire book, embodied in the closing piece:

This dawn-light is
ember-thin, it
quickens and

             dismembers
me

I am fading
into the bleached
bone-beauty of

          poems

I am everywhere
photographed in the
darkest rooms

I am the
passionate statue
in each of your parks

I am the
poet in his pure

             air

(remember and

          beware)

Gutteridge's writing career, academic and literary, moved on. He recalls in his bio the publications of his books: "... *published... by Oberon, the most successful small literary publisher in Canada at that time. I felt I had arrived as a poet (and a minor novelist)... I continued to publish papers on educational theory and practice in English throughout my twenty-five-year career...*" *(Refer to his biography at the end pages for more titles and publications)*

During what he terms "... *a full life,*" Don has kept on writing and printing his work with different publishers: Oberon, Brick Books, Black Moss Press, Bev Editions, Moonstone, and Borealis. After retiring in 1993, he devoted himself to feverishly write: *"I retired in October 1993. Bored with retirement, I started in on what became a twelve-volume mystery series, The Marc Edwards Mysteries, with four publishers over a twelve-year period (2003-2015). These would be the last prose I would write. But I started writing poems again…"*

First Choice Books reissued Don's *The Village Within*, an original 1970 Fiddlehead Books publication, in 2017. The book is subtitled "poems towards a biography," which gives us an exact notion of the themes approached in it and the book's general tone. Some of the original poems were removed from this print, a decision made by Gutteridge because *"not all of the poems now live up to my standard." (Taken from Note from the Author in the book)* He settled with the remaining ones, reproduced untouched.

Within the rich variety we find in the book, we have "This Maple in my Fallen Yard," a piece Don recalls as his *"first poem published in a real magazine…"* From it, an excerpt, the last stanza. Readers will absorb right away the solidity of a poem that stands the test of time and shows a rapidly maturing poet:

This maple in my fallen yard
dies a thousand lives
that old bones unmarrowed
on the cross of fallen leaves
can pull yet another spring
from the harrowed earth
of this my fallen world.

A brief, grave poem, made of various pieces, is "Some Thoughts for November." I chose the closing one, number 6, for its shortness yet also for its Emily Dickinson ring in mood and compactness (Gutteridge quotes her at the book's beginning, whom he considers a transcendental poet):

When winter comes
there will be time, perhaps,
for lesser deaths.

In 2014 *Lily's Story* was published by Don's agent under the imprimatur of Bev Editions. In 2019 he revised the novel and it was reissued as *Lily Fairchild.* Tablo Publishing, as Gutteridge said to me, *"did the honours."* An unquestionably outstanding and well-established poet, Don Gutteridge shows the rich tessiture of his writing in this superb, heart-touching piece of prose. The novel is an ode to sacrifice and endurance, to determination and courage, to freedom of thought and act, to faith magnificently worded in one of the book's final meditations: "… *belief is a hard flame to extinguish…*" In his words, *"I wanted to write an historical novel (that abiding interest) from a woman's point of view…"*

As a reader, I don't need a more suitable way to connect with a book than the one chosen by the author, as he starts by describing Lily's childhood settings, packed with family details:
"Lily was glad to be in the comfort of the trees' canopy. It was cozy here, like the cabin with Papa's fire blazing… While outside, heard only by her, the snow sang to the wind and no one in the world was lonely… She would surprise Papa at his work, celebrate another tree felled, and laugh when he swept her up and twirled her around, saying 'Lady Fair Child, may I have the pleasure of this dance?' "

The opening line in the book, *"Something stirred in the darkness ahead,"* can be considered premonitory of what would befall Lily - prefaced in her Mama being sick. I value the allusions to Old Samuels' mumbled stories, a thoughtfully depicted character in both personality and language, an element that is appreciated in Gutteridge's choice of all dialogues, idioms, turns, graphic representation of speech, etc., which speaks highly of his meticulous studies to write the novel. Furthermore, at the threshold of Chapter 6 Gutteridge displays still another ominous act,

"I'm…Lily… Papa sent me… Sensing the bewilderment in the woman's face, Lil's heart sank. She fought against the faintness and vertigo as best she could, but it felt as if her bones had melted outright in a treacherous sun."

Exploiting these factors, Gutteridge prepares the reader for the avalanche of events unfurling from his pen. In many ways those early chores and experiences Lily, seven years old, had to assume and learn from molded her charisma, and may have given her strength to face the hardships and setbacks she would encounter along the way.

Two especially tender-sad moments come to us with the mother's *"Let's-have-tea,-little-one"* instant when she tells Lily of her and Papa's previous life and how they came to a new country, and the scene with the cameo pendant with a silver chain that Lily's mother showed her:

"With a start, Lily recognized her own eyes. "Your grandmother." Mama's eyes filled with tears. She reached into the box again. "I saved this, out of the storm." She held up a gold chain on the end of which dangled a slender cross no more than half an inch long. Instinctively Lily leaned forward and the crucifix settled on her throat as if it had always expected to be there."

Auspiciously, this moving minute comes back to us at the end. *Lily Fairchild* finely chronicles, in its status as historical fiction, a period – rather a succession of periods – in the Canadian past that approaches natives' life – stylishly accompanied by the use of words coming from their languages, what brings the reader closer to the textual atmosphere – and sketches crisscrossing seeds that grew into the Canada we have today.

Alongside, Gutteridge remains loyal, and constantly refers to one of the central motifs in Canadian writers, nature. He is faithful as well to his excellent treatment of family themes – skillfully addressed too in his poetry – placed either in the 1850s or in more contemporary contexts.

Another welcome virtue in the book is place references constantly being made – a tribute to Al Purdy's devotion to Canadian geography? –, which play an important role throughout the novel, not just spatially but also from a historic-contextual perspective. More significantly, Gutteridge's accounts are the result of deep research to recreate locations and situations accurately.

Despite Lily's misfortunes and hard times, Gutteridge does stimulate the reader with some high peaks in her life in the form of her Aunt Bridie –

family – "*Bridie wanted to be severe but couldn't manage it...*" (Her Aunt enrolled Lily in Common School, giving Lily up as help around the house), and

"Don't you fret about it, child," Bridie soothed. "Not much learnin' goes on in schools anyway. Come September, we'll teach you to read proper.

She was looking at Lily now. "Remember this: We're not gonna spend all our life chewin' dirt."

(Bridie gave Lily consolation after humiliation in school).

Once more, Gutteridge leans confidently on family ties to channel these two emotional instances in the novel. A most delicate matter becomes the centerpiece in the story when Lily gets pregnant. Such occurrence in the late 19th century would certainly be critical for a woman, given the epoch, which I won't advance here, of course. From this incident up to the dénouement, readers will be taken on a carrousel ride, going up, going down with Lily's predicaments. Were it not enough, Gutteridge gives us a soul-rending scene in Chapter 12:

"I do love you, Tom."
"Then you'll marry me?"
Lily looked away, then back. "I can't," she said.
"But why?"
She felt the full weight of his hurt and her own. "I can't marry a soldier."

This is *Lily*. The book is masterfully filled with wise dialogue and monologue, with profound reflections, introspective and clear intentions to teach and leave an imprint on the reader. I have enjoyed Gutteridge's way to deal with history in the making blended with memories and an intensely personal story. These ingredients will please the most demanding of readers.

2018 was the year for Hidden Brook Press to print *Home Ground*. While I cannot go over each poem, I will focus on those that more strongly appealed to me and my own memories. This is what I call a close significance approach. I comment on poems that stimulated evocations of my life and my own transit from childhood to adulthood. No significant experience and anecdote escaped Don, positive or negative, blissful or hurtful.

Significant means to me that something leaves a mark; it teaches and encourages learning and channels what is learned towards an education and an attitude for life. Don Gutteridge opens his book with "Black Lake." There is light in the poem, quietness and peace: *"unruffled, silvered surface,"* *"ravishing red dot,"* *"a pair of loons undulated,"* *"sunny butterfly fluttering."* The poet praises the painter, Gerald Parker (*"so you added...,"* *"to subvert the scene you...,"* and adds his personal poetic "strokes" by detailed descriptions for the reader. While the title includes "Black," there is overwhelming beauty beyond blackness achieved by painter and poet.

We notice instances of alliteration in the poem: *"lustrous light to lavish on Black Lake's...,"* "silvered surface, so," *"loons ululated on the cusp of lust and the little stream..."* Alliteration builds a melodic effect into the utterance and creates an emotional atmosphere, very much in line with the poets' purpose. *"Alliteration in the English language is deeply rooted in the traditions of English folklore... alliteration as a structural device... has shown remarkable continuity. It is frequently used... not only in verse..."* (Taken from I.K. Galperin. Stylistics. Moscow Vyssaja Skola. 1981) Let's read the entire piece:

After a painting by Gerald Parker
One alabaster moon
was not enough lustrous
light to lavish on Black
Lake's unruffled,
silvered surface, so you
added a ravishing red
dot above the very
spot where a pair of loons
ululated on the cusp of lust
and the little stream feeding
filigree never slackened

its pace, and just to subvert
the scene you drew a sunny
butterfly fluttering
on monogrammed wings
over the outcrop
where we stopped to wonder
if this was all a dream.

"Moon Over Monk" shows instances of alliteration: *"Mara's lamp…
mellowing its light along…,"* *"gently gendered,"* among others, plus other
stylistic devices that embellish and give emotional connotation to the
poem: a simile, (*"the moon sits in the horizon"*) *"like a serene replica of Mara's
lamp."* The moon is a leitmotif in Don's poetry and imagery, and accom-
panies his memories. This time, it reminds him of Mara – both lights will
now show the way, together or alternately. The poet reminisces of his
childhood games and *"the sacred place where we play."* Here, the full poem:

The moon over Monk Street
sits above the horizon
like a serene replica
of Mara's lamp, each
mellowing its light along
the sacred place where we play
our gently gendered games
in embossed luminosity,
like miller-moths thrilled
to be illumed and shadow-
free: we think of Artemis
and her Grecian bow, bent
wise and unneutered
by the night.

In the poem "Match," Gutteridge photographs life as it comes. He de-
picts life the way it happens – and it can happen to anyone. Down-to-earth
occurrences that send even the consecrated ones into doubting: ("The
Reverend Bell") *"wondering… whether God was on his side."* Job, the Biblical

character, comes to the picture (*"Why have you made me your target?" "Have I become a burden to you?"*) *(Taken from Holy Bible, 1984, Zondervan Publishing House. Job's words in Job 7:20).* However, it is implicit that Gutteridge presents facts and narrates them for the reader to ponder, but also to smile. Let's enjoy it:

The Reverend Bell came home
one afternoon, flung
his cellar door wide
and, though less than wise,
lit a match: we found him
sitting in a singed patch
of his grass: surprised,
a touch unhinged,
and wondering how such
things come to pass
and whether God was on
his side.

My father smoked a pipe and long cigars when I was a little boy. He quit many years ago, more than forty-five, but I still remember the aroma of cigar and smoke and I still keep a wooden box where he placed his cigars. It is deeply registered in my emotional memories. "Helm" made me remember how essential scent (or sound) is for people. In reading *"a lozenge of elm or oak"* I instantly felt wood scents coming from a carpenter's work-shop, and I was transported back in time. Gutteride then blends scents with sounds: *"through the burr and bite of the band-saw."* There is a floating sense of onomatopoeic echoes, direct and indirect, in the combination of the sound "b" in *"burr... bite... band."*

Alliteration escorts the scene: *"a particle of the puzzle he was perfecting piece by filigreed piece."* I could not help noticing a gentle balance between the heavy work carried out in a work-shop: noise, sawdust, probably the logical mess of a place like that, and the child's full involvement (*"I nuzzled in closer"*) with his grandfather's work, finely ended with *"knowing I would be cherished and thrive here with this man at the helm"* and preceded by *"the unspoken tousling of my cowlick.*" It was a heart-caressing memory where the poet does not remember his exact age; but he does remember wood names! An indelible experience, voiced in his bio: "*I spent a lot of time in my grandfather's workshop, and adored him.*" Enjoy the poem:

I might have been five
when I first wandered into
my grandfather's workshop, and watched the hands
I loved guide a lozenge
of elm or oak through the burr
and bite of the band-saw,
a particle of the puzzle he was perfecting
piece by filigreed piece,
and I nuzzled in closer,
waiting, in my need, for the pause
that preceded the unspoken
tousling of my cowlick,
and knowing I would be cherished
and thrive here with this
man at the helm.

Gutteridge serves us fond memories in "Apostasy." Feelings and human values are kindled in the furnace of human connection. From there emerge convictions and attitudes for life. Gutteridge praises his grandmother for her devoted undertaking of pie preparing and baking. As I read, I feel like I am right there watching her. The poem:

My grandmother baked
pies on Sunday mornings
(cherry and rhubarb
in season, raisin for my
Grandpa's bucket), an echo
away from the Anglican nave
and apse she had no
reason to give the nod
of approval to nor taste

its soothing pieties, for she put
all of her love and outsized ardor into the gentle
kneading of her dough and braving
the wrath of a hairy-jawed
God, while we feasted
on her pastries and praised the Lord

Gutteridge relives two experiences: unique home-made food and religion. One is body-provider; the other, soul-provider.

"Rare" offers another touching memory for us, and awakens our own. Alliteration is present (*"on the sand in his Sunday suit," "even dove under like daring dolphins"*). Gutteridge leaves no memory/experience/anecdote in the darkness of forgetfulness. This time it is the beach, which most children adore. I understand the sensation of water, of being "perfectly safe" in the hands of my father, of *"venturing up to our waists and even dove...,"* of *"(he) smiled at us and we smiled back at him."* Happiness is ripples, splashes and adventure in the beach.

A transition from innocence to an awakening from the "gender-free" games is reflected in "Chums." This is presented in the first stanza, as it dilutes into "– *until the day.*" From that moment on, it was, *"I took a fancy to her burgeoning beauty."* Don depicts falling in love, that first-time butterfly in the stomach together with: *"and felt my heart hum."*

Nancy and I were chums,
playing our garrulous games,
gender-free, in Withers
field, festooned with sun-
light in the long summer
afternoons or under
Mara's lamp in the usurping
dark of Monck Street,
superintended by a marinating
moon—until the day
I took a fancy to her burgeoning

beauty and felt my heart
hum and a voice inside
singing Olly, Olly
en-fray.

"Abide" is another experience/anecdote illuminated by "*a sun-stunned meadow.*" There is some rituality and solemnity to this particular day: "*but there is this day no game to be got.*" The child admits the pleasure of the adult's company. The poet regales us with wonderful imagery: "*our guns as silent as the thoughts we share.*" No need to talk, really, the "*love that abides*" keeps them connected.

My Uncle Potsy and I
go hunting cottontail
in a sun-stunned meadow,
and, if we are lucky, spot
a jackrabbit anteloping
speed in an open field,
but there is this day
no game to be got,
but all I need is striding
side by side with my uncle,
our guns as silent as the thoughts
we share, with a love that abides

Memories, experiences, stories are not always pleasant. So, Gutteridge wants to "redeem" himself by recalling that sad incident from years ago. He confesses he "*became something I was not: a bully.*" This poem, "Bully," is an I-am-sorry postcard to Susan.

The poet/viewer is enraptured by his surroundings in his poem "Dark": "*we skated on glazed meadows.*" He remembers what and *who* was there, "*clove bloomed,*" "*wild mustard throve,*" "*larks buffeted the air.*" The moon, so significantly recurring in Don's poems, cannot be left out this scene: "*amazing the moon as we moved…*" Magnificent imagery to give us a landscape, one Canadian poets are so good at describing, which Gutteridge uses to remember his school crush, Leckie:

When Leckie's field iced
over after a thaw
and quick freeze, we skated
on glazed meadows
where once clover bloomed,
wild mustard throve
and larks buffeted the air –
as if the globe had hewn
one raw rink
where we left in our wake
filigreed meridians,
mittened our hands in gendered
pairs, and unmuffled
our carnal cries – two
abreast lest we fall
off the world: amazing
the moon as we moved through
the lustrous rendering
of its light towards the star-
flecked obsidian dark.

A second title for the book could be the poem "Towards the Light." This poem does not mention the moon. There is no need for it: Mara's lamp is there instead. Gutteridge sent me to my 1970s childhood when my sister and I would cast hand-shadows, silhouetting from background candles, on the walls during power outage nights in my hometown... Pablo Neruda, the Chilean poet, knew we must walk towards the light. He said, *"... I walk towards the light." (Taken from Palabras de Pablo Neruda. Neruda 2004, pp. 34-35 (post mortem)*

While Don's poem reads about *"nightfall," "dread of darkness," "inked shadows,"* he ends it with a clear passion and confidence of *"knowing full well that, like every living thing, we all grow towards the light."*

Nostalgia and remembrances come in "Together." How many times do we all go over our old family album? Those past days, those memories rekindled when we flip page after page – smiling, tears flooding our eyes, re-living... I have a picture with my parents just like that one.

In this photo, my mother
and father, standing tall
on my grandfather's lawn
in the their Sunday suits,
hold me up high
between them for the camera's
loving eye, like a prized
doll for all the world
to see, their hands tethered
to steady me on my maiden
shoot, as happy as they
will ever be, and I still
regret I wasn't enough
to keep them together.

"A Birthday Poem" is warm, intimate, sweet. The poet leans on love, "*our abiding love.*" The line between brackets ("*your hand in my glove*") defines, for me, the mood of the poem. Together, poet and wife, Anne, "*have eased into our age... gracefully.*" Notice the verb, "ease," which implies comfort, calm. That is how the poet sees their love and life together. A constant emphasis of the "we" and the "our": "*We have stopped counting our birth-days... our say-so...*" In the end, they have their ("our") "*abiding love*":

For Anne
We have stopped counting
our birthdays, but the years
glide on without permission
or our say-so, but we have eased
into our age as gracefully
as Time and Earth allow
(your hand in my glove),
and whatever fears
we may have for the future
are flouted by our abiding love.

I have shared my views about some of the poems in *Home Ground*. In doing so, I have visited my own life, as I have been mirrored, so closely, in his poems. They have brought happiness and homesickness to my mind, and as Gutteridge himself expresses it in his last poem, "Defy," *"poetry is both bliss and consolation, a way of speaking to the world that subsumes both shy and defy."* He has spoken to the world. The world has replied: Erin Nichol Cochrane said, "… *a poetry collection that will knock you off your boots in the sweetest of ways." (Taken from praises to Home Ground on the back cover of another Gutteridge book, Village Dreaming)* Let's have "Defy" full:

For Stan Burfield
For more than a dozen years
you were surrounded by blooms
in your shop, a long way
from Alberta's unlyrical
land, and when you tried
your hand at verse, were
your first poems for poppies
and their roaring red, sonnets
for sunflowers a-burst
in lavish light, haiku
for hibiscus and their passionate
purple, or pentameters
for peonies and their kissing cousins?
Did you let them speak
for you, go soaring through the
petrified petal of your fear?
For poetry is both bliss
and consolation, a way of speaking
to the world that subsumes
both shy and defy.

Hidden Brook Press published more books by Gutteridge in 2019. *Out of the Blue* is a collection of his poems (selected by James Spence) from 1983 to 2011. About it, Erin Nicole Cochran was emotionally truthful, *"It's only a handful of words but I felt this inside of me as though it were an epiphany of sorts.*

There is a classical instrumental quality to every poem…" and she finishes her comment, *"Don Gutteridge's soul is on every page"* *(Taken from the book's back cover)*

Some of his poems echo his earlier works and solemn style, like "Indian Summer On a Farm Near Preston" and "Riel":

(excerpt from "Indian Summer")
"… where stones have stood
a hundred autumns
and kept their true till spring,
and underneath the quiet earth
I hear November voices
singing of the deep fallow
where all the Indians lie.

(excerpt from "Riel")
There is no
eloquence to
blood running
from the mouths
of wounds and
battles lost,
the eyes
of the dead
at Duck Lake
and Batoche…
or will this
prairie be
a coffin
for my voice
a dwelling place
for
        two
        white
            stones?

One particular piece I was fascinated by is "First Steps" (dedicated to Katie-Anne). We perceive innocence expressed with tender pen and candid heart fallen for an image of a toddler. We are pleasantly caught up in the sweet imagery and the soft touch pervading the whole poem. John Barnet shares this thought with us: *"When Gutteridge turns to the subject of his grand-children, his poetry is lovely and lyrical, and dances"*:

Your toes tingle the broad
pool of air and a leg
steps strident into its
smooth immensity,
the body follows with a feel
of floating,
      then you grin
to let us know it's okay
to applaud.

The poem that entitles the collection, "Out of the Blue," is an ode of remembrance and optimism, of recognition of truth and unavoidable fact but also of capacity to hold on to what is cherished *(excerpts)*:

Out of the blue a call
from a boyhood chum…
I am back in King
Edward Public School…
and nothing is ever lost:
not even the pain of what
we can never fully
regain.

Village Dreaming is another Hidden Brook Press 2019 production. "Dunes at Canatara" *(a poem I talked about when I reviewed Point Taken)* is a "Purdian" gem as I commented then for its extolling voice to greatness before the human eye and feel *(excerpt)*:

It took a million years
to sculpt these dunes,

grain by grain of wavewashed sand whipped
by seasoned winds into
voluptuous curves
and bevelled runes.

Another superb piece is "Ruthless," a sustained elegy to poetry, how a
poet strives to pursue "*the truth*" and is fully engulfed by such "labor":

And me composing poems:

inklings I tease
towards some sense
in words whetted upon
the wheel of memory
and swerving askance
upon the page where they lean
upright, enlinked,
ready to be swallowed whole,
raw and ruthless
in rhythmic pursuit
of the truth.

"Au Revoir" is a heart-breaking poem. We see a high poet in love, deeply
in love for his departed wife. Everything reminds him of her. Torn in pain
and nostalgia, he weaves scene after scene, image after image, glued to the
physicality of her memory. Despite grief – and/or fuelled by it – he manages
to erect a monumental piece here and in other poems, "*elegies for my beloved
wife*" as he told me:

I do not empty this house
of your presence: you are here
in every room we shared
breath in, your clothes still
hang where they belong
in their closets, and every painting
that adorns our walls is a reminder

of your artist's eye, and the chesterfield,
your bête noir, still
bears your imprint, and a novel
lies where your fingers last
lingered, nor am I made
forlorn on entering the space
now vacant of the woman
I cossetted and cradled with
love in its essence, for we are taught
that death is not an ending,
not goodbye but au revoir:
I refuse that platitude,
preferring your haunting hover
and the remnants of the things you touched
with such tenderness.

Also in 2019, Hidden Brook Press gives the readership *Inking the World*. The book's essence is superbly sketched in the opening piece, which entitles the book.

Whenever I think of my demise
I try to remember the day
my mother, still a girl,
unwombed me and I swallowed
a village whole and kept it
tucked inside the little
room of my mind for eighty-
one years, and I have grown
gracefully old and somewhat
wiser, embracing my age
and inking the world with poems.

"Be" traps the reader in nostalgia, illusion and cravings. The poet longs for what is gone, wants it back in his life yet channelling his thoughts into a possible tomorrow, into being "*born again / in the place where I could merely / be.*" The verb BE acquires hues beyond a simple residence in space. It implies an existence in temporal terms, in physical terms that would allow him *"to feel one more time / the brush of a breeze...":*

I have such a longing
to see once again
the lush lavender of the lilacs
that hugged grandfather's lawn
and to feel one more time
the brush of a breeze combing
the leaves of our Manitoba maples
and to know the warmth of a home-
kitchen, love-tugged,
and to tingle with the touch of fingers
so tender I could dream
only of being in their embellished
embrace and I have such
a longing to be born again
in the place where I could merely
be.

The height in the book's general tenor is, in my view, "Blessed." Gutteridge summarizes how he feels in those classic words he has been able to forge during his poet's life. He is *"blessed by fortune, / embossed by the gods, passionate / and true."* Starting on a rhetorical question that is answered line after line, we walk with the poet's enumerations and "itemized" aspects of his long life besides his beloved Anne, to whom the poem is dedicated, finding shelter in beauty, love, truth, a rose, mementoes, being optimistic and objective in his understanding of life:

Does anybody know how deep
love goes or how radiant
a rose can be in the luminous
light of a June morning,
for we are born to love
and beauty, despite the odds,
and we suffer heartbreak

and loss like heroic stoics,
and I have known it all
since you first flowed
into view and we fashioned a life
together, blessed by fortune,
embossed by the gods, passionate
and true.

The book closes with "Village Dreaming," a poem included in *Point Taken*,

the big Gutteridge collection.
Rocking in my chair I dream
of the village where I was breathed
into being by the athletic lusts
of my hockey-heroing father
and the girl he deemed his paramour,
when my world was as new as a
chick picking at the shell
and a blank page I wrote
myself upon with words
wrestled from the womb, and a town
surrounded me with folks
to people my poems and startle
the stories I would create, in the
mortar and pestle of my imagination,
of their forgivable follies, the hustle
and bustle of their Dickensian lives,
and those childhood
chums I turned into combed
prose, who made my days
worth the telling and strummed
the strings of my memory, leaving
me to dream, rock and sing
the song of myself.

Gutteridge's *The Star-Brushed Horizon* came out in 2019 as well. It must be
read as a story, the poems within visualized as chapters. Each poem is a

different yet strongly interconnected memory lane – interdependent synapses – the poet walks up and down in his rewarding recreation of characters, events, emotions and moments Jack Magnus calls *"these still breathing moments of memory." (Taken from the book's back cover)* because they are alive in the poet's brain.

Allusions, people, places, names, echo back and forth, skip across the waters of a frequented pond, skate under a summer sky, or bask on a familiar beach. Gutteridge travels and takes us with him back in time, to a past that may well be our own pasts: his stories and ours will meet at many crossroads, coincide and link up these synapse-poems in our minds. Emily-Jane Hills Orford stated: *"Each one* (poem) *captures a precious moment, a cherished family member or friend, a glimpse of beauty in nature, in the skies, or at night and so much more." (Taken from the Press Release by Hidden Brook Press)*

The general theme in the book moves from *"… nature themed work to the memorial pieces celebrating friends and golfing companions…" (ibidem)* From the first poem, "A Butterfly for Anne," we feel the light elegance of symbolism. The poet dedicates it to Gerry Parker, the actual muse being, as in so many wholehearted pieces, Gutteridge's Anne.

You send this exquisite
green butterfly in lieu of
a visit, perched poetically
on an amaze of lines,
alabaster moons and a dazzle
of dots fancied afresh:
a master's art that says
how much you loved my Anne,
that utters its grief through
its breathless beauty.

My eyes could not avoid noticing how often the poet employs a classic expressive means I have noted in this paper in earlier analyses, alliteration. It builds a melodic effect into the utterance and creates an emotional atmosphere, very much in line with the poet's state of mind and the poems' mood.

This is perceptible in many of his poems, a feature he referred to in his emails to me: *"… my recent work (since 2012) is structured around internal rhyme, assonance and alliteration…"* Notice it in "A Butterfly for Anne":

"perched poetically," "dazzle of dots," "fancied afresh," "breathless beauty."

Cuban Apostle, José Martí, spoke highly of one of Cuba's 19th Century teachers, Luz y Caballero, and his profession: *"… he ambitioned nothing yet became everything, because he was a teacher…"* *(quoted from memory)* Our next poem pays tribute, directly and gratefully, to teaching in the person of Ian Underhill, whom it is dedicated to (see the constant reference or allusions to family and friends):

"Purveyor"
For Ian Underhill
You spent a lifetime
purveying poems and stories
to generations of students,
reading aloud with alliterative
ease in your sturdy baritone
until the rhymes chimed
and the consonants collaborated,
until the metaphors stood
up and mentioned their meaning:
you gave them Munro and Purdy,
Atwood and Lawrence,
and all you asked for in return
was their passionate attention
and some small acknowledgement
that teachers, ungloried
as they are, really matter.

Achievements are condensed in three aspects, *rhymes chimed, consonants collaborated, metaphors stood up and mentioned their meaning,* and contribution concretized in the legacy of the names he calls as homage: *"… you gave them Munro and Purdy, / Atwood and Lawrence…"* Gutteridge's key statement comes at the end: "… *all you asked for in return / was their passionate attention / and some small acknowledgement / that teachers, ungloried / as they are, really matter*." The poem is an ode to a man that turns into an ode to teaching.

"Jury" stands as a mature understanding of life, philosophically approached, a happy reconciliation with what it has been and how it turned out for the poet. In between, an apt Shakespearean line, "*I've had my day*," and his effective pet tool, alliteration: "*like a lark lifting*," "*last lick of light*," "*fuelled my fury*." Here, the full poem:

It's been a long and satisfying
life, and I intend to go
gently into Dylan's Good
Night: after all,
I've had my day, weaned
my soul from strife and woe,
eased myself into age
like a lark lifting into air,
content with what has been
allotted me, but the jury's
still out: as the last lick
of light flickers in the dark,
I may shout "Nay!" – bent
by bravado, fuelled by fury.

We see what Jack Magnus termed as a "… *world ostensibly simpler but so much richer…*" *(ibidem, Magnus)* in "Reach." It is a piece where Don depicts simplicity and richness together; splendor that feels exuberantly idyllic. Read these lines, in which alliteration continues to amaze us (particularly in "*we watched the wind-wafted waves*"):

On sultry summer afternoons
we watched the wind-wafted
waves of Huron, as blue
as morning glories stroked

by lasering light, break
upon Canatara's
fabled beach, and we also
found time to cast
an unrighteous eye
upon the girls who once
were merely our chums
as they lay now full-
frontal on the sun-infused
sand, knowing all
along with our penultimate breath
that these creatures, lazing
there, feigning boredom,
would be forever beyond
our reach.

On the book's back cover, John B. Lee, in characterizing another Gutteridge book, *Home Ground*, refers to a recurring theme in the poet's work, "*… the reader is presented with insight into the precocious child coming of age, engaged in imaginative play, experiencing the sexual stirrings of his gender…*" When we read "Fury," we understand universality in Gutteridge's poetics.

It is a poem about the awakening of sexual interest, colorfully narrated, story-like. Even in the semantically vehement shades of the word *fury*, I imagine an "innocent fury," rather an energetic drive in line with the intense emotions shooting through the young boys' brains.

How many summers did we while
away the days on Canatara
Beach, where the sun hummed
on the **heat-soaked sand**
and girls, **new-breasted**,
smile-beguiling and **thigh-
shy**, stretched out
before our **salacious gaze**
(hoping to be pursued perhaps),

but all we could do was shout
something rude
and plunge, **unfazed**, into Huron,
where we stroked each wave
with **mammillary** fury.

The rhetorical implication of the poem's first line, "*How many summers did we while…*" finds an "excuse" answer to reminisce, therefore, enumerate, play with original epithet-charged animate-inanimate references (go to bold-letter italics in the poem). I was amused by an interesting element in the last line, "*mammillary* fury."

The more common meaning of the attribute used by Gutteridge is "*of or pertaining to a nipple, shaped like a nipple*" *(Babylon English, Digital Dictionary)* yet according to the Concise Oxford English Dictionary, digital, the word has two more technical entries, one related to minerals, the other to anatomy, "*denoting two rounded bodies in the floor of the hypothalamus in the brain.*" The hypothalamus is a region in the brain involved in emotional activity. This validates my previous remark about the energetic drive and intense emotions shooting through the young boys' brains.

However, we look at the poem and will invariably find peace, sound reminiscence and a realistic proposal resulting from the "*studied attention in life to the past preserved in memory…*" *(ibidem, John B. Lee)*

Don's poetry grows memorializing, as I said, people, events, feelings, places – and pets. So is "Stranger," a piece written about a dog, Moochie, and about a kid, the poet, who is concerned about the dog's future. In quite an imaginative spin, the boy wonders, "*what dog-thoughts / went whistling through his head…*" attributing human qualities to the animal. Let me share the entire poem with you:

When our dog Moochie
fell ill with distemper,
my father drove him into the
countryside and dropped

him off, and I've always
wondered what dog-thoughts
went whistling through his head
as, confused, dazed,
abandoned, he started up
the nearest lane, hoping
some stranger would call
out, "Here, pooch!"
and show him more love
than we did.

Now read this poem,

"Roan"
For Grace Leckie
I watched you galloping
across the fallow field
on your stalwart stallion
with a thigh-gripping ease,
and waited while you went
coursing by, your hair
bountiful in the breeze,
the roan tight-lipped,
nostrils a-flare, and I wasn't
sure whether I loved you
more, or the horse.

We encounter plenty examples of alliteration, hints of vim and movement
to enhance scenic effects – *galloping, fallow field* (flat terrain that would
allow free rein), *stalwart stallion, hair bountiful in the breeze, nostrils a-flare*
(suggesting breathlessness and speed) – and the end line closing with a
touch of comicalness the picture the poet has sketched in our heads.

This poem is a poetic urge emerging from Don's school days. He recalls
it this way: "*I became entranced by a grade 7 girl, Grace Leckie, who occasionally
rode to school on a chestnut stallion...*"

Moving along with memories, we come to the piece "Exalted." Reading the first two lines is enough to understand a man's allegiance to his love: "*Loving you is an act / of remembrance.*" The poet might as well say "remembering you is an act of love," both expressions valid in his committed voice, in his dearest recollections. The poem is a "*celebration of moments,*" as Magnus tells us *(ibidem, Magnus)*:

Loving you is an act
of remembrance, a recalling
of all those days when we were
too young to be tempered
by tactful touch or the soft
collision of lips, when being
amazed was our common fare,
when I knew such jolting
joy at a glimpse of your hair
haloed by juddering sun-
light or your eyes as blue
as crystallized cobalt
or the effortless allure
of your youthful gaze:
in truth our love was too
exalted to be nipped
in the bud.

Deeper into the book we find a biblically resounding poem, "Desire." It is a parable of sexual awakening, amusement and re-visitation of emblematic themes in Gutteridge (also treated by the other poets I review in this book).

When God ripped Eve
out of Adam's ribs, what
he saw was a mirror image
of himself: with breasts
unsuckled and an extra
cleft and hair that hung

like flung flowers; he felt
no fire in his loins
as hand-in-hand they strolled
the groomed sod, until
Eve purloined an apple,
and Adam, smitten, came
unbuckled with desire.

The poet's high muse, Anne, lives in the following piece,

"Loving You"
For Anne
Loving you is as easy
as breathing, and our long
lives have not diminished
the intricate dance of our
separate selves,...

Intimately simple, dialogic and revelatory of the mutually responsive inner bonds that sprout gently yet unbreakably out of an acknowledged "partnership" of two people who have loved each other. It is best worded by the poet as "*the separate selves*" in an "*intricate dance.*"

The closing lines, as the whole poem, are premium statements of love:

... and above
all else we touch
each other in ways
that have no need for
anything other than a
knowing nod or a con-
junctive squeeze
of the hand.

Thus we come to the end of the book with "Eventually" which is a hymn to the futility of things and life yet in calm, pensive tones reassuringly asking the reader to partake in the balance he has achieved, in the remembrance stage we all reach, eventually. The last two lines are an axiomatic fact of life.

When we were young and easy
in our own skin, we let
our bodies be as they pleased,
happy to find a home
in one another's arms,
and as we grew wiser
we met thigh to thigh
and our love sprung anew
with each familiar sigh,
and when age surprised
us out of the blue,
we let ourselves be
content to sit side by side
in abiding repose, knowing
that everything kith
and kin eventually goes.

Finally, "Pendulum" closes a book with five stars in its horizon. It is a superb piece where the poet challenges the old saying, "You know what you've got only when it's gone." Gutteridge knew since day one what he had, and beautifully admits it in this poem. Imagery fills its lines from the very beginning, as the poet likens his grief to a pendulum and his pain both subsides and surges back as he looks at the things that are monuments of remembrance, a yellow rose, the chesterfield, the halls. Let's have the poem,

My grief, like a pendulum,
comes and goes, the sight
of a yellow rose, emblem
of our long loving years,
can overwhelm or the chesterfield
where you lay during your last

days can amaze tears
I had thought forgotten,
but mostly it is the ghost
haunting these halls
above and below, but it's good
to mourn what we have lost,
for it tells us how far
love has come.

Point Taken (Hidden Brook Press, 2019), a huge, welcome undertaking, puts together most of Gutteridge's previous work. I must say that those early years in his life when he was *"consuming the small library there (at Point Edward and nearby township) and writing both his first poem and his only play"* *(Taken from Gutteridge's Bio)*, were such a strong influence for his career, and a reminder of my own childhood.

Those were actually career-defining moments: "… *he spent his first eleven years in a childhood enlivened by schoolyard chums and summers spent sunning on Canatara beach and paddling in the chill waters of Lake Huron… pristine days of his boyhood… There he spent three idyllic years…"* *(Idem)* that furnished Don's budding formative period and left marks on what would be his exceptional style and ability to recreate the past and lay it down freshly, strikingly and kind-heartedly. It also built a foundation for his gallant, brave and confident attitude towards today and his being at peace with tomorrow.

This book has the rare touch to make me travel. While on my spatial-temporal voyage, I have been led into my own soul, my own memories, dusting many of them out of an almost forgotten past. I thank Gutteridge for it. It unveiled gently, completely, a universe of shimmering words and images to replenish the soul. Jack Magnus tells us of Don's craft *"in making his images sing…"* *(Taken from back-cover comment on Home Ground, a previous book by Gutteridge also included in Point Taken)*

The book is divided into self-standing yet mutually-cohesive titles and dates that feel like sections, hand-guiding the reader across its over seven hundred pages. Despite its length, Gutteridge has succeeded in collecting poems that will stay with us long after we have finished the book. John B. Lee tells us about Gutteridge and his poetry: *"we might carry these poems with us where we go…"* *(Taken from back-cover comment on Home Ground)*

We will put the book down with a mixture of states and feelings wafting about us. We will feel a bit of fatigue from the long, edifying journey, but also a generous pinch of satisfaction for being witnesses to the extensive high-polish oeuvre the author has compiled throughout his prolific writing career, magnificently displayed here. We will be proud for sharing in the message and scope of his work, sincere acknowledgement to the merits of the book and the poet, and a sense of belonging to that group of people who are now in possession of an extraordinary volume.

On *Home Ground*'s back cover too, Jack Magnus's impressions about the poet's work cannot be more commendable: *"… instilled in me a sense of wonder and presence at his memories…"* and he goes on to say: *"the reader can't help but be affected."*

In my view, this book is to be approached with spirit and an open will to walk down the roads Gutteridge paves for us. You will need time, which you can profit from alone, or in the company of beloved ones. The poems in the book are heartening, inviting and embracing. John B. Lee best coincides about the effect of poetry when he says: "kissing the darkness / when the pages are closed / and silent / as a dreamer's mind…" *(Taken from Lee's poem "Kissing the Darkness When the Pages Close")*.

The book gives us a latent past, a defining present and a future that may well be anyone's future. That is how I felt regarding this book and its lingering aroma after reading it.

The book's parts are *The Way it Was, Tidings, Peripheries, Inundations, The Blue Flow Below, The Sands of Canatara, Inklings, Cameron Lake: a Suite of Poems, Home Ground, Night Skating, Days Worth the Telling, The Breath of My Being, The Star-Brushed Horizon, Foster's Pond, Mara's Lamp and Inking the World.*

A review of this intense-extensive compendium of colorfully-varied images and aesthetically-carved proposals must attempt at revealing its straight-to-the-heart poetic vision and stylistic precision, masterfully evidenced by the poet. To this end, I will make reference to some of the poems in some of the sections. It will help me illustrate my analyses and clarify my criteria for the readers.

Gutteridge presents his formidable book in a chronological arrangement of his literary production, 2014 through 2019, fanning out his most intimate nexus with syllable, word, rock-solid meanings and indelible metaphors, which are finely expressed in his poem to John B. Lee in *Home Ground*:

… the inheld breath
before we say the syllables
to ourselves and dream
them onto the page.

In *The Way it Was* section, the author embarks on a trip to his early reminiscences, and he gives us a free ticket to follow him. His poem "Blue-eyed," for example, abounds in tender phrases that depict moments and scenes familiar to everyone, thus creating links that we cannot break *(full)*:

For my Grandmother: 1888-1957
My grandmother: shaking
dust-bunnies out of her mop
in a willing wind, and me,
at five, hopping in a onefooted dance at her side,
the serene sun alive
in her hair as together
we breathe easy in the April
air, crisp clouds
clustered above: her glance
a blue-eyed barometer
of her love.

The two instances settle comfortably in our mind's innermost recesses, playfully activating our personal experiences, positively connecting us to this and the next pieces.

"Letters" follows up in the trail of the previous poem. Earnest lines worth quoting for the reader, where Gutteridge displays his seasoned skills to give us his grandfather (I touched upon Don's love for his father earlier in this paper – and bring us ours:

For my Grandfather: 1892-1955
I am now the last one
who will remember my grandfather, and so it is
I try again to catch
that fleeting face in the prism
of a poem, to see it
again with the clarity of crystal
and feel that benign smile
in the serendipity of a simile,
knowing that he will survive
as long as these letters
linger and thrive.

I could not avoid recalling Shakespeare's "*When in eternal lines to Time thou grow'st.*"

"Dunes at Canatara" shows us a poet of deep thought, of concerned meditation about time and land, which he gracefully blends with his own life. The poet does not detach himself from the land; he rather admires such creation and paints himself, and peers, into it:

It took a million years
to sculpt these dunes,
grain by grain of wavewashed sand whipped
by seasoned winds into
voluptuous curves
and bevelled runes.

It took my pals and me
an afternoon to put
our imprimatur upon
the shimmering concavities,
our bodies pressing
their wry signatures deep
deep into the sun-stunned sand,
feeling the heat of a hundred
centuries oozing through.

I pick Purdy echoes in this poem: *"I lay with my ear flat against the monstrous
stone silence..., listening to the deep core of the world – silence unending and
elemental, leaked from a billion-year period before and after the season of man."
(Fragment by Al Purdy taken from Al Purdy. Essays on his Works. Edited by Linda
Rogers. Essay by Stan Dragland)*

We enjoy sound humour in "Career":

Oscar and I boxing
in the home-built ring
suddenly my chin...
too close to the gist
of Oscar's toxic fist,
and down I go, sprawled
on the cellar floor, knocked
here and everywhere
at once, and contemplating
the demise of my illustrious
career.

We smile in half-closed-eyes gratefulness with "Nightfall" as we roll back
to our childhood:

When night came down
upon the village verge,
we gathered around

the intergalactic glow
of the streetlight like
marauding moths, and it
was hide-and-go-seek,
as, in our pulsing panic,
we combed every ell
and alley to burrow in;
then ululating allyally-in-free, we
rocketed out of
our hiding holes, triumphant,
until something
darker than night called
us ineluctably
home.

In the section Tidings I was deeply moved by "The Way Home":

The way home is thru
the heart, every bloodbeat hums with remembrance,
the village at the nub
of our being runs deep,
keeps our aloneness
at bay wherever
it finds us: estranged
as we are and listening
hard for that
emphatic thrum.

This is a recurring leitmotif in Gutteridge, sweetly handled and firmly setting in our minds. Then again in "Home-grown" those Purdy vibrations that speak of the land, how Gutteridge mentions places of special connotation during his growth:

... the curve of Canatara's bountiful beach,
the infinite surge
of Huron Lake, the marshes

below the angular Bridge
spanning the blue cadence of our River,
while meadows bounced
with bobolinks near a park
where we played until
the evening evaporated
– these were all of God's
geography I would need
to track the terrain of a story
or the swerve of a poem
with my cartographer's eye…

This is continually singularized in the poems "The Lake of my Childhood" and "Pleasure." One particular poem of endearment is "For my Grandmother." He had dedicated a previous one I presented above. This poem reaffirms Magnus's axiom: *readers will be affected* by Gutteridge's words.

When grandfather died
your world was abruptly halved,
all those little rituals
that bound you one to one
now ended, you could not bear
ever again to sleep
in the bed you shared for more
than fifty years, your dreams
entangled through the long night
until morning woke you
with a new day; I remember
you best in the evenings,
you knitting in the kitchen,
Gramps snoozing through the news
a room away, but both of you
linked by love.

The axiom applies also in "Allies":

Nothing abides like love:

for fifty-odd years
side by side we have
weathered the world and not
grown weary, two
souls allied as one
since that moment so
long ago when we eyed
one another and satisfied
something wistful
inside; and here, now,
riding out our last days,
we smile and, knowingly,
nod.

These lines confirm my assertion about the poet's attitude in regards to
what is ahead, his confidence and mature stance. He portrays his life poem
after poem, his family, his fears and joys; and we gently ease into them
and feel on our skin what he has felt.

Peripheries is a section of little jewels as well. "Letters" speaks about the
emotions stirred inside the poet. He enumerates them slowly, as if to
imbue all the homesickness they inspire, as if to relive the past that now
passes before his eyes:

It's a long way home
to the place where the heart lies:
the village that superintended
my birth, that gave me space
in its eyes to grow under
its lavish light...
a place where the heart lives,
etched in perpetual Spring,
unravished by Time.

The last line tells us of the durable tie between poet and place.

Gutteridge is loyal to the Canadian tradition of writing about nature and the elements. In his poem "Gloaming" he impresses us with a splendid, eye-caressing feat of images, similes and metaphors *(excerpts)*:

… floated
like a drunken dolphin
… as the dark
deftly descended and the moon
lurked aloft, a-glimmer
in the gloaming…

This is equally valid for "Eternity," a brief, passionate and nostalgic poem I quote fully:

My Lake was bigger than the
salten seas with no
horizon but a blue blur
where the sun would sequester
each evening, with a
kaleidoscopic squeeze,
and when we dipped a toe
into its chilled solemnity
and felt its heavenly breeze
upon our chastened cheeks,
it was is if we were touching
Eternity.

I praise the poet for his delicate, well-outlined images and epithets: *"kaleidoscopic squeeze," "chilled solemnity," "heavenly breeze," "as if we were touching Eternity."*

"Unsayable" closes this part with the poet's musings about poetry writing. John B. Lee seeks answers to the mystery of writing: "… *to feel the fertile germination / of a sentient breath / transforming / tight-packed syllables / of in-*

terlocking words...” (Taken from Lee's poem “Kissing the Darkness When the Pages Close”) whereas Gutteridge explores possibilities and offers explanations:

I've spent a lifetime
seeking the reason for rhyme
in pursuit of the perfect poem
where dactyls dance until
they make indelible sense
in the midst of metrical meaning...

He does not give up (*“I've spent a lifetime”*) and certainly does persist in the act, *“in pursuit of the perfect poem,”* while his metaphors waltz: *“where dactyls dance...”*

Yet, “Silence” epitomizes this quest towards the why and the mystery of writing:

For sixty-odd years
I've been a wielder of words,
my pen propelled across
the page, metamorphosing
into three-beat iambics
enmeshed in metaphor
and circulating into sense;
when I can no longer be
a purveyor of poems,
I shall leave it all
to God and silence.

We see the deeply religious man, poised and assured. Few poets spend so much time and sculpt such excellent pieces of poetry in dealing with this topic, and few achieve such heights in their attempts.

Inundations is a section that recaptures the scenes the poet so adores: family, context and childhood memories, sprinkling these with poems to nature, seasons, places and experiences like falling in love. Seasons, for instance, reverberate miraculously in his “Dappled”:

When I die I want
it to be in the Spring
when the crocus erupts,
tulips tantalize
the sun, my maple's
leafage abruptly
levitates and the hedgerows
are hung with berries ripened
by light, when apple blossoms
blow blizzard-white,
and I may lie in some
dappled shade and dream
of being young.

A sense of belonging and a bond with nature are noticeable in this poem, as much as in "Birdsong" – and many others. The notion of poetry writing is revisited by Gutteride in this section too. Here we find "Wit":

Once more I sit
down to compose,
amazed again at the
limned linkage
between the ink-dark
word and the flush of feeling
induced…
dazed with knowing: words
are both weapon and wit;
"The Game":
I'd like to write a poem
to take your breath away
but words have a will of their own…
they may
be read in a dozen different ways…,
and "Rhymes":
In my advancing age
let me still be the one

wrestling with words to wield
the world anew, to send
them dancing on some
distant dais, sylvan
with simile: the page
where all my rhymes ring
true.

Shakespeare's line *"All my best is dressing old words new"* echoes magnificently in Don's "Rhymes": *"wrestling with words to wield / the world anew."* In the modesty the poets show, we realize how concerned they are with the continuity of what they write; in Don it explains the role he wants to keep investing his words with, a strife to effect change around him.

The Blue Flow Below, The Sands of Canatara, Inklings, Cameron Lake: a Suite of Poems, Home Ground, Night Skating, Days Worth the Telling, The Breath of My Being, The Star-Brushed Horizon, Foster's Pond, Mara's Lamp and *Inking the World* will show the reader a Gutteridge nurtured by his past, charmed by his present, and in concord with what the future holds for him. This notion is visible in my next analyses. I especially remarked that in *Star-Brushed Horizon*. Don's penmanship can be explored further in my detailed analysis of *Home Ground*, available in the above pages.

I have gone back on my own life, as I have been mirrored, so closely, in Gutteridge's *Point Taken*. His collection of poems has brought happiness and homesickness to my mind. Even when Point was taken, it was I, reader and admirer, taken too into the glorious poetic knitting Gutteridge has done for us in this book. About it K. C. Finn said, *"… it's fair to say that there is something for everyone amongst the many themes and influences of the poet's life… a powerfully penned collection of sentiment, nostalgia, emotion, and observation… I really enjoyed the theme of capturing memories that will last long after us and recording moments and people from the past." (Hidden Brook Press Release)*

K. C. Finn's words help us grasp the book's worth: *"Don Gutteridge writes most of his verses in a similar style of rhythm and pacing, which offers a kind of comfort to readers as you begin to feel that flow and pacing of his words in a very natural way. I really enjoyed the theme of capturing memories that will last long after us and recording moments and people from the past. It gave many of the works the feel of a loving tribute and a recreation of a glorious past for us to step into for a moment. What results is a powerfully penned collection of sentiment, nostalgia, emotion, and observation that takes a traditional look at verse in the best possible way. Every poem you pick from this collection feels like an instant classic, and overall I would highly recommend Point Taken: Collected Poems 2014 – 2020 for poetry fans looking for a deep and meaningful collection."*

Christian Sia says: *"These poems are filled with the humanity of the writer and readers can easily relate to the emotions evoked in the lines… While the collection features poems written over a span of six years, they explore recurrent themes like life and love, family, nature, humanity, the meaning of death, and many others. Each poem reads well, each has hidden importance, a unique meaning. The work is filled with vivid imagery, from the elements of nature to strong feelings inspired by genuine human contact and thoughts on reality. Don Gutteridge writes in a pensive style and the poems are a powerful testament of the poet's consciousness of life within and around him."*

As he hoped in his poem "Eternity," I can state Don has been able to memorialize his life in this book and leave for us a recorded legacy thus touching eternity. His books are poetry and autobiography. They reach out to people and remind them of their own lives. Who best words it is Shrabastee Chakraborty, *"I can truthfully say that reading this book has enriched me. I heartily recommend it to any reader who appreciates poetry or simply loves looking back on a life well-spent."*

Point Taken is the book of books of Don Gutteridge. It should be among the top recent poetry books a reader must have and hold, go to for inspiration, for enlightenment, for pleasure, for the sheer elation of reuniting in time and space with family, friends, remembrances, then place it back on a treasure-keeping bookshelf feeling complete, always willing to return to the book for feedback and spiritual enrichment.

Thus we come to 2020 with another Hidden Brook Press publication, Don Gutteridge's *Invincible Ink*. This is a 111-poem volume loyal to the themes and style that have made Gutteride one of the best poets in the Canadian poetdom.

The first poem, "Litmus," honors the craft of composing a poem. The poet states fluently, tastefully, what poetry writing is all about. I do not see an attempt to limit its definition; it is rather a preamble, comprehensive one, to what each individual may feel. It gives us open territory to roam free after *"the brink of begetting."* Nonetheless, there is a statement in the poem which may well be a definitive reference when it comes to declaring the urges, aesthetics and boundless realms of poetry, *"for a poem, ancient / or newly honed, is really / a surging of the soul towards / the litmus of light or the mind."*

These are epigrammatic lines. Whatever we pursue poetically can be sparked by reading them. Let's enjoy the whole piece:

The urge to pen a poem
is as old as the lullaby sung
to ease the sleep of a fretting
child or the heartfelt hymn
to an ungrateful god or a
soliciting psalm to the setting
sun, for a poem, ancient
or newly honed, is really
a surging of the soul towards
the litmus of light or the mind
on the brink of begetting: words
stirred afoot, seasoned
with invincible ink.

Nature will never part from Canadian poets. The next poem I present bathes in it, finds nourishment in beauty and the cycle of seasons, motifs we discern in all five gems I have discussed in this book. "Wintering" is a seasonal passage as the poet moves slowly, in detail, across seasons. Nothing escapes him. Even in the leaf's grief, *"Bereaved of its leaves, this / maple in my fallen yard / stares bare-boned / into a sky,"* Gutteridge acknowledges the power of nature, of the earth's renovating magic. This faith can only endure in the poet's reassurance of life's constant renewal:

Bereaved of its leaves, this
maple in my fallen yard
stares bare-boned
into a sky, clotted with cloud
in the wilting light from a sun
bereft of its summer heft,
and in this time
of fallowed fields and the fringing
of frosts, we trust in the Earth's
rebirth, when bulbs bulge
with soon-to-be blooms
and robins throb with the nurturing
need and April rains
seize the sleeping seed
and waken it whole to the world,
but it is come Autumn now
and, ever a sinner, I must
winter over my soul.

The same feeling pulsates in "Wings," the poet's necessary shelter in tomorrow:

Outside my window
the trees are de-leafing,
there is an autumnal hum
to the wind and all things
summer come undone,
and though I have no heart
for what Winter brings,
I remain steadfast
in my belief that Spring will glide
into bloom on welcoming wings.

The elegance and tenderness we enjoy in Gutteridge's heartfelt poems overwhelms us when we read "Furious Felicity." The title hints two expressive means of the language, alliteration and oxymoron. Gutteridge has been showing his skilled employment of these and other means throughout his work. The repetition of the consonant "f" echoes classic poems of yore (Poe's "The Raven," for example, *"For the rare and radiant maiden..."* (the "r" recurrence).

But the title also carries a basic opposition of meaning between the noun-modifier, "Furious," and the noun "Felicity." This semantic-stylistic clash is noticeable in the poem's mood. Above all, we sigh with the profound sensitiveness and dripping melancholy the poet words in his oniric dialogue with his beloved one. While we perceive grief and bits of irony, they never outshine the intimacy and love flowing across the lines. Let's have this heart-touching piece full here to close my comments:

I wake in your arms once
again, unforsaken,
and even though I know
I'm dreaming, I hug you
like the last Adam in Eden
offering Eve a paradisal
pass to the celibate sun,
and I want to tell you
there are gods that keep us
from harm's way, from being
a delegate to Death, and that love
with its furious felicity redeems
us all, but that would be
a luxurious lie, for such
deities let me love
and you, die.

As I said in my final words about *Point Taken*, for feedback and spirituality we must always go to the classics. Don Gutteridge is one of them. I have been on a voyage across his vast ocean, my life illuminated by this glistening Canadian gem.

GLEN SORESTAD

Six Reasons I Write Poems

A poem empowers the child in me
to emerge and show me the way;

I've discovered through poems
what I otherwise wouldn't know;

Each of my poems is a small tile
in the ongoing mosaic of my life;

I like the state I'm in when a poem
takes hold and won't let go;

I love the subtle way words can map
their own path through the forest;

Poems allow me to share with strangers
moments of intimate intensity.

Glen Sorestad

In my Introduction I said readers *"must be prepared to go deep into each poet's core, frown, open eyes wide, laugh, cry, interpret, learn, grow, sigh, lean back, lean closer and, upon returning… see the world differently."* Glen Sorestad's life and work are palpable proof of my assertion.

Sorestad has been a steady figure in Canadian poetry. His books have been published for years. His themes reflect life in all its manifestations. Poet Caroline Kennedy (author of *She Walks In Beauty*. Hyperion, 2011) commented *(Taken from https://www.npr.org/2011/04/13/135383019/caroline-kennedy-walks-through-favorite-poems)*: "Poems can even make ordinary moments seem extraordinary," Sorestad honors this – I must state all the poets reviewed in this book do it – by writing, without repeating himself, excellent pieces that tell us of his acute capacity of observation and of internalization of what he sees and feels. His sources of inspiration are varied, as is life and the world around him.

In an interview he said that ""*My inspiration comes from all around me, from the people I come into daily contact with, from books, photographs, from my interaction with the world around me, both the animate and inanimate worlds, from what I see and hear in my perpetual eavesping on the world, from memories of things done and not done. Inspiration can come from everywhere, from both the expected and the unexpected sources." (Taken from https://canlit.ca/canlit_authors/glen-sorestad/)*

Sorestad published *Leaving Holds Me Here: Selected Poems* (Thistledown Press) in 2001, for which he received the Saskatoon Book Award. The book's back cover comment presents the great writer to the readers: *"Known for his ear for the delicate nuances of language, Sorestad's poetry delights in the natural world and its many revelations. While angling in the streams and pools of family, friendship and memory, Sorestad lures the reader with a compelling imagination that is accessible, as well as personal and universal."*

(Taken from the digital version:
https://archive.org/details/leavingholdsmehe0000sore/page/n179/mode/2up)

One particular poem called my attention, "We Need These Silences":

the spaces that lie
between moments of sharing,
those times when it is
enough to feel the presence
of the other, the knowing
that this silence, too,
is a gift;

the silence of the mountains
or the dark forest,
or the plains at night,
reaching out to touch
some part of us
that craves time alone;

the moments before sleep,
or after waking, when the world
rises or falls into order,
finds shape and meaning
of its own.
We need these silences
as we need the words
we must first learn to say
and then forget
as we come to know
silence.

We feel as we read a soothing rhythm, a lullaby-like cadence that flows gently, engagingly as the poet gives us, if you will, *his* arguments of silence. The value of silence is revered in this poem, "*the knowing / that this silence, too, / is a gift*," even in company – which is not at all rejected by the poet, only invited to the communion of the silences he evokes.

We are touched by the "*natural world and its many revelations*": "*the silence of the mountains / or the dark forest, / or the plains at night…*" while the poet plays with spaces and time, with the innermost corners of the human being who "*… craves time alone.*" The poem is an intimate call to partake in moments that restore and make existence complete. Notice how axiomatically expressive the poem is in the last stanza. Silence complements words; it is as articulate as they are, and equally enriching. Silence, in Sorestad's acute perception of the world around us, brings balance to that "*part of us.*"

Another arresting poem is "When the World Disappears." Sorestad impresses me by depicting a singularly responsive and extreme moment in it. His lines, "*We are, all of us, blind pilgrims / groping for some distant shrine / lost from our view…*" mirrors an anticipation of what the poem deals with. Hyperbolic expressions support the poet's intention (*… the world disappears / horizon, buildings, trees, traffic, / the road itself, all gone. Snow, / blasted by a fierce south-easter, / obliterates equally land and sky.*")

The use of zeugma contributes to the general fineness of the poem in terms of language techniques and those "*nuances of language*" the poet knows well how to handle (*"clinging to the steering wheel, / clinging to frail threads of reason, / clinging to little more than blind hope"*). Let's have the whole poem.

 Driving through a flat-out prairie
blizzard is a classic struggle between
terror and faith. Between Paynton and
the Battlefords the world disappears
horizon, buildings, trees, traffic,
the road itself, all gone. Snow,
blasted by a fierce south-easter,
obliterates equally land and sky.

On this two-way stretch of highway
we drive into the snow cloud.
As vehicles behind and in front
vanish from my sight, so too have I
from them, my hands iron vises
clinging to the steering wheel,

clinging to frail threads of reason,
clinging to little more than blind hope
as the white-out erodes confidence
and panic probes below
the thin skin of logic.

We hurtle through nothingness,
my silent prayer willing that whatever
lies on the other side of this void,
whatever other drivers are steering
the margins of their own misery,
their paths do not intersect mine.
We are, all of us, blind pilgrims
groping for some distant shrine
lost from our view, alive only
in the minds that will them.

Blood and Bone, Ice and Stone (Thistledown, 2006) is a collection of poems with a previous appearance in numerous formats. Among them, the following literary magazines and online journals: *Arc, Day Poems (U.S.), Grain, Grey Borders, Kaleidoscope Journal, It's Still Winter, Mesquite Review (U.S.), Mukkula (Finland), Nashwaak Review, The NeWest Review, The Norseman (Norway), River King Poetry Supplement (U.S.), Shampoo (U.S.), Sodobnost (Slovenia).*

Also, several of the poems appeared in the limited edition chapbook *Dreaming My Grandfather's Dreams* (Frog Hollow Press, 2002). "Kvikne in Rain" and "Dreaming My Grandfather's Dreams" both in the anthologies, *New Century North American Poets* (River King Poetry Press, 2002) and *Nose Mountain Moods* (Smoky Peace Press, 2002).

The same two poems were filmed by Incandescent Films as part of the "Story Albums" television series for SCN television network. "Horse-radish" appeared in the anthology *Henry's Creature* (Black Moss Press, 2000), "Ice Fishermen" appeared in the anthology *Mocambo Nights* (Ekstasis Editions, 2001) and "When the Hands Sleep, What Do They Dream?" appeared in the anthology *Body Language* (Black Moss Press,

2003). "Rivers" appeared in the anthology *Reading the River: A Traveller's Companion to the Saskatchewan River* (Coteau Books, 2005).

Sorestad's varied presence in the media speaks highly of public acceptance and reverence. He is a poet of reference in his country, and has been translated into other languages (Spanish, Italian, Finnish, Slovene, etc.)

This is what is said about the book and the poet in the Web: "*Glen Sorestad has been publishing poetry for thirty years and throughout his distinguished career he has relied upon the central themes of family, history, nature and friendship to guide his readers through his ever-expanding desire to name, and remember. Blood and Bone, Ice and Stone continues Sorestad's poetic journey. Whether seeking his family roots in Norway, capturing the small epiphanies in nature as he travels, or shaping the memories of those whom he has met and befriended, his poems deliver a supple wisdom and unfettered honesty.*"
(Taken from https://www.amazon.com/-/es/Glen-Sorestad/dp/1894345975)

In *Dancing Birches* I remarked how the poet understood life's course unfurling in the wild. He watched and saw beyond the mere surface of things and motions. "Amazing," for instance, was a landmark in his progression from my viewpoint. In *Blood and Bone, Ice and Stone* he reenters the magic of water, juggling with metaphors and overlapping comparisons, bestowing imageful powers to what catches his poet's eye. The poem below acquires cosmic proportions in the poet's gentle etching, entwined in the cycles of life:

"Rivers"
> *... for Myrna Kostash*
The river flows one way
and in its passing, swift
or slow, you feel
the weight of time,
the lunar pull, the turn
of seasons. Go with
the current and it takes
you where all things

come at last together.
But there is another way —
turn against the flow
and brunt the mystery
leading you where things
begin, where a river is
just a notion wrought
from sun and ice and stone.
The river flows one way,
but in the wonder of its
passing, we choose.

Next poem I wish to comment is "Blue Heron at Sunset":

The sun falls through spruce
on the western shoreline, paints
woods dark as night, the lake
a murky green mirror, the boat
a giant water beetle. From reeds
a great blue heron launches
its graceful arc of flight,
seeking its own private space
where it can lead a quiet
heron life and stand
stock-still in shallows,
a vigilant statue, poised
and waiting. Darkness settles.

We easily perceive the poet's facility to describe the heron's awesome routine molded upon a spectacular backdrop. The bird's trajectory is *"a graceful arc of flight,"* the boat (human allusion) is built in but pertinently tempered, and transformed under Sorestad's wand into a beetle, in the magnificent painting he offers.

On a similar chord runs "Flying With Snow Geese," the human eye bewitched by prettiness around, caught in the allurement of moment and view:

We swim the warm blue sea of sky
as August's hold, hour by hour,
releases and September nears

with frost-nailed fingers. Below us,
a ragged string of snowflake geese
ride their own airy flight path,

high over rock-rimmed lakes
while conifers beneath them wave
adieu to summer's last visitants.
Our Cessna turboprop leads
this white squall of beating wings
south to the fields of plenty.

"Semantics" is a piece I could not resist including. To attempt an explanation is unnecessary: there are as many interpretations as readers of this attention-grabbing poem. Its intrinsic *semantics* allows infinite between-the-lines, stylistic construal. What does remain is its revelation of multiple paths towards a message, its subtle witty tone, and the poet's fluent, fulfilled discourse, which succeeds in amazing and piquing our curiosity:

That night
when you asked me
to tell you
what I meant
when I used
the word,
          friend,

somewhere
along the road
of my anecdotal
illumination
I lost you.

I close my voyage through this book quoting another fascinating poem. It reveals a pensive onlooker, capitalizing on all the potentials of life, and his sharp appreciation of these, to produce refined fresco-like pieces such as "Angel of the Afternoon." Strengths in the poem: epigrammatic lines (*"dreams are what keep us all alive," "some good things never change," "dreams and faces are like time"*), which expertly compact good sense and counseling:

Afternoons find them gathered, these
aged and aging lovers – their willing wit,
their sage and salty sayings drawn
from days in diverse worlds of work.

To this neighbourhood bar they're drawn
by a shared illusion, so shrewdly spun
by the woman who serves their drinks –
that she favours each one above the rest.

That sultry smile shines just on him
and on no other of the table's crowd;
the soft fingers that linger on his arm
as she leans in close to serve his drink

Convince each, if only for the moment,
that had that old Nemesis, time,
not disqualified him from the chase
he'd be undoubted ruler of her heart

And in this fantasy he wears his crown.
That all of this is dream matters not –
dreams are what keep us all alive.
She knows this in each of them,

knows, too, some good things
never change, that her dreams
and theirs will never converge,
that dreams and faces are like time.

Michael Ondaatje, in reference to Al Purdy, defined two of the most crucial duties of a poet: to map and to name. One of Sorestad's books, *Road Apples* (Rubicon Press, 2009), does precisely that. The chapbook is a continuous sequence of poems following Sorestad's wife, Sonia, and him on an autumn driving trip that took them down through small town and rural Midwestern and Southwestern America. It becomes a useful, practical guide for the reader, drafted in poem-form, integrating geography and nature.

This is a book Sorestad likes to think of as a "poetic travelogue." It is travelling with the poet and his wife and reading their shared experiences in poetry that is sometimes anecdotal, sometimes lyric, but with a focus on the landscapes encountered and passed through, the stopovers made, the people spoken with:

From Plentywood to Culbertson
in mid-afternoon we roll
                                    past bales of hay
and fields of ripe wheat.
                        Cattle loll
in lush grasslands,
                    combines chew
and spew their gritty way
                            through swaths of grain.
A sprightly pheasant cock
                            hotfoots across
the asphalt ahead
                    pursuing a pair of hens.

Sorestad chronicles his trip, imbricating landscapes and socialscapes with photographic detail:

Williston. North Dakota oil patch
in 24/7 frenzy. Every hotel room
occupied. No matter. We sleep well,
tucked into our Pleasureway.
Under down-filled duvets, we

drill down into deep wells of dream,
lulled to sleep by the throbbing
diesel engines of rig workers
in the parking lot of the El Rancho Motor Inn.

Nature prevails, enjoyed by the poet, captured by his "poetic lens":

The Can-Am highway south
from one Dakota into the other
rolls through luxuriant green range.
The lushness amazes us.
September and we are accustomed,
especially at this time of year
to faded duns and tans —
the austere notes of autumn
on these great central plains.
Scattered clusters of pronghorns,
as sleek and content in their grazing
as the prized black Angus herds,
marbled flesh rippling as they
munch and chew towards
the looming slaughterhouse.

Sorestad had brought us to the realm of sound in poems to his grandfather.
Now he kneads color, taste and scent into an appetizing piece:

Rapid City. O the aroma!
Poblano peppers fire-roasting
in a revolving drum!
Nostril-seizing wafts drift
from a greenhouse parking lot
where they insinuate their way
in every direction to tantalize
olfactory senses and appetites
of even those poor unfortunates
who have never in their lives
eaten freshly roasted peppers.

Thus, the poet shares his traveling experiences with the reader. The book flourishes with names, places, people, happenings. It is a poet's diary open to the public eye.

In 2010, Glen Sorestad publishes *What We Miss* with Thistledown Press. This book contains fifty-three warm pieces that actually move towards the light. I am no expert but I do distinguish an emphasis on nature poems in the book's first part, **Moving Towards the Light**. I see titles related to birds (and other animals), the elements, the cycles of day, seasons, months, etc.

The first poem is a display of color and sound, typical in birds. Sorestad uses distinct imagery to recreate what he sees and shares with us. For example, "*… gaudy orange breast / spinning a small sun at us…*" or "*its operatic presence* (the bird's) */ an aria we've waited / months to hear.*" Wholly, we enjoy this overlapping nature in the poem; a feature the poet knows how to express in his style. Let's have the poem full:

"The First Robin"
is perched atop the roof peak
this April morning,
gaudy orange breast
spinning a small sun at us
as it trills its thrushy tune,
declaiming its territory
for all to hear,
its operatic presence
an aria we've waited
months to hear.

The next poem, "After Five Days of Wind," remains faithful to the poet's personal approach to the acts and creatures of nature. Like many Canadian poets, he engages in brief yet detailed narratives allowing readers to feel they are witnessing what is depicted.

We can feel the bird's impatience and joy to be "*freed from rigid north winds.*" Sorestad draws a resemblance between the bird's "feelings" and ours. As we do, it shivers under winter's blanket and stirs back to life as winter slips away into a welcome spring. Let's see that narrated by the poet:

the red-winged blackbird has
emerged from deep in the reeds
where it has alternated shivering
and calling out its springtime greeting,
albeit with less conviction;
and now its songful stage
is a new-leafed aspen
beneath an azure dazzle where,
red epaulets aglint it bursts
its fierce, flutey melody,
as happy now to be freed from
frigid north winds as we.

An interesting element in these two previous poems is that their lines start with the very title. Reread them so you can perceive how the title introduces the poem as an entire unit but also begins the text flow.

In my appreciation of A. F. Moritz's work (see my paper on this poet after Sorestad), I quoted the following: "*Marvin Orbach's daughter, Ariella, introduced her father's Redwing (Hidden Brook Press, 2018) saying*: "… *these poems speak of… the power of observation, of sitting still and connecting with the life that flows around us… They speak of the simple beauty of insects, of a tree, and of course, of birds.*" Moritz himself stated in an interview: "*People don't even appreciate them* (reference to animals in the city) *or say thank you.*"

Our next poem made me go back to these opinions. "What We Miss" speaks of a poet who "*passed the gnarly poplar on* (his) *morning walk…*" and "*heard a tapping sound above.*" This is the "excuse" to present us a richly elaborated piece where image, sound, and "flickery" description emerge when the poet realizes that "*I'd passed a hundred times, but never / stopped to stand and view…*"

Sorestad uses onomatopoeia to round off the poem's result, which evolves from an apparently routine stroll to a call of attention to the beauty Orbach's daughter and Moritz refer. This expressive means heightens the aim sought after by the poet, "*Tap-tap-tap-tap-tap*" (extra resounding effect in the /r/-recurring words "*jackhammering*," "*percussion*" and "*drummer*" conveniently located in separate lines in the poem), blending observation with hearing.

The way Sorestad structures the poem and the semantic-affective weight it carries, plus the end fact that he finally sees a Flicker, are the factors leading me to talk about a "flickery" description. Let's have the poem:

I passed the gnarly poplar on my morning walk
and heard a tapping sound above. I stopped,
expected a jackhammering woodpecker,
percussive probing for early grub.

My eyes moved up and down this tree
I'd passed a hundred times, but never
stopped to stand and view as distinct
from its companions in this aspen grove.

Beak-wrought holes, up and down,
fierce handiwork of strong bills. Why
had I never noticed? Why the steady
beating of a beak above to see?

I saw no bird. My gaze scoured every
foot of trunk and branch. No drummer.
Had my ears misread the message?
Tap-tap-tap-tap-tap.

The beaking was inside; within
the dying: a Yellow-shafted Flicker
poking its head from a hole,
then disappearing again.

Canadian poets have a gift we Cubans do not: the seasonal cycles. This is motive enough to write sensitive, highly perceptive pieces like "The First Yellow

Leaf." Despite Sorestad's unawareness of the change, I remembered Patrick Connors' line, *"There's beauty in the change of seasons."* Because there is beauty in them, and Sorestad points it out to us in an original manner.

Let's read his well-set definition of beauty: *"I am a writer whose life-long passion has been poetry. So much beauty for me therefore exists in words and language. I love how words come together, or even collide, and the beauty that is found in the clash or melding of sounds, the unexpected turn of phrase, the surprising pleasure that fills me when the juxtaposition of two words seems absolutely perfect, the beauty that lies in what we see as the perfect expression of an idea or a feeling. The poem itself can be a creation of simple beauty in the same sense as a painting or a musical composition can be. The writing of a poem is a quest for beauty." (Taken from https://peacockjournal.com/glen-sorestad-two-poems/)*

The poet placed in crucial time and place to come to realize the transmutation of seasons, change dawns on him in vivid words. The *"omen"* is critical in introducing the reader to the slow but inevitable process the poet memorializes. Once more, the nature-poet "umbilical" bond I have mentioned is so rooted in Canadian poets. The end line reflects an understanding and a philosophical attitude before the wheels of time and season. In many ways, this is the attitude the poet assumes too as a person. The poem:

I was not ready for it. The elm leaf lay
before me on the cement walk. An omen.
I glanced up to chastise the offending tree
and noticed there were more, many more,
a decided gilding of what had been green,
this single fallen leaf just the precursor.
As much as I may be unprepared,
as much as I may object, seasons turn.

The book's second part, **Now That I'm Up**, continues the nature theme and adds other powerfully crafted pieces. A poem I briefly mentioned (quoted first stanza), "Autumn Burial," in my comments about Glen's presence in the CCLA *The Ambassador* magazine as Guest Poet, is included in this new book. I was impressed by its solemnity. The burial-cemetery-loss-death themes have occupied quite a few pages in many poets' books. Here, I quote the full poem. It floats in the sadness of the *"words / that commit to the earth in this graveyard... my first cousin and boyhood friend..."* but somehow lessens the pain thanks to the beauty of *"Canada Geese and Snows* (that) *stroke the sun-fired sky..."*

Fine lines that brought to me lines from two poems I wrote, *"a prayer drifts / settling on every grave / our hearts lighten / so we can move on"* and *"Silence, silence / of farewell and tear, / the graveyard... the loss / so searing, so near."*

Let's feel and relate – we, mortals bound to bid farewell to our beloved ones, and part eventually – to this poem ended beautifully with hope in the human need for spiritual shelter above the gloomy fences of a cemetery, *"My heart grows wings / and lifts, following down the sky"*:

Head bowed, I shuffle to the grave."
The clergywoman utters the words
that commit to the earth in this graveyard
holding those many shared common kin,
my first cousin and boyhood friend.
Distant, then growing to a clamour:
waves of Canada Geese and Snows
stroke the sun-fired sky. Scriptures are
no match for this strident airborne din,
nor can the pastor's voice be heard.
I try to focus on our shared boyhood,
my first cousin and childhood friend.
But the blue beckoning of geese will
not let me be. My heart grows wings
and lifts, following down the sky.

From part three, **There Was a Time**, I enjoyed a remembrance poem, "Snow Tunnels." Ease at penning and placidness in revisiting memories, Sorestad applies strokes of *"hard-packed snow"* on the winterscape he presents. Similes surprise us, *"... like frenetic Richardson ground squirrels..."* or *"like wool-clad field mice."*

Metaphors arrayed before our implicated eyes: "... *how joyous we were / freed to claim snow as our domain, / those tunnels, too small for the foes / of joy, a Lilliputian winter world...*" The experience plays out and stays with the poet, an indelible adventure he goes back to – like Tom Sawyer and Huckleberry Finn had – and would now write about. See the import of what Sorestad relives in these lines: "... *a room we all could gather in, / out of sight and hearing, where / we'd never be summoned.*" Let's enjoy the whole poem:

We burrowed hard-packed snow
like frenetic Richardson ground squirrels
awakened mid-hibernation to find
a strange world of white,
crystals of ice the only medium,
and we were now transformed into
tunnellers crazed with snowblindness.

If there was an unsullied snow bank
we claimed it for our own.
We dug into it to create, below
the hard glazed surface and within
the insulating warmth, a warren of passages,
snow caves we traversed on all fours,
like wool-clad field mice.

In this long looking back, what still
lingers is how joyous we were
freed to claim snow as our domain,
those tunnels, too small for the foes
of joy, a Lilliputian winter world
where all that existed was what we
brought to it. It was whatever
we deemed it to be.
We moved snow, below the skin
of the world, claustrophobia unknown
to us, in search of perfect snow,
the perfect grainy drift that would allow

a room we all could gather in,
out of sight and hearing, where
we'd never be summoned.

The implication of winter echoes in many of these poems. We read
"Christmas Oranges," a religiously blessed poem:

Each was a succulent treasure
wrapped like a tiny round doll
in its Spring green tissue jacket,
packed in a compact wooden box.
The arrival of Japanese oranges,
sweet summer suns of winter cold,
was one of the most anticipated
Yule season joys the child I was
remembers. Magi gifts from the Orient,
quick-peel treats to highlight morning's
ransacking of Christmas Eve's stockings.

No other fruit could compare.
We seldom gave a passing thought
to the miracle their mid-winter appearance,
how they travelled half the world
to reach us on a remote farm in
equally remote Saskatchewan, how they
survived mind-altering cold to be
a part of our Christmas memory.

We hurried apart the delicate segments,
swallowed them, piece by piece,
heedless of anything more
than that these small marvels were
ours to enjoy, as children will.
As I still do.

Sorestad succeeds in attracting us to the magic of Christmas since lines
one and two,

Each was a succulent treasure
wrapped like a tiny round doll.

The poem, like the tasty treasures, is now part of the *"Christmas memory"* he writes about. The "resilience" of that memory has remained ingrained in the poet's visual-affective mental corners – and that is the *raison d'etre* of this poem. As he claims, categorically, he enjoyed those moments then, *"as children do,"* yet they cross time and bring him pleasure he declares at the end: *"As I still do."*

Because of its meaningfulness, I wish to end my voyage through Sorestad's book quoting fully his poem "Map of Canada." The poet has succeeded in blending personal recollections of his younger years with a touch of what I deem as Purdian appreciation of his *"home and native land."*

For doing so, Sorestad bases his poem on culturally defining food tidbits and sweets, spread across the whole poem, writing a finely accomplished "documentary" piece of refreshing school days and homage to his Canada. This is history penciled from a perspective that makes us smile as we read and "sail around" geography, history and culinary delicacies *"somewhere off the western coast... | those chocolate bars that made | of our nation a delicious confection"*:

My vision of Canada has always been
chocolate-flavored. The country school
that steered me through seas of learning
had only one large wall map of our nation,
prominent, at the front of the classroom,
the map supplied by a candy-maker.
Apart from the predominance of pink
that transformed the Arctic North into
a gigantic midway candy floss, I don't
recall much about the different colours,
except each province had its own hue
and Saskatchewan may have been green,
which we all knew to be appropriate.

I can see the four Neilson's candy bars
tucked in the map's four corners,
subliminal treats encouraging us to regard
Crispy Crunch or Jersey Milk as
valid cartographic rewards. I was
not only inculcated in sensual pleasures
by Neilson's map, but all through my
adolescent years into my twenties,
my fidelity to Neilson's chocolate goodies
remained unshaken, undiminished.

Whenever I have cause to create in my head
the Canada I know, even now, over fifty years later,
it's hard not to see Crispy Crunch or Jersey Milk
or Malted Milk somewhere in that image
and I know that I am not alone. I also know
long after the last Neilson's chocolate bar
has been eaten, no matter that some
multinational corporate food giant has
eaten and excreted Neilson's for good
and the name disappears into
the commercial limbo with Lux and Ipana,
there will still remain a few of us,
scattered over this chocolatey nation
who will retain forever on their image
of our home and native land,
somewhere off the western coast
of Vancouver Crispy Crunch Island
or in the Beaufort Jersey Milk Sea
or off the Grand Malted Milk Banks
or Cape Breton Jersey Nut Island,
those chocolate bars that made
of our nation a delicious confection.

Sorestad shared very interesting thoughts with me in an email about "Map of
Canada": "*Sometime following the Second World War ended, Neilsons' Company,*

one of Canada's largest candy makers, decided to give every school a large paper wall map of Canada. The school I went to certainly had one and so, I think, did almost every school. They were a form of advertising because the map had one of the Neilson's candy bars in each corner of the map. So while we were learning about Canada from this map, we were also learning about Neilson's four chocolate bars which, of course, we all desired fiercely because we seldom actually saw real ones. While schools were getting a free map, they did not realize the school was unwittingly advertising Neilson's candy treats to impressionable children. I was one of the children who grew up to think Neilson's candy bars were the ultimate dessert or reward or pleasure."

In 2017, Canada Cuba Literary Alliance (CCLA) Founding President, Richard Marvin Grove put in my hands a fine book, *A Thief of Impeccable Taste* (SandCrab Book, 2011) (English-Spanish), by Glen Sorestad. The front cover was enough to lure me into the adventure of reading. The back cover gave me the preliminary why of reading.

The introductory words by Velázquez, former CCLA VP, eased me gently into Sorestad's poems, whose imprint I now try to present to you by commenting some of them. He stated (in "On the Art of Making It Last"): *"The first surprising thing in Sorestad's poetry is that scenes are illuminated by a luminescence that comes from understanding... Maybe that is why the poetic reconstruction of what has been lived is impeccable, faultless."*

"Looking Back" is the poem I have always wanted to write; but I have not been able to. Sorestad made me remember. There are memories latent somewhere in our minds, memories that time fades yet poets like Sorestad salvage them, give them shape and enriched meanings putting them in perspective, because it is good, it is enlightening to remember. He made it a principle to look ahead and go on. There is no staying in the past. It is just a round ticket, which takes you there, amuses you, makes you cry, suffer, love, recall.

Sorestad narrates seamlessly his innermost thoughts. He is, in this opening piece, telling me a story in flashback. The phrase *"Never bored"* clearly voices what childhood meant to him. He claims that there is no act of foolishness in nostalgia.

Obviously, family is there, innocence, "*a vast sky.*" The poet, feet set on the ground of objectivity: "*time past will not return,*" knows it, so we marvel at what "*lies ahead,*" it is ok to look back in time "*at the road we've traveled.*" Let's enjoy the poem fully:

Sometimes I am shaken
by a desire to return
to that child I was –
endless days under a vast sky,
sun omnipresent as the mongrel
that dogged my footsteps.

A half-century and more
removed, I remember each day
bloomed wonder. Never bored,
I did not realize how poor
we were, having so much.

On second thought, it's possible
my retrospective vision is
blurred, selectively smudged.
Perhaps it is our nature to hold
hard to what causes least pain?

To indulge moments of nostalgia
is no act of foolishness. Though
time past will not return,
we still can marvel
at the road we've travelled,
at the one that lies ahead.

It is not surprising that Sorestad opens his journey with this poem. But beware, "Streetcar Passing in the Night" follows, keeping us near his childhood. He handles the past resorting to sounds. Key words are "*listen,*" "*rumbles,*" "*clatters,*" "*squeals,*" "*groans,*" "*vibrations,*" "*purr,*" "*sound.*" These words appeal to sounds and to motion. Onomatopoeia reaches our ears, propped up by two similes: *"like a diesel tractor,"* *"like a giant cat."* Velázquez comments: *"… the streetcar that still passes at night, leaving vibrations that go from the walls and the floor to the body."*

Most kids are drawn to tractors and cats, cars and pets in general. Sound and movement are central to a child's universe: he/she is either affected by or producing them! Sorestad depicts everydayness crafting words and images that story-tell us farther than pictures would. Read these lines *(excerpts)*:

… I let my mind idle
like a diesel tractor at a truck stop.
I am back in childhood, lying awake
and waiting just as I am now,
but what I am waiting for is
the rumble and clatter of a streetcar,
metal on metal squeals and groans
shuddering the wooden walls

"Stanley Park" is a detail in the larger painting. The poet takes our hand (don't forget *"father's hands"*, a recurring image in his poetry) and, using direct second person plural/singular discourse, leads us across the "jungle." If sounds, movement and cats is what Sorestad deployed in the previous poem, here he stresses the animal part:

But it was animals you came here for –
the stuff of storybooks. Only these
were real beasts – well-fed lions
lolling in heavy-barred metal pens,
edgy black bears pacing cement cells,
their long claws clicking dangerously
on the concrete pads, their cubs nosing
the bars for treats, spider monkeys
trapezing back and forth in their cages
like acrobats beneath the circus tent.

If Archimedes told us, *"Give me a place to stand and with a lever I will move the whole world."* (*Translated version taken from* https://en.wikiquote.org/wiki/Archimedes), Glen Sorestad tells us *"Give me a Zoo and I will conquer children!"* Zoos bustle with noise; Sorestad knows it and uses it, wonderfully. These are not photos; this is a movie, cameras going from cage to cage, from site to site. The last stanza is where the poet assures us memories will stay and stand the test of time. Now I know Stanley Park sensorially and emotionally *(last stanza)*:

You and your younger brother clung
fiercely to your father's hands as you
moved through a world of fur, claws
and smells that would insinuate
themselves forever into your memory.

A poem that left me "hanging" was "Suspension of Belief." A visit, again, to childhood. Sorestad is set on rekindling our own by reminiscing his. The poem's last line flashes maturity mixed with fear. Last stanza is an exquisite "swinging" metaphor: *"faith and trust teeter and sway"* (like a bridge does). These words pave the way towards the final, definite *"No," I say."*

Cables, ropes and wooden slats
create a seemingly fragile
sagging arc high above
the crash and dash
of Capilano Canyon.
I am five.

In my eyes this is not
a bridge – but rather,
some adult deceit
designed to instill
fear in a small boy.

Father takes my hand,
envelops it in warmth,
strength and security

a child comes to accept
as truth. "Come on,"
he says.
I step forward.
Beneath my feet
faith and trust
teeter and sway
side to side,
nothing beneath me
but a void
my fear has filled.

"No," I say.

Bittersweet tang comes with "Painting." In his answers to my survey,
Sorestad wrote it is one of his favorite poems. The father figure recurs in
the poem's mood. The poet acknowledges what his father did for him.
Family love fills the poem. Sixty years do not suffice to erase such vivid
memories from Sorestad's mind – nor has Time been able to wane his
painting habit: *"I've never stopped painting" (excerpts)*:

Just keep painting, he said.
So I did. I didn't much like it,
but I did. How they adhered,
Father's words, good enamel
sealing me with a lasting coat…

… My right wrist ached, I wanted
to quit. We were not finished.
My father would not relent.
Just keep painting, he said.

That day is sixty years past.
Each wall, window frame, door –
we made them glisten in the sun,
walked away proud of our work.
I've never stopped painting.

When my mother died, 2005, I wrote her a sonnet on my first Mother's Day without her. Sixteen years later I wrote a remembrance piece, "Burial Day." (Evocative of Sorestad's "Winter Burial," included in this book, and "Autumn Burial," in another volume). Sorestad has the ability to make me tremble in recognition of the feelings stabbing the poet in "Ten Years."

It is an ode to a mother, a thoughtful prayer. Sorestad uses a soliloquy skillfully bound around a son-mother dialogue that leaves a painful yet tender sense of closeness, an intimate conversation as if his mother were sitting next to him, with her "*easy laugh*." Edgar Allan Poe knew the feeling well too: "...*among their burning terms of love, None so devotional as that of "Mother*."

My father always emphasized how important mom was to all of us, how she made us what we are. Sorestad sides with my father's insistence: "... *how a mother is heart and core of what a son becomes*." Here, the full piece:

It is now ten years since you left.
After the mini-strokes, the path
your body wobbled down
as it slowed to a final stop,
after the final stroke unworded you
and shrunk your world
to the size of a hospital bed,
your heart unwound until nothing
and no one could wind it up again.

Ten years now I have missed you
daily – the desperate reaching out
for what was so long a part of me,
belated recognition, with its constant
reminder, of how a mother is
heart and core of what a son becomes.

How I miss your easy laugh,
the gentle accord you fashioned

with the small world you knew
and neither demeaned or questioned,
but accepted and lived with as though
it held either everything or nothing
of how life's mystery unfolds.

I heard a poet say once that we link memories to songs, oldies. Sorestad validates that in "All The Sweet Songs." Sound is at the core of the poem, music and musical instruments playing a "*bittersweet remembrance*." Even if these memories are "*Silenced*" and "*waning echoes*," the poet keeps them here for us. He moves from "you" to "we," a gathering of family members that expands on father-mother allusions of previous poems.

Sorestad allows no memory to collect dust. Now his friends are called in, remembered in "Elegy for Good Friends Gone." We read rhetorical questions that the poet poses; partially answered in the second stanza. I kept thinking of "In my Life," the song by The Beatles: "*I know I'll never lose affection / for people and things that went before / I know I'll often stop and think about them…*" The poet knows death lurks. However, he does not ask for sparing; he simply and maturely asks for peace. The last words of the closing line tell us that for Sorestad life is a dance – a final one but a dance. It is a lovely, brave way to see it.

What happened to those friends of my youth –
those for whom life was an endless party;
the ones who prattled hours of riches,
always elsewhere; the ones for whom a laugh
was an answer, life a bawdy joke;
the ones who sang away their nights
with joy – where have they gone?

They have fallen into earth, so many now.
Time is cruel with some, gentler with others.
But I think of them all, from time to time
count the fallen, count those times memory
still holds, count each new sunrise a blessing.

I chronicle our days, give our lives a chance
of not being swept under history's carpet.
Death grant peace to good friends gone
and those still with me to the final dance.

Sorestad's "Loose Lock" raises the simplicity of a hair lock above the
ordinary (I have pointed this out before in the book). He places it in the
thick of the poet's plot: "*At once my heart was haunted… / all because of you,
your hair just so…*" In an array of stanzas, he gives significance to the hair
lock thus reaffirming his skill to heighten simple things' beauty: John
Keats' "*thing of beauty*" that stirs memories and makes us sigh.

Sorestad reminded me of a poem I wrote, Poljot," to my paternal grand-
parents sparked by my finding an old analog watch ("*Today I found my old
analog watch… / it was in my lowest chest drawer / dusty cracked glass, opaque
green hands / … My heart leapt. // It was a gift from my grandparents when I was
nine…*" In "Loose Lock" the magic is struck by a lock of hair. Here, the
poem, full:

I dropped by.
Knocked on your door.
No one answered.

It doesn't matter.
All that I wanted
to tell you was

the lock of hair
that tumbled awry
and fell across

your left brow
reminded me of
my favorite aunt.

At once my heart

was haunted; slid
back through years,

all because of you,
your hair just so,
that loose lock.

Another of Glen's favorite own poems is "The Thief Reflects." It is an elaborate and sustained metaphor. The poet reveals a message piecemeal, proposes the reader to jump from the *"inessential fragments"* to the most important whole: "you." A love poem, a loving poem, putting *her* in the spotlight, finding the best of excuses for the thief to steal/choose her. The poem is a deliberate declaration, elucidated by Velázquez: *"There is a necessary space for confessions, to the loved woman first. It seems every thought and act, conscious or unconscious, was for her."*

A line from this poem titles the book. Thanks to the poem's perspective, we perceive one of those moments in which primary meanings of words like *thief* are miraculously ameliorated in proper, well-framed contexts. By the end of the poem we empathize with the contention that the poet cannot *"be dismissed as common thief, nor as cheap trickster."* Let's enjoy it fully:

Tell me, what have
I stolen from you
that you have missed?

Surely you know
I have taken only
inessential fragments
you would have shed
without my help.
I can in no way be

dismissed as common
thief, nor as cheap
trickster. You must

agree I am a thief
of impeccable taste:
I did choose you.

The importance of friends, "*fellow travelers*" (those who accompany his life), group synergy that makes Sorestad be "*at ease*" is what we have in "Journey".

As he said to me, "*My second main motif* (his first one being the natural world) *would be my fellow human beings in all their infinite foibles and unusual gifts. People are an endless source of wonder and of rumination and of ongoing delight for any writer and I am no different in that sense. Human dynamics, those exchanges between people that can be the source of either pain or laughter or all the feelings that range between laughter and tears, is a huge and all-encompassing range of human expression.*"

Camaraderie and motion, as in the poems about childhood, escort the poet. Perhaps it is that sixth sense telling him movement does relate to life, to breathing. "*That we are sharers all*" offers a partaking Sorestad who knows the social aspect of sharing, how it lessens burdens and enriches lives – sharing is a soul provider. "Journey" is worth-quoting:
I move in ever smaller circles. It's not that I am doing
so much less. My pace befits the point I have reached.

As the circles diminish in size, there's a contradiction
of satisfaction looking back and anxiety for the road ahead.

But in the company of my fellow travellers I am at ease,
knowing that we are sharers all, still moving and moving still.

"*The mask is not the substance*" is not the poem's title; "This Morning Mirror" is. But the line captivated me for its judicious connotation. It is essence what counts, unbridled, timeless spirit: "*Love still burns deep, glows deep inside.*" That is what Sorestad is telling her – us – about old age. In my view, the fact that he chose "morning" to modify "mirror" is a reflection of how confidently and bravely will the poet face life: mornings come and go, it is only the mirror in the morning. The man takes it from there into the bright side. As a mirror freezes an image for a few seconds, so is the apparent, initial negativity in the poem's fleeting start waived aside in the last stanza.

The battle of telling the truth is unveiled in Sorestad's poem "To Have and To Hold." I agree with him: sometimes we must just keep silent. Do notice that Sorestad never tells us to lie. Simply to "*keep* (your) *mouth closed.*" In a selection of thought-out metaphors: "*truth is a tale,*" "*knowledge can be either the thorn or the rose, or a rising bile,*" and with supporting rhyme, he offers this poem as advice. Be wise, those "*we love most*" are "*The injured so often.*"

"Presences & Absences" is white/black, joy/fear. I would have expected Sorestad to start with the "negative" stanza and leave the "positive" one for the end, to please the reader. But then I read the poem a couple more times and noticed that in writing the poem the way it is, he empowered the last stanza with all the beauty and significance displayed for the reader – and for the person it is dedicated to. Her presence fills with "comfort;" her absence then would be "*the spear of fear.*"

That is how he sees the presence-absence formula. Loving someone next to us is easy and comfortable; loving from a distance is a test of endurance! Deep reverence to poem and poet.

Once more The Beatles ("*All you need is love, love is all you need…*") sing in "Offering," reminding me of a past Sorestad goes back to so much. Social issues are also addressed:

What am I to offer
this day, or any day –
add my voice to the shrill
wail and rail against
the permanence of injustice –
against being either man
or woman in a world that treats

either with equal disdain?
Add my cry to the decibels
of anguish, to all hearts
that cry out their messages
of lost hope and despair?

There is nothing I can offer,
but love. Let me say it again:
there is nothing I can offer
you, or anyone, but love.
Love is all there is
can save us from what we are.
Only love redeems, now
and ever more.
Only love redeems, now
and ever more.

In "Offering," Sorestad summons to the act of loving. Hear him out. He comfortably sits among Canadian poets who embrace the beauty surrounding them, a feature I have analyzed in previous essays, with his piece "Make It Last." It is Sorestad as a narrator again, presenting out-door worlds (his foremost writing motif):

A flash of orange and black
through sun-splattered aspen leaves,
the faintest glimpse of Baltimore Oriole;
or the brilliant scarlet shoulder sheen
as a Red-winged Blackbird warbles
from its wind-bent cat-tail perch;
or a high-above dissonant clamour
of a passing startle of Snow Geese
etched white on unmarred blue:
rare moments the willfully blind
view as commonplace, or do not see.
Beauty surrounds us – no charge,
no previous experience needed.

Stand awhile. Look and listen.
Make it last.

He alerts the *"wilfully blind"* to open eyes and see, be filled with that grandeur in landscape, flora and fauna. It is environmentalism, but above all admiration for life and realities that he wouldn't want us to miss.

"The Watcher" follows this fresh shower of awesome nature, so do "Winter at Emma Lake," "Mourning Dove," "Paper Birches," and many others. Let's look at the latter:

The clump birches
beside the lakeshore
are slowly peeling off
their papery attire
like well-practised
lovers intent
on sustaining that
delicate tension
between fantasy
and reality.

"Six Reasons I Write Poems" closes this *impeccable* book. The *"small tile"* Sorestad has bequeathed to us is material for a canopy of pleasures. I quoted one of its lines in a poem I wrote trying to convey what I feel when I write. Sorestad said: *"I like the state I'm in when a poem takes hold and won't let go."* In his answers to my survey, he wrote: *"Once I begin to write a poem, I feel that I am in a state that blocks out any thoughts about the mechanics or structure of poetic craft."*

A poem empowers the child in me
to emerge and show me the way;

I've discovered through poems
what I otherwise wouldn't know;

Each of my poems is a small tile
in the ongoing mosaic of my life;

I like the state I'm in when a poem
takes hold and won't let go;

I love the subtle way words can map
their own path through the forest;

Poems allow me to share with strangers
moments of intimate intensity.

Glen and I, two strangers, shared *"moments of intimate intensity."* He is no longer a stranger to me. He has good reasons to write and charm us. *The Thief of Impeccable Taste* has become a giver of aesthetic values and wisdom.

In Glen's words, *Along Okema Road* (Rubicon Press, 2013) is "... *a chapbook I am very fond of and poems from which are also in the Dancing Birches selection, I feel very close to many of the poems of this book and maybe you will be able to decide why that is so."*

The poems of this book were all written over the past half-dozen years while he was staying on the Kenderdine Campus of the University of Saskatchewan at Emma Lake, one of Saskatchewan's beautiful parkland lakes north of Prince Albert. As some of its poems are included in *Dancing Birches*, I choose two I did not approach. They are:

"Fickle Weather"
Today, the meteorological gamut.
Early morning, cloudless and still,
a blue plate overhead. Then wind
tosses in a handful of clouds,
reaching out to clasp one another,
and the sun hides behind them
as greyness settles like an old cat.

Distant mutters as dark thunderclouds
loom. First rain, soft as sprayed mist.
Then raindrops ricochet off shingles,
chatter-clatter. Sudden burst of blue
as clouds part company and leave.
Wind flees into the forest and the lake
falls asleep in its reflection.

and "Leaning Birch"
Across the grassy bay a paper birch
leans fifty degrees out over the marshy island point,
its wan whiteness in fast falling light
a bony finger pointing the way to somewhere,
I know not where. Is someone responsible
for the tree's pronounced tilt –
some attempt to mark a visible bearing
for boaters, a waterways inukshuk?
Or could it be nature has managed this
of its own accord, this leaning birch
now gleaming pale under a rising moon,
pointing to a distant star?
Who has never fancied a star shared with another,
or singled out one special light in the starlit night?
Often we accord to stars our hopes and our dreams.
Who has never sought a galactic talisman,
some light in the dark bearing its own message,
a marker we can fix upon to untilt our own lives?
How responsible to hold a dream, to ponder
the unimagined? All this about a birch
become a finger, a ghostly signpost leaning,
pointing somewhere in the night.

The closeness Glen feels for these poems, which he invited me to explore, can be traced back initially to his personal bond with the inspiring contexts in which he wrote them (Kenderdine Campus of the University of Saskatchewan at Emma Lake, one of Saskatchewan's beautiful parkland lakes north of Prince Albert).

Reexamining the poems, I venture in saying Sorestad's spirituality shines in them, an element that may stem from the above-mentioned environment. "Amazing" pops back with singular force as I state this. Likewise, Canadian poets have an "umbilical" nexus (a term I have used before) with nature. Let's not forget Canada's pioneer poets and their nature poems. Herein is found another reason for his fondness towards these poems and the themes that inspired them.

In addition, Sorestad is a sharp beholder. Nothing escapes his eye, everything is worthy of perusal and notation for writing about. A glance at his list of favorites throws light too on his affection for this book. They were motivation and model to write.

Nonetheless, we could detect another underlying factor, a time-based, intimate one. This is what he advised in his answers to my survey: *"I also believe that poetry is intensely personal, that a poem that one reader finds especially engaging or moving or illuminating may not have the same impact at all on another reader. That is why time is the greatest factor in determining the lasting power of a poem or a poet."*

This conception corroborates his station in Canadian poetry and is applicable to his dedication to every book he has written.

As I expounded before, the Canada Cuba Literary Alliance, founded in 2004 by Richard Marvin Grove, was created to promote friendship, culture, literature and art. It opened formats to publicize the work of Canadian and Cuban writers and artists. One of these is the official magazine, *The Ambassador* (English-Spanish). Poets from both countries have filled its pages, some of which are dedicated to a Guest Poets section. The magazine's 11th volume presented Glen Sorestad as Guest Poet.

The magazine's editors introduced him to the readers like this: *"... As one of Canada's most celebrated poets today, we are honoured to have him as our feature poet. Much of Sorestad's poetry lances though lived experiences, trails through the bushes of memory reviving what is distinctive, what has skin and marrow, what throbs and lives."*

Richard Grove's opinion about the poet is rightly adjectival: "... *another inspiring, stirring, moving, stimulating feature poet, Glen Sorestad...*" Let's trail beside Sorestad through the bushes of memory with some of the poems he published in *The Ambassador*:

"Aide Mémoire" *(From Leaving Holds Me Here: Selected Poems. Thistledown Press, 2001)*

The world begins and ends in memory;
what I remember is what I am.

Did that blade of grass I plucked
as a boy to vibrate with my breath

really burst the air with shrillness?
A remembered world holds truth

and realities far clearer than echoes.
In the cupped hands of remembrance

the thin green reed of what we are
trembles with a sound so rare.

Mnemonic by title and content, the poem invites to the act of reflecting. The poet ponders, and suggests we do. Beautiful imagery abounds in the poem. I was charmed by

In the cupped hands of remembrance
the thin green reed of what we are
trembles with a sound so rare.

The metaphor crafted at the beginning of the line branches comfortably out through the remaining fragment. I am briefly unsettled by the closing line yet I reconcile my short-lived confusion with the sweet tones of the poem as a whole, educated in its lore.

The second piece, "Moon Thoughts," inherits the metaphorical richness of the previous one:

It might have been
something in the soft
flush of moonlight
as it slid cool
fingers through your hair

reminding me
                         decades later
of you

                  when moon thoughts
first crept across my mind

The poem is a trip of recollections flashing back from *"the soft / flush of moonlight"* in a web of decades and moon thoughts. The *"something"* Sorestad proposes pulses with intimacy and mystery. It is the excuse to write and memorialize those mementos.

The gravitas surrounding "Autumn Burial" floats respectfully in the airspace between the text and my eyes *(excerpt)*,

Head bowed, I shuffle to the grave.
The clergywoman utters the words
that commit to the earth in this graveyard
holding those many shared common kin,
my first cousin and boyhood friend.

The trail continues with "The Beauty of Silence." A discreet plea is felt as we read, intertwined with soft melancholy and the discovery of *"the beauty of silence,"* which struggles with *"the need to speak that wars / with our desire to hear silence…"* These are impulses colliding inside the poet:

I think I am beginning to understand,
to come to know why it was you said

so little to me then, much preferred
to write a letter, send a book.

I too have lost the will to say
again and again what must be said.

I too know the beauty of silence,
know the need to speak that wars

with our desire to hear silence
say all the things that we can not.

So many times I've looked into myself
and found your silence there, Father.

To conclude, we read the intense piece "Ancestral Dance" *(From Leaving Holds Me Here: Selected Poems. Thistledown Press, 2001)*. It is one of his favorites. The recurring idea of the *"final dance"* we had in "Elegy for Good Friends Gone," comes back to end this family-poem, this trip into memory lanes of sounds and nostalgia. Like Sorestad's grandfather, we are *"Caught in the mystery of the past"*:

The violin my grandfather
staunchly called a fiddle
but refused to play for us
held for him some magic link
with the man he was.

Left at home alone when we
were safely distant for the day
he'd uncase the fiddle,
rosin the bow with trembling fingers.

Caught in the mystery of the past
he delayed death, bowed the fragments
of a life that was always private,
even on a crowded dance floor.

In the gathering silence
of seventy years
with fumbling recall he
became the dance.

Hazards of Eden: Poems from the Southwest (Lamar University Press, 2015), a book of poems from the American Southwest, also holds a half-dozen of Glen's favorite poems within his oeuvre, "The Dancing Man of Santa Elena" and "After the Fall" being among those favorites. About the book, Sorestad says in the Preface, "*… thus began my long and continuing fascination with the Southwest, call it a love affair if you wish, and one I'm happy to say is still flourishing.*"

For its self-explanatory character and clarification, I quote more of his comments in the book: "*When I travel anywhere, I write poems. That is just how it is with me. It's what I do and it's how I respond to things that capture my attention, that stimulate my interest and that pique my curiosity. I can no more avoid writing poems during my travels than I can avoid breathing. It's just who I am. I don't pretend to be anything more than an interested observer as I move through the Southwest.*" We are still disclosing the poet's strong ties to his poetry, one he views as his offspring.

One piece immediately validating the poet's statement that "*The poems are the written manifestations of what has captured and held my attention, even for a moment, of things that have impressed themselves upon me,*" is "Life is a Highway":

We drive the interstate towards San Antonio,
and I am enjoying being behind the wheel
of this rented German road machine that clings
to the road and purrs contentedly to itself.
A sign announces the next exit as COMFORT.

I pass without comment, but I do note
how appropriate it feels, here, this moment.
Inside the Passat all is well. Comfort indeed.

Further along the concrete another sign says
the next exit, believe it or not, WELFARE.
Only in Texas, can one forsake Comfort
for Welfare and still be on the right road.

From man-made infrastructure and signaling, Glen gears swiftly, dexterously,
to nature themes. He revels in its purity:

"Hard Scrabble Clouds"
Beneath this unmarred blue
the only clouds today

lie just above the russet soil
on stems of ripening cotton.

In "Big Bend Suite" Sorestad surrenders to the awesome desert rendering
superb haiku pieces. Here, excerpts from it:

1.
Chihuahuan desert:
spring is a horseman fording
the Rio heading north.

2.
The mountain lion
turns darkness into danger
high in the Chisos.

3.
Santa Elena:
canyon carved by Rio Grande
to sheer sandstone walls.

The Purdian legacy, mapping and naming, is felt in this poem:

"If Place Names Mean Anything"
then how fortunate
the New Mexico poet

who lives in a house
at the very foot

of Dragon Mountain
in Owl Canyon

Dancing Birches: Selected Poems (Impremix Edizioni Visual Grafika, 2020), in the poet's words, "*draws upon poems from several books, including A Thief of Impeccable Taste, Along Okema Road and Water and Rock, as well as a few earlier poems and a few poems from Cuba that make their first book appearance in this volume.*" It was published in English-Italian.

Sorestad offers the beauty of the landscape, wildlife free to roam, nature prevailing in metaphorical dabs, in the poem "Evening Settles on Okema Road." How he absorbs reality and pens it is told in his words: "*Sometimes a visual image is just so appealing and illuminating when you see it for the first time, that you want to capture it in words before it slips away, or before memory loses its grasp of it. Sometimes, for me, it is not visual, but verbal, or musical, but essentially you want to preserve the initial sensory experience for later, when you can enjoy and consider it in quiet contemplation. As a lifetime writer of poems though, I have learned to rely on moments of sheer Inspiration...*"

We will understand what he means and how he transits, masterfully, from theme to them; or combines them, by reading the poems below, starting with "Evening Settles on Okema Road":

White-tailed deer emerge to browse from deeper woods where
their days are free from prying eyes and human intrusions.

In falling light they are insubstantial, one with the forest,
moving in utter silence, hesitant wraiths, cautious but curious.

Sunset glow languishes; trees and undergrowth blur to oneness
in this slow merge into black night. For the moment,
in this twilight, otherworldliness descends on Okema Road,
upon the forest that holds the road and all along it, everything

and everyone, in a glow, not of ominousness, but of wellbeing.
This is the time when to walk along Okema Road is to move

through a story of your own making, a story you may or may not
choose to share, one that will lie in the mind like a dormant seed.

A stylistic device intermittently encountered in poetry, onomatopoeia,
greets the reader in the especially long "Early Morning Owl" *(excerpts)*:

I was awakened about five this morning
by the persistent calling of an owl.
Whoo-hoo, hoo-hoo.

I don't know whether it was horned or barred,
grey or white, long-eared or earless —
I did not see the owl at all.

Whoo-hoo, hoo-hoo,
it seemed to call straight to me through
the open window of the cabin.

Was it an omen? I ask myself this now,
later in the day when the hooting returns
to resonate loudly inside my mind.

I'd rather not see this as omen or a premonition.
Nothing in the articulation or tone made me
think for a moment it was my name

on the creature's tongue, nor that the bird
intended its message just for me...

But then, but then…
if I am recalling this early awakening
with accuracy and not creating specifics
in the aftermath of the creature's presence,

something any writer might well incline to do,
I seem to remember the owl hoo-hooed at me…

Sorestad handles the owl's sound as a direct onomatopoeia yet takes a leap
beyond through linguistic conversion using it as a verb, stylistically
coloring his intent. There is no doubt in me that Poe's "The Raven"
reverberates not just in the onomatopoeic interplay of sounds in both
poems but also in the atmosphere the two poets create. In Sorestad's case,

… Whoo-hoo, hoo-hoo,
it seemed to call straight to me through
the open window of the cabin…

Was it an omen? I ask myself this now,
later in the day when the hooting returns
to resonate loudly inside my mind…

I'd rather not see this as omen or a premonition.
Nothing in the articulation or tone made me
think for a moment it was my name…

But then, but then…
if I am recalling this early awakening
with accuracy and not creating specifics…

I seem to remember the owl hoo-hooed at me…

Onomatopoeia is revisited in the poem "Suddenness of Squirrel," where
the poet combines both types, direct ("*CHIR-R-R-R-R*") and indirect
by repeating strings of the sound /r/, its echo starting three lines above
with "*squirrel*," emphasized in the verb "*shrilled*," then "*spruce*" and rein-

forced in the lines "… *struck a note of near panic / somewhere… / through the Sonoran desert… / maraca of a diamondback rattlesnake…*":

I am not sure where my mind had gone to hide,
or whether it was chiseling away at some large grey stone
in the sub-consciousness, unapparent images or sounds
bursting like fireworks, but whatever may have been
happening on an intellectual or even aesthetic level
was abruptly obliterated, the sculpture image toppled
and zapped into the void, the precise moment the red squirrel
shrilled loudly from its spruce limb just above my head.

I lurched sideways, taken aback by the stridence of its sudden
CHIR-R-R-R-R, which struck a note of near panic
somewhere deep inside me, as if I had been walking
through the Sonoran desert and had been stopped cold
by the chilling maraca of a diamondback rattlesnake.

I was not ready for it. But why should this tiny, harmless
creature have triggered in me, rational animal, such instant
fright-and-flight reflex? I am at Emma Lake, for godsake.
I know I share this space with squirrels – and I am
more than happy to do so. Is it because we want nature
on our terms and not on its own? I can now laugh
at my ignorance and my unseemly fear, shrug it off
as an aberration, though I know it's nothing of the kind.

The poem "Amazing" is indeed remarkable. Sorestad is a keen observer who decodes in words the impressive, optic-musical manifestation of life playing out in the wild. He watches and sees beyond the mere surface of things and motions:

1.
The way the soft
first light of dawn
feels its way

through needles
of black spruce,

as water pries
its inexorable path
through dense
hardness of bedrock.

2.
The way a slab
of granite becomes
a garden where mosses
and lichen precede
birch and pine,

the way roots will
themselves to gain
a hold, then
drive upwards
to court the sun.

I cannot close my comments on this book without addressing Cuba-related poems. "Finca Vigia" is especially close to me. I studied Hemingway in college.

His house is now a museum. You can look,
but you can't touch – photos, if you wish,
may be taken from cordoned doorways
or through open windows in this home
where he and Mary lived, where he wrote,
where they entertained movie stars and statesmen.
Pilar, his fishing boat, stands weathered,
high and dry, alongside the swimming pool
where Ava Gardner is said to have stroked
lengths, adorned with that famous sultry smile,
and so the rumour goes, nothing else.

Everywhere in Havana that Hemingway
ate or drank, worked or played, is remembered
by fresh generations of those he lived among
and loved with a fierce tenderness, people
who loved him back and love him still –
an American hero in a nation blockaded
by his own people — this place he came to live in,
where he will never die, but be forever Papa,
a giant among the people who welcomed him,
who took him into their hearts,
not the man who also lived in Idaho
and hunted pheasants, who one day
took his shotgun out and wrote the end
to the story he spent a lifetime telling.

Dancing Birches: Selected Poems is, as I said, a compilation from other books. From *A Thief of Impeccable Taste*, which I presented before, I pick one piece I did not comment, "Nocturne." As in earlier poems, we enjoy its call, pieces of advice and astuteness compacted in its lines:

1.
Night is never dark enough for some.
There will always be things to hide.

Cold speaks its own language. Listen.
The deafest ear will hear something.

Fear not the night, the dark, the cold.
It is ourselves that we need to fear.

2.
An open heart will always be hurt.
Close it if you must. All hearts die.

Open hearts know the joy of yes.
Closed hearts only the pain of no.

Only a fool tries to stop the wind.
The same fool tries to stop hurt.
The open hand feels good about itself.
The closed hand always wonders why.

I conclude my journey through this book with "Sounds." In "Aide Mémoire" we read about *"the thin green reed of what we are / trembles with a sound so rare,"* and I was briefly unsettled by its warning air; in "Early Morning Owl" we heard the vibrations of an ominous tu-whoo. Now "Sounds" is a plunge into the labyrinth of quiet resonance, indirect onomatopoeia murmuring in the /s/-/ʃ/ sound configurations across the poem, specifically perceptible in *"a soft-shoe shuffle of wind"*:

There. That is the sound
I have missed – the sound
that stirs my dreams,
that comes and goes in the night:
a soft-shoe shuffle of wind
moving through birch and aspen,
scratching its sides
on spikes of spruce and pine.
Welcome back, it says.

If I were to delve into Sorestad's closeness with onomatopoeia – his stylistic soulfulness in general and his penmanship – I would start with three (surely more) crucial factors. First, family influence: *"As I've mentioned before, my parents kindled my passion for language, rhythm and musicality by reading to me as an infant. They promoted a love of language that led to a love of poetry."*

His earliest recollection of poetry goes to his mother and father reading to him: *"The rhythms of nursery rhymes though, my earliest memories, instilled the elements of poetry into my blood while I was still an infant. How could I not become a poet?"* Evidently, seeds were being planted. The plentiful harvest would come eventually.

The second factor was school milieu: *"I had the good fortune to go to school in a small rural school where independent learning was necessitated and fostered. That left me free to explore poetry well beyond what the curriculum required. I memorized dozens of great poems and can still recite them today, poems like Frost's "Stopping by the Woods on a Snowy Evening" or Tennyson's "The Lady of Shallot". There are countless fragments of classical poetry – from lines and stanzas to complete poems – that I have carried with me…"*

Factor three lies in the list of favorite authors he would read as he grew: *"I have many, many favorite authors and over the years of my writing life, many of these have changed, or been superseded by others that I have "discovered". Longtime favorites of mine include Robert Frost, Carl Sandburg, Alden Nowlan, Al Purdy, Pablo Neruda, Stephen Dunn, Naomi Shihab Nye, A. E. Housman, Mary Oliver, John Newlove, Billy Collins, Keith Wilson, Miller Williams, Lynn Knight, Tom Wayman."*

This is how I end my stroll across Sorestad's magnificent poetry. In my Introduction I quoted Sorestad, who emailed me these humble words: *"I have always believed that when the writer has finished the poem and has sent it out into the world for others to read, the writer's job is done. Now the poem exists as a piece of art and like any piece of art it is subject to literary criticism. I have always believed as well, that at that point, the writer should be silent because he/she has had his/her say."*

Well, Sorestad's job is done in every single poem and book he finishes. Let's have hope there will be more to come. As he says, his poetry is a piece of art. We wish to continue reading it.

A.F. MORITZ

Poem

The unheralded mystery of spring
forces its will again on the herald flower.
In the thicket I pause to remember.
February was my mentor in misery,
that hollow pamphlet from yellow skies,
basin of dead sparrows.
I am a glove on an absent hand
and speaking, writing are nothing but the dream.
Don't try to say they are anything more than dream.
Whether or not there is such a thing as time,
I am this window on night's senseless palette,
which is already the portrait
more perfect than the face.
Across the torn darkness
I am this anarchic scrawl,
this wake of a restless scalpel.

A.F. Moritz

An approach to USA-born Canadian poet A. F. Moritz should start with his own words. He referred to a poet's "job" in an interview as *"To write well: creatively, authentically, powerfully, beautifully…. poetry is partly self-development…"* We are talking about a multi-awarded poet concerned with the role of poetry from a moral and socio-linguistic standpoint: "(Poetry)… *is duty, belonging to a community… poetry's role is as the guardian and developer of language.*" *(Taken from an interview on the Web)*

In talks with Richard Grove and James Deahl, they have always been emphatic on my approaching Moritz. Both have said he is a figure I cannot overlook in a review book. James has stressed on the fact that any poetry anthology must have his poems.

A. F. Moritz has been called *"one of the best poets of his generation"* by John Hollander and *"a true poet"* by Harold Bloom. He has received numerous awards and honors in North America: the Award in Literature of the American Academy of Arts and Letters, the Guggenheim Fellowship, Poetry magazine's Beth Hokin Prize, the Ingram Merrill Fellowship, and the Griffin Poetry Prize.

His favorites and influences are vast: *"The English Romantics, and the German Romantics, are my Ur-writers in many respects. The great mid-twentieth-century poets were my school in writing a modern idiom and verse form: the English language poets, yes, but especially the European and Latin American ones, usually in wonderful English translations: Ungaretti, Quasimodo, Montale, Pavese, Zanzotto, Luzi; Jiménez and Jorge Guillén; George Seferis and Cavafy; Mandelstam; Celan; Rilke, Benn, Bobrowski; Breton, Bonnefoy; Neruda and Vallejo and Paz; Czeslaw Milosz. Those are a few… I love and am very influenced by Beckett, Jonathan Swift, Alfred Tennyson, Hölderlin, Vergil, Sappho in the translations by Mary Barnard and Willis Barnstone. Lucretius, Catullus, Aeschylus. Whitman, Emerson, Poe's dozen or so best poems, in which he' a great poet Emily Dickinson. Wallace Stevens. John Ashbery, whom I knew. Derek Walcott. The mid-to-late nineteenth-century French poets are essential to me. There are many more I should mention."*

My study of Moritz started with *Song of Fear* (Brick Books, 1992). It is one of those awe-inspiring books we put down with care after reading them, feeling they have refocused our entire existence. Already established as a poet, Moritz shows full artistry in description and elucidation of thought-provoking realities laid out before him. The poet is in a long moment of ecstasy.

Regarding the realities and motifs that inspire him, see what he said in his answers to my survey: *"I don't know. Perhaps I don't know on purpose. I think it's not good to be too studiously aware and calculating, about such things as motifs. I believe that my awareness of them arises as I write, as part of the writing. Perhaps I become aware, for instance, that seeing a bird is a typical inspiration for me. Then the poem becomes both a direct response and creation based on this encounter with a bird, and a poem about the fact that birds, and the apparition of birds, customarily move me, and customarily happen to me. In other words, birds and their appearances—their crossing my path, coming into and out of my vision and my life—both belong to some characteristic of my responsiveness with an obscure origin and purpose within me, and belong to the "outside world", to the birds themselves, who come to me for what we call a reason."* This bird element will be with us throughout his entire work.

The opening poem, "Evening," mirrors a brooding man. Events and objects, thoughts and human undercurrents unfold in metaphorical feats *(excerpts),*

... eyes chained to dusk,
chained in pleasure to the ash-golden going light... //
... where night
already welled up roots and trunks...

The poet admits the kaleidoscope of ideas trooping into his mind, allowing him to word them in a cascade of reasoning and prickling sensations *(excerpts)*:

... I wondered again how joy...
... could come and always does
from this lessening of things, of colours, movements,
number and speed and happy confusion of thoughts...

The poem is gently dense, simultaneously deriving images into tropes, musings into imagery; shades of stories weaving out of the text *(excerpts)*:

… the leaf-fall thickening night, night deepening the fall,
the placid evening swallowing the hot autumn noon…
… the brief watch of his presence here: and so he dreams
on the hillside, still hearing the young footsteps
dying in the cellar…

Unavoidability of loss is evident in our next poem, "A Philosopher." The society-aware poet pulses in the first lines. He has said, "… *I have a great interest in society and a great desire to participate in society…," (conversation with The Sunday Edition's host Michael Enright)* commitment surfacing *(excerpts)*:

To love the people and each woman, each man,
to fight for their freedom when the enemy
                    comes with his guns…

The seeker of truth and beauty resonates too:

… this is truth
where nothing true can be.

And the man who clings to a shaft of relief, courage and proudness, self-salvaging his place under the sun *(excerpts)*:

And I was proud to live on this last tiny fragment
from the decaying body
of the son that never rose,
proud too of being myself a fragment
in the earth that covered him.

Moritz is fascinated, like many poets (and definitely the other four poets I reviewed here), with time and aesthetics: "*A recurring theme is the passage of time and evanescence… Beauty is also an enduring theme. Thus Moritz celebrates the 'never-to-be-exhausted/fascination of sunset, 'symbolic of the cycle of day and*

night — which in turn is linked to the cyclical nature of life itself."
(Taken from Wikipedia:
https://www.thestar.com/entertainment/books/2020/04/23/water-fountains-books-
heart-surgery-the-unexpected-feature-in-al-moritzs-new-poetry.html?rf)

Regarding both time and beauty, the poem "Something Else Must Come" is, in my view, one of the most stirring pieces I have read by Moritz or any author. It is a concert of images, sound, colors, softly arranged and lovingly laid upon a metaphorical stave, on which sensuousness and tenderness are gracefully drawn *(excerpts)*:

The hours when you were naked by
the still more naked ocean
will die. The sand will stretch out…
its warmth will lick the breasts
pressed down on it. High engines
will drone softly, as once to you,
from the blue sky or water,
more softly than bees in a red flower.

Enjoy the last lines. As we read, we almost gasp drowned by sizzling subtext and immeasurable scopes, laced with hyperboles and metaphors:

But I know the dark of each day
would bring you, with humiliation,
with slavery to anyone who deigned
to serve you an exhausted hour,
ecstasy also, nervous ecstasy
that would crest higher even than the sun,
if it left you more alone. Then find,
find someone from within this very dusk
that's thickening to love you. Morning
won't come again, the earth
rolls you ever deeper in its shade.

In this book we have "April Song of Fear," a poem (also "Song: It Does

Not Matter") the reader may approach later in this paper in my study of *The Sparrow*, which is a compilation of pieces from Moritz's books, personally chosen by him.

"Song of a Traveller" is a poet's introspective wandering down the paths of existence, implicated inwardly and outwardly while baring his thoughts elegantly *(excerpts)*:

If I could be the air that fills my lungs.
It enters all their dark tunnels, their branch-roofed roads
and comes to every end, fills all ends with itself,
and goes still farther, changed…

The poet declares his admiration for the air's "suppleness," how it is capable of filling *"all ends,"* how it is capable of change and how it *"goes farther."* It is his aspiration too: he wants to break free; he wishes to have the gifts of the air *(excerpts)*:

And not be what I am: a tiny wanderer
along the forking paths and streams of my own body,
with always a new turn to face, a new decision…
… envy of the air
that gently possesses everything – but not
as my hope does…

Moritz will forgive my saying that the poem's last five lines reminded me, in rhythm and epigrammatic weight, of Shakespeare's Sonnet 116, specifically *"Love's not Time's fool, though rosy lips and cheeks / Within his bending sickle's compass come; / Love alters not with his brief hours and weeks, / But bears it out even to the edge of doom."*

Let's see Moritz's lines:

… that gently possesses everything – but not
as my hope does, which drags its horse behind it,
and when sometimes it arrives at a place it loved from far off,

it can't bear to stay there even long enough
to cry or sleep, but trudges onward that same night.

As Moritz has stated, *"I truly enjoy life,"* so he proves in his poem "Reckless April." The bond with nature, a sufficiently argued regularity in Canadian poets, emerges in this "landscape painting," or "motion picture." Both perspectives surely express what the poet is trying to convey, the seasonal lure *(excerpts)*:

… a sapling breaking
into bud under wooded slopes, and one clear ray
from the sun breaking from the pure sky
of spring's first pallid warmth, finding
a way through a dark mass of leafless branches,
reaching the sapling, touching it alone.

Colors are suggested, movement and scent too; meticulous images either dabbed from the scene or videoed for posterity. Personalization prevails. Life enjoyed by the poet, captured by his poetic eye, he closes the poem in a rapture of happiness, as he realizes the harmonizing magic of the month:

… a point of clarity, freshness, of fiery green
dazzling and calm, where frigid April, reckless,
fuses the warring elements of joy.

"They simply fly with the sparrows" is a line from the poem "Results of One's Research." A pet motif in his poetry, Moritz gives us his sparrow element in a piece when,

There are times when one is wholly confused with the voices
paid homage to so carefully and so long. It's then
they say least of all: they simply fly with the sparrows…

Now we have a thinker, sharing what he perceives and turns into words aiming at the comprehension of all, trying to grasp beyond the obvious, the literal:

... And space is lovely, bright and deep, but memory
is only the dead sound of this last step,
there is no history here but the natural one
that shines all around in blue houses and gold trees.

Again Moritz will have to forgive me for connecting this poem (the first line in the previous snippet, which ignited my recollection) with Frost's "Stopping by Woods on a Snowy Evening": "*The woods are lovely, dark and deep, / But I have promises to keep...*" Notice the poems' similitude in pace, coincidental key words like "*lovely*" and "*deep*," and the conjunction *but*, plus the close-rhyming echo of "*deep*" with "*step*."

 I felt happy to know Moritz does have Frost as one of his earlier experiences in reading: "*... My father made up and told fanciful stories a little. In my late teenage years, I discovered that he loved the essays of Charles Lamb – beautiful but far from easy reading! – and the poetry of Robert Frost, because, he said, "It sounds just like prose" – he was thinking of the narrative poems, of course.*"

Sparrows recur in the poems "Death of a Sparrow" (considered as "*... one of those perfectly constructed, perfectly expressed and unforgettable poems that some of the finest poets succeed in writing once or twice in a long career.*") *(Taken from Wikipedia)*, "Sparrows with a Sentence" and "Sparrow," besides other bird/insect-related poems, explanations of which the reader can refer to further down this paper.

From "Death of a Sparrow," let's have some of its descriptive lines that pass on to us the bird's – and the poet's – anguish:

The twisting dance of the sparrow, delicate
agony, as it tried to bite its wounded shoulder:
circular flurries, brief trembling flights
and fallen landings – then the wait, panting...
... When I approached,
a fury of terrors possessed the sparrow...
... The next day, the sweet body in the grass
lay there..."

While I was working on this book I was asked to write a review about an anthology edited by John B. Lee. The poems in it were dedicated entirely to poets' traveling experiences. I comment this because Moritz's *Mahoning* (Brick Books, 1994) is about a unique kind of traveling. While it is impossible to cover all the poems in this volume, it is my intention to navigate across some of them; those which drew my attention as I read, the way Moritz's poems did in *The Sparrow.*

The first poem, I, is a spatial and a temporal journey, affections underlying the poem's tone. Childhood reminiscences are told by the poet, which merge with geographical environments. See what he has said about it:

"The possibility of childhood and that freshness that you can always go back to and renew yourself — that remains..." (Taken from an interview on the Web: https://www.thestar.com/entertainment/books/2020/04/23/water-fountains-books-heart-surgery-the-unexpected-feature-in-al-moritzs-new-poetry.html) (all excerpts):

I wake up. And it seems to me I am
in childhood's place again – or still:
that the far-off Mahoning flows nearby,
while heat and floating water gather
and thicken in September's night.

The poet's themes (natural cycles, insects) resonate in the poem; they show us his drives and devotion:

... summer should be over, dead,
but it rages one more time, and in the fever
that starts in summer's sleep and breaks its dream...
the crickets are vibrating, their steady drills
not music but something older, cool
and clear: sweet water at its source...

Intimating, dazzling metaphors garland the thoughts. There is a fast-moving trepidation in the enumerations, as happens in life, creating the sensation of multiplicity; perhaps to bewilder – as life does:

… It's as if the wall
that the world is were a graceful labyrinth
of leaves and branches, inviting
endless transgression: openings, entrances
everywhere, and numberless winding ways
leading to forkings into other ways, the same…

Poetry occurs as life does in Moritz's conception of creativity. When I asked him what would lead him to sit and write, he replied: "*When there comes a flow of the words. It's the upspringing of words in their musical or melodic dimension that creates an irresistible attraction and momentum in me. What we call meaning is always there, but the essence of poetry is the musical and melodic element, just as music and melody are the essence of life…or rather, the type of unity that life and existence possess, that type of unity and identity within perpetual change, is best thought of in terms of melody and harmony… So when a series of words comes to me that is already a line, or a line and a half, or a small group of lines, with a unity and a movement, which includes but dissolves, as it were, and carries the meaning, them I'm eager to get the whole structure that will emerge from this seed… Poetic inspiration is constant, is a constant dynamic presence, but for a poem to occur, it needs a certain provocation, which cannot come except by something happening in the world and our being open to it, sensitive to it, response to it. Wordsworth said that we must be "a sensitive and a creative soul"."*

The surrealistic style we have seen in many of Moritz's poems is present in piece X. He wades through the density of the images, pushing on, coalescing reality planes:

… And near us was the sizzling of one last word
in an ancient neon sign, almost burnt-out,
the glowing of one light through silver maple leaves
on a street of unpainted houses.
Your lips brushed the sunken drum in the marsh,
the smoke, corroded mills…

As a reader, I can almost feel the flickering illusion caused by the "*almost burnt-out*" sign. It glows with both the metaphorical construct and the actual physicality of the "*maple leaves.*"

"Along the Rails" speaks of continuation; nonstop feelings reeled out in the lines. Creation is the center piece, explication the key that turns and leads to a place of origin,

Along the rails, between grass plant, brick plant, steel plant
and the dark banks, there grew and flowered the ideas,
science, medicine, song.

The scenes described undulate among images and insinuations of a reality that by instants is; by instants is not. In the end, home the way the poet sees it; earth, where it all occurs:

The town crept on the earth, dripping
a dripping fire, clouds that sink in darkness, and always
new cars and old drove through its simple designs.
Who needs another thing? We are home...
the waiting earth
that keeps us busy, that buckles the concrete.

In a poem I wrote I say, "*Southbound on a bus coming home / I see illusions of stillness where land meets sky / hills zigzagging... / miscellaneous past filters into / this moment of returning: / how many days burnt out...*" Moritz brings it to me in his "Visit Home":

Returning, I saw that land still burnt
under the highway's lash – more than ever. And driving on
I saw it burning now too form the sun...
Mahoning land: its flesh was cracking open
and falling away, blowing in yellow grass and disappearing...

I utterly enjoyed "Evening," an idyll gently told by the bard in which he seeks peace and solace from hectic city life:

Huge evening, calm, surging
fresh in the oaks, their green
darkness thrust up

swaying to touch steel-blue
and molten-iron colours flying higher
into blackness…
Then orange windows
and white stars came out…
the children race amid lighting
bugs densest
in the dark under maple trees…

The poet blends symbols of movement and pause; tropes enabling his hand to dip us, readers, into the vaporous settings. See how Moritz treats the sleep notion:

Water
and sleep were gathering
where leaves cupped the slender
bases of the stems…
But sleep
grows strong, its moist hand
indistinguishable from tears
brushes the young brow
closes the eyes, and their sight
grows indistinguishable
from not knowing…

"Founders" is one of those poems that stay with you long after the reading. It is overwhelming and encompassing. The poet travels through the whole spectrum of life vibrating before him. He goes to the essences, to the roots – nature first and foremost – as seen by the human eye, safeguarding and sheltering,

Beautiful in its distance
the day burning down and flight of stars,
quiet in your eyes, disaster so far away…

From the natural, to the manmade world; however, laced with the sparrow element:

Incomparable, this human world: the vast
plain of vast roofs,
light and music at the quiet crossing where five streets join.
Full of joyous prophecy is the flight of heraldic sparrows
in shifting rivers, childish, self-willed
flocks unraveling among elms at dusk…

At this point, the unreal seems to build itself into the text:

… Women decay
and houses stand open, orange light
streams from the torn eyes and mouths. Others are dark
as though ruined, abandoned this century
or this afternoon: in the distant day of the founders…

Anticipated in *"disaster so far away,"* the poem closes facing what Moritz
refers to in his interview, *"I experience all the stresses of modern society…" (ibidem).*
Read these lines:

… The whole injustice of the earth — isn't it here? —
the whole failure of the blessing, in this wooden calm
of faces, walls, obscure
spaces…
… where childhood stream
bleeds from the ground, you still were blessed with peace
by the one unknown.

As I leaf through Moritz's *Rest on the Flight into Egypt* (Brick Books, 1999.
Third printing in 2000), I bow at the rich intricacies of the English
language unraveled and turned to advantage by the poet. About him, a
Wikipedia comment states: *"Moritz is not an easily digested, standard-issue
poet… Consistently through the years, he has built complicated patterns of
diction…"* Creativeness at its highest is what defines text and style in
Moritz, noticeable as we enter and linger in this book.

Moritz pushes through mazes of content and form, inviting readers to a
journey that will not be easy: elaborate mental products; thoughts

sweltering, provoking, challenging. *Rest on the Flight into Egypt* allows no rest actually. The book's solid wording sets a bar that will be reached or overcome by those familiar with the author and those ready to pause and be enlightened reading a monument to language and poetry. No wonder a comment on the book's back cover states: *"This is poetry of extraordinary depth and intelligence."*

Moritz proposes factual-oniric inter-planes in "Manifestation," for example, juggling like a warlock with polysemous word arcs and subliminal image cues. Take this excerpt, which opens the poem introducing a symbol of French *avant-garde* and founder of the *théâtre de la cruauté.*

As in the poem, the core idea in Artaud was to thrust spectators (in the poem it is readers) into a medley where *"gestures, sounds, unusual scenery, and lighting combine to form a language, superior to words that can be used to subvert thought and logic…"*
(Taken from https://www.britannica.com/biography/Antonin-Artaud):

Antonin Artaud in the middle of the night…
was rooting up
my garden. Breaking off fingernails,
fingertips pouring blood… dog-eagerly he scrabbled
in the lilies of the valley. Whenever he found
the rhizomatous root cords he was after,
he'd haul them up, straining his skeleton: I could hear
the vertebrae cracking…

Across this surrealistic scene, we trek down to the end. The dreamlike sights and sounds Moritz has deployed for us now seem to slow down, as the poet builds into the text autobiographical reminiscences of his childhood, still pasting onto them colors and scents. As is commented on the Wikipedia, *"… he is not overtly autobiographical, though from time to time he does seem to let drop decipherable hints of his past and provenance…,"*

In the morning I found the lilies of the valley
entirely undisturbed, and just beginning to bloom, and just beginning to bloom —
a flower I've loved since childhood,

when I would weed around it in my mother's garden
and live the day in its perfume…

Yet, in the end, Moritz returns us to the primary moods and modes that he knotted us with at the beginning, reiterating words (an adverb, *"relatively"*) to effect semantic-stylistic contrasts:

… I was relatively content. But this is fiction.
In fact it was late autumn. In the morning I saw the lilies
nothing but brittle, tattered, colourless leaf scaffolding,
and I was relatively filled with hatred
for weather, season, and earth.

I venture to disclose the reason of this abrupt step back into the *"brittle, tattered and colourless"* context based on the very ominous "Artaud" foundation at the poem's onset.

Moritz's theme-refrain with sparrows flies back to us in "Ballad of the Sparrow and the Goddess." The poet insists in the need of harmony and a degree of closeness between humans and nature. I have referred to his position regarding this issue in this paper. Let's turn to illustrative excerpts from the poem where we clearly discern gist and Moritz's point. Touches of nostalgia, criticism and environmentalism I have examined before in his work also run through the lines:

A sparrow passing through in fall
came to my tree to look
for the bird-feeder I once had
but now have taken down.
A neighbour feared the birds it brought,
a divorcee…
… And how to reconcile…
the careful anguish
she, brittle goddess, felt?…
… I watched the disappointed bird
turn on the branch and gaze

on the new-empty space…
… and I saw that if I just…
and took him in my hand,
he would consent to be comforted
and learn to understand.
But then the vision passed. Again
it was obvious if I
made any movement fear would make
the baffled sparrow fly.

"*O holy night, the stars are brightly shining,*" a line from Nat King Cole's
"Silent Night" crosses my mind as I read Moritz's poem "Silent Night."
The descriptions in the first stanza, despite their variety, give me the illusion
of nothingness, as might be the poet's intent. My supposition is confirmed
on the book's back cover: "… *ecstatic lyricism that knows evanescence is the only
enduring truth.*":

Bronze pages scattered on the open ground.
No shadow of a house. No plan,
no picture scratched on a broken tile.
No voice can give the agitation of wind,
Honed where it moves nothing…

The opposite of that nothingness seems to exist only in the poet's mind:

What do I remember? A city
in these mountains erased, a tree
by a brick wall…
sometimes sparrows…
In the shadow of the house, the family lived…

Again, the recurrent sparrow detail; again the poet skilfully toying with
alternate realities, natural vs. manmade, "*a tree by a brick wall*" and throwing
in ghost-memories, "*In the shadow of the house, the family lived…*"

Finally, a two-line coda sculpted, in my view, with outstanding Moritz-
made imagery to close the poem:

… just as the great forest, the star-wood, burns again
on earth when finally night comes.

"The Door" is an appealing "aperture" connecting the poet's mind and
the outer world, he is fascinated by the cycles of day and night (I discuss
this elsewhere in the paper) and addresses them in his poetry. The poetic
text pans like a video camera from daytime to nighttime and insufflates
human qualities into these cosmo-natural events. I have humbly done this
in my own poetry, likening the cycle to an eye:

"… *the wind recalls the gentility of their crowns / … its whistling as lovers' murmur
/ spelt straight into the beauty of the day's blinking eye… // An elder sun departs
from earth… / as soon as dusk / whispers through the cedar grid / and naive
creatures venture / into the day's closed eye.*" Let's enjoy Moritz:

All day the day had hardened…
a day tightening self-annoyance over the skin
with noises of clashed metals filling thought…
Then night, how you opened it. You let
a first planet be glimpsed as through the black narrow ray
of a door drifting open in the dark…

At this point, the world's metaphorical vastness floods the poem:

It slowly swung so wide,
the whole field beyond the sill imperceptibly came in,
and the room was now worlds shining…

The poet is caught in the dreamy visions he is having, as he moves along
the day-night cycle, and pens spectacular imagery sprouting in epithets,
tropes, personification:

Later – before dawn – I stepped outside
and saw the sun's slow light
erase the weightless stillness… watched
hungrily…

as night's old freedom now was cancelled again…
so the door close
and it again be day.

Once these separate stanzas are integrated and reread, I have the tingling sensation of human smallness before the immensity around, singularized through the poet's eyes yet overflowing towards every reader's experiences and individual ways to face things. The poet won't fail at implicating us, after all on the book's back cover we read:

"Moritz sings to our selves — our failures, our cruelties, our stupidities, and beauty which even now astonishes and leaves us breathless…"

House of Anansi published in 2012 Moritz's *The New Measures*. Anyone with second thoughts about the role of poetry I have discussed in the pages of my paper and how effective it is in bringing mental awareness and change, will be either silenced or motivated by the comments made on the book's back cover:

"… bold collection of fiery, passionate, visionary and fiercely singing new work… And they insist on the hope… perhaps impossible, yet never extinguished–for the perfection of a world both natural and human."

If visionary is what we want to read in Moritz's poetry here, the piece "Simplicity" is useful. Nature lives in the poet's proposal, roots (and *"homage to the simple"*), the elements from which *"blood and action"* stem *(excerpts)*:

The first and simplest things were best.
Light, and then darkness and wind.
Water, which is light with darkness
for its body and wind
for its blood and action. Then trees
arise on its banks: complex things
and implying complexities, implying
a whole earth, but staying where they are,
at home to pay homage to the simple.

Uncertainty develops then in the last lines, the poet's lesson implied:

Next comes one
traveling, eager, a dread of what comes next,
who stops under them awhile,
imagines their lyrics, and imagines
himself abolished in simplicity.

If we seek bold, fiery and fierce, enjoy "The Idea of the Flood," where
"tender and forceful, terrified and assured, grateful and enraged" take turns to
flood the reader *(full)*,

Scum of life on the ponds
clearing as it dies off in autumn
so they will stare up, bright, black and still
amid the last crumbs — a few towers
of leather, copper, and flame — of the first wonder
of the world. Many eyes with one gaze
waiting for never to rise. The angel
who brought us the idea
is always here, nude winter and summer,
unmovingly wandering in the fields and weeping by the stream
under the willow tree, whether they are fields,
stream, and willow, or later desert. The angel
is always right here, as we are,
when the sun and the planet swing away
and leave us in black space. We make
love to the angel ceaselessly,
monotonously: the body
all sex and every sex with no insides,
our love that never moves
while we desert and revolve.

Biblical and daring, Moritz speaks about "Eve" with his very personal
seal. With crossword play of mystical images, he leads us – or lets us
up momentarily – through the poem's plot and plan where *"the freedom of*

imagination," "The prayers of Eve," "three sparrows plumped and shivering" and
"wild grape vines, junk trees, and milkweed" are kneaded into a socio-naturalistic
mental picture. Let's read a few fragments:

The freedom of imagination is
a matter of the weather — the inner
and the outer weather. Is it possible
to sing of summer in the winter,
spring in autumn?...
 to look at the three sparrows plumped and shivering
in a cedar bush, sole and rifled cottage
against the horizontal howl,
fails to reveal if in their hearts is the image
of a better time or only the ongoing
of an engine not yet off. The prayers
of Eve, who once talked with God, are similar.
She who went naked through the day and night,
inspired a lust that was the pith of cleanness,
bathed in the river and the seeing of the sun,
patted the phallus eels and fishes
and the tiger's nose...
The overgrowth of wild grape vines,
junk trees, and milkweed makes the fence
a perfect screen and beyond it
he sited the parkland where she played.

"Song: How Softly It Rains . . ." is a hymn to a moment of balance; that
"perfection of a world both natural and human" the back cover comments refer
to. Moritz sings to simplicity and directness with less complex wording in
this poem, he rejoices in the nakedness of skin under the rain yet also of
his feelings, tenderly outpoured. Let's have the poem fully:

How softly it rains and how well
my nakedness understands it.

I was perfect alone in the sun,
o my son who loves the rain,
o my daughter who loves the rain.
My heart stammers with excitement,
the soft rain rolling down
on my face, chest, and sex.

How my nakedness understands it.

Wet leaves and petals now
are eyes, hands, and feet for me.
These are tears and this is pleasure.

My breath and pulse skip and stop,
human at last with the vanishing
visit of the rain.

O children of my children, how well
my nakedness understands it.

The poet fuses with nature, *"Wet leaves and petals now / are eyes, hands, and feet for me;"* he takes *bared* delight, *"These are tears and this is pleasure."* He feels his humanity, which surfaces and heals as he is cleansed by rain.

On the book's back cover we read that *"These poems make unique music."* Such feat is achieved not just in the poem's fluent pace: it also rings in the use of syntactic expressive means (repetition) structuring of the poem. Repetition is stylistically handled to endow it with an unmistakable musicality: *"... my nakedness understands it."*

This phrase stands as a refrain through the poem. Semantically, the echoing of *"understands it"* steps beyond the mere comprehension of something. It starts at some open-heart moment in the poem to sound like acceptance, a progression from the epidermic to the mental recognition and belief of what is going on between the vulnerable man and the outwardly simple act of raining, what revelations surge.

Stanza arrangement contributes additionally to supplement rhythmic tempo to the poem. As a final point, the pertinent use of a recurrent interjection (*"o my son who loves the rain, / o my daughter who loves the rain… // O children of my children"*) complements and completes the poem's musical format; also its affective content. Interjections are "… *words we use when we express our feelings strongly and which may be said to exist in language as conventional symbols of human emotions… are direct signals that the utterance is emotionally charged…"* (Taken from I. R. Galperin. Stylistics. Moscow Vyssaja Skola. 1981)

One of Moritz's landmarks is his symbolic wording. As complex as it has been considered, once readers grasp Moritz's symbolism, they can *understand* his poems as much as he understood rain in our previous poem. An intensely appealing piece is indeed "Symbolism." (The book's front cover displays a maize plant).

Moritz plays with meanings and shades of meaning. His thought-stirring lines propound a singular dialogue that sets our brains in motion. How far the poet goes in mind-bending can only be truly measured by how capable we are to decipher his genius in this poem and all his work. We instantly sense the eagerness to belong, to harmonize, we sense "… *the hope… perhaps impossible, yet never extinguished—for the perfection of a world both natural and human…"* (ibidem) (excerpt):

This cob of corn — is this
your transformation,
your earth-change? Having
eaten you, do I
hold you again? Did
you drop into the land
as a seed to come forth
a blade of grass
like a tree, with kernels
that are teeth, cool
close-packed suns, drops

of a golden ocean,
nuggets of sugar? And
can I talk to the blackbirds
and the spiders that
cling to you, making you
some part of their worlds,
as if they are syllables
meant in friendship and
gathering to a sentence
intelligible to me?...

Ironic and forceful, Moritz leaves us one of his infrequently brief pieces. Our next poem is self-explanatory. Metaphors plus a tidbit of humor make it a fine almost-haiku *"thing of beauty"*:

"Noon In Our World"
Time was still.
To stop that nonsense
a helicopter
beat the sky.

This short poem reflects the urge in Moritz to write upon inspiration, be it a short or a longer format. He simply cannot hold his hand. Read his reply to one of my questions (*"What guides you in terms of poem structure?"*): *"Once a poem starts, it should continue to be a flow of inspiration, and it should stop when this stops... I'm always in search, in each part of the poem—in each phrase, line, group of lines, turn from one line to the next—of a sense that it is a fluid unity, that each part continues to encompasses a vibrant diversity."*

Moritz's *The Sparrow* (House of Anansi Press, 2018) is impressive. One of the book's back-cover comments refers to *The Sparrow: Selected Poems of A. F. Moritz* as a book that *"surveys forty-five years of Moritz's published poems, from earlier, lesser-known pieces to the widely acclaimed works of the last twenty years. Here are poems of mystery and imagination; of identification with the other; of compassion, judgement, and rage; of love and eroticism; of mature philosophical, sociological, and political analysis; of history and current events; of contemplation of nature; of exaltation and ennui, fullness and emptiness, and the pure succession and splendour of earthly nights and days… The Sparrow is more than a selected poems; it is also a single vast poem, in which the individual pieces can be read as facets of an ever-moving whole. This is the world of A. F. Moritz — a unique combination of lyrical fire and meditative depth, and an imaginative renewal of style and never-ending discovery of form."*

In this context of highly valued appreciation of the acclaimed author, I assumed a huge undertaking: selecting poems that would embody – from my perspective – Moritz's powerful style and make me vibrate. Reducing the analysis to a few poems seemed difficult: his work is vast and classic in many respects.

However, when I started reading, it fortunately dawned on me that *any* poem I picked would suffice to illustrate the poet's greatness. That is how I decided, initially, to start with "Shade" (*Here*, 1975), "Morning Fragments" (idem), and "In the Dead of Night Only" (*Sequence*, 2015). My deliberate choices are two early poems and a recent one. Once I expose my views on these three pieces (which were my first approximation to Moritz's oeuvre, we will embark on a longer voyage with *The Sparrow*. These three poems helped me profile my preliminary construal of his work.

On the book's back cover, John Ashbury says that *"we seem to hear shattered echoes from the Bible…"* I was also privileged to hear other voices. I began my review by quoting Shakespeare. How serendipitous I was initially drawn to "Shade," our first piece. Moritz's technique flies, like a sparrow, in a polished range of multi-styles held in *his* concentrated style. The Toronto Star recognizes it as *"polished turns of phrase and fluid cadences." (Taken from the book's back cover)*; integrating an encompassing gamut of influences and flowing trajectories.

Here the poet introduces the reader into beauty and fantasy, hazy realms and visual-mental explorations:

Before you were born, summer's beauty died.
Now at times it brushes you
with its abstract wing.

I pick a brave, ingenious variation from Shakespeare's Sonnet XVIII, *"Shall I compare thee to a summer's day? / Thou art more lovely and more temperate... / And summer's lease hath all too short a date... / But thy eternal summer shall not fade..." (Taken from Complete Works of William Shakespeare, Volume XVIII, Philadelphia David McKay, Publisher)*

Moritz creatively eases from a second stanza describing metaphorical-concrete realities altogether:

The sounds of the beautiful ideas...
sit looking down through mist
at leaves...
and on both sides of the window the water
slowly condenses and rolls earthward...

From there into the third stanza where more figurative, imaginary proposals are unleashed:

... a thought of time dwelling in a timeless place
will fall, if a tree dares to dash across the sun.
A blow of shadow strikes your sleep in whitened light.

The next stanza is the meditative poet, caught up in the endless, fathomless well of time, asking the questions so many poets ask themselves, inquiring about existence, this enigma we were headlong-born to:

Again the image: days passing beneath oaks
to nothing but further days, further knowledge
of the sky held in fingered leaves:
it empties you into confusion.

Is it a poet lanced by pessimism? Or should we rather discern an inquisitive man probing the entrails of living? His wise choice of language remains unaltered, metaphor-charged: *"days passing beneath oaks," "sky held in fingered leaves."*

The finale tends towards a possible recalibration of events and states of mind, of attempts at charting one's cosmic bearings, physically and mentally – bodily and psychologically:

And that ancient being, you, sole citizen
of the shadow, waits, echoing with muted light;
alone, cannot pronounce itself alone
expecting someone, expecting pleasure...

The last line reminds us of Shakespeare's Sonnet XVIII, *"Nor shall death brag thou wander'st in his shade" (Taken from Complete Works of William Shakespeare, Volume XVIII, Philadelphia David McKay Publisher, no year)*, to give us a Moritz whose resourcefulness renders an imaginative deflection in his own poem:

"...nor shall you brag it wanders in death's shade." Two transcendental poets addressing similar issues.

We perceive how the poet handles the notions of that *"... sole citizen...; alone, cannot pronounce itself alone..."* and the social – the sharing – element. In his own words: *"I think [solitude] fascinates me because it's a condition of my own personality, and I'm always looking for its roots. On the other hand, I have a great interest in society and a great desire to participate in society ... To participate in society you ought to be a full citizen, and you've got to go out and join a party and campaign or whatever you're interested in."* Here we see the *sole/full citizen* contrast he refers to. We are in the presence of a solid poet even in his beginnings back in 1975.

Still focused on the marvel of life and time, Moritz displays more captivating images in his poem "Morning Fragments." This particularly philosophical poem brought to me the work of another iconic contemporary poet, John B. Lee, his poem "Morning Expectation": *"hope's expectations of longer days / birds will soon return / insects waking / life's cycle renewed / in this morning of change..." (Taken from Two Thousand Seventeen, Sanbun Publishers, 2018, New Delhi)*

In his poem, Moritz targets morning in "tropeful" insinuations of how it slowly glides in, the morning theme being an excuse to ponder over deeper questions:

And the morning fragments,
growing visible, seem to rebuild themselves
out of twilight, mildew, and melancholy
towards an edifice still darkened in you…

Somehow the poet invites to the search for answers, or provides them after posing firstly rhetorical questions: *"And were you here yesterday already?... were you following / faint prints of a day before?"*

Then the answers, cosmic, as I said before, delving into and out of doubt, a point made by the use of the conditional *if* (there is no *absolute* certainty):

You will know at last if the sun ages
or is created every dawn
out of nothing at the surface of the sea.
You will know if this dayspring is eternal
or lies on a heap of others,
a page just turned, reversing all.

Through his poetry, Moritz leads the reader to a fumbling limp towards an ultimate truth – if there is one. He places layer *after* layer, layer *beside* layer, layer *against* layer, of denotations and connotations of meanings that flit among syntactically engineered word-loops. Take this example:

And meanwhile night has sunk as a hedge
sinks into distance as you walk away.
Voices were making explanation behind it,
something you might have understood, some secret
of a former life…

You stumble from your present into "a former life" and fall back into uncertainty:

... so that now you will never know what was being said,
if something is lost forever,
or if much, happily,
is put behind you and forgotten.

As much as poetry is an act of solitude, the final product evolves into a dialogue in this poem. The use of "you" very much assists in this. Moritz is aware of the powerful tools of language at his disposal as a poet. In one of his answers to my survey, he commented: *"When speaking of such elements as metaphors and phrases, the only "process" I use is to observe what has come to me as I try to compose the poem, and then to working on that*

And this process with regard to metaphor-making and phrase-making is the same one that applies to expression of sensations, perceptions, emotions, and the like. The development of the phrases and the figurative language is identical to the expression of these things..." I will be highlighting his bond with metaphors along this paper.

The third poem I chose is "In the Dead of Night Only." The poem is a substantial, sustained metaphor, overlapping with another expressive means, personification. The first stanza's last line is illustrative of this:

"... *night exhausted, dawn not yet.*"

The poet puts together the idea of color with the idea of feeling; he equates them with an accomplished symbolic treatment:

... a darkness blacker than the young night's
beautiful colour, known at last
now in nostalgia.

The last stanza is definitely surrealistic, a detail worthy of a Magritte or a Dali easel:

Then you recognize
the journey in which your bed is an evening's pause:

it's the house of this moment
in which the journey is a dream.

P. K. Page commented that *"Some of [his] poems are… full of portent, with the gravity and power of myth." (Read the book's back cover) and the Toronto Star deemed them "… subtle, far-reaching… spiritually revitalizing." (Idem, previous reference).* Thus we return to Moritz's axiom on how poems must be written:

"creatively, authentically, powerfully, beautifully." His forty-five-year fertility in poetic production has honored that principle and made the poet transcend in content and form, in time and space.

After these introductory analyses of Moritz's work, I will try to present to the readers a further study of his poetics, taking as reference *The Sparrow.* From my perspective, I will attempt at "illuminating" readers through the forty-five years comprised in the book.

The book opens with a *Prelude* for which the poem "We Decided This Was All" (*The Tradition*, 1986) was chosen, and closes with a section, *Coda*, with "The Last Thing" (*Black Orchid*, 1981). Obviously, these two poems are milestones in Moritz's long, fruitful career.

Part I offers a spectrum of nine years in the poet's work (1974-1983). Thirty-three poems were chosen by Moritz to represent this period in his writing. From this section I already talked about two pieces. Let us then read "In Winter" (*New Poems*, 1974) *(excerpts)*:

… The spring
is coming, will turn to a dawn-coloured
broth these brittle sculptures
the motorcycles left us as a sign
for our conversion. You look across…
… If you are caught, it isn't
within walls, behind windows, in the flesh.
It's in the seeing that already finds
beyond this another winter, where

the changes, though noticeable, are not
of the least importance to anyone.

This is a poem of contemplation where the poet reminisces of the seasonal leitmotifs so at home with Canadian poets. It leads us through personal glimpses, a ride in time and space, with past and present spiraling into words that denote observation-retrospection. The following quote throws light on this: *"Moritz is engaged in making something that is memorable and freshly meaningful rather than easy. Consistently through the years, he has built complicated patterns of diction that draw on sobriety and intimacy." (Taken from Wikipedia)*

There is a firm gentleness in the poem "Here" (*Here*, 1975). A concerned poet watches, pensively, *"… the stones that will live almost forever,"* contrasts them with our lives, *"… we are as old in shadows as the stones…"* As he muses and weaves metaphors across realities and thoughts, he tells us of the inevitable cycle of things, of the images and colors and sounds, which seem to open a portal to dimensions only he can word *(excerpts)*:

… Amber lights
open from time to time in a mask of cloud.
Between are brown moments in a coal-dust air.
To cease is not permitted here.
To complete something is not permitted.
Out of the river climb elongated musics,
oddly shaped shrieks of light…

The quest of life the poet craves is illustrated in his "Ulysses en Route" (*Black Orchid*, 1981). It is an epic poem where Moritz displays his intricate thought-dreams, his elaborate incursions in *"dusty spring" (excerpts)*:

… So I retain the image of the meagre world
that now amid crowded flotsam
in shipwreck, in absence, I desire:
not as relief but as
the true adventure, dusty
spring…

Mythology bubbles and intersects the subjective-temporal planes he designs:

... It is to be unborn
in branching tunnels,
this custody of the wind's treasure
that must not be touched, this knowledge
of swine born of the intercourse
between men and the sun's power...

And still, I am an idea,
this is a breath of envy
to men who hear of these adventures...

Called a *"master of metaphor,"* Moritz shows his penmanship in "Poem" (*Black Orchid*, 1981). Seasons become animate beings under his hand *(excerpts)*,

The unheralded mystery of spring
forces its will again on the herald flower.
In the thicket I pause to remember.
February was my mentor in misery...

The metaphysical collides with the oniric as he questions all around him, sensorially, substantially. A string of metaphors is unleashed, prophesizing, inquiring, doubting, as much as Poe did in "The Raven" ("*Deep into that darkness peering, long I stood there wondering, fearing, / Doubting, dreaming dreams no mortal ever dared to dream before*"):

I am a glove on an absent hand
and speaking, writing are nothing but the dream...
Whether or not there is such a thing as time,
I am this window on night's senseless palette...
Across the torn darkness
I am this anarchic scrawl,
this wake of a restless scalpel.

Part II (from 1986 to 1994) presents seventy-four poems. Loyal to his principle of questioning and probing reality, Moritz travels into history and past. That is when we find an absorbing piece, "The Tradition" (*The Tradition*, 1986), filled with a rightful denunciation and stern approach to the issues he addresses. The first lines define a witty canvas of what we will encounter *(excerpts)*:

I think we are the heirs of slaves,
a race of water bearers to the patient herd.
But whose memory reaches so far back?
We can see how quickly the children of our day
forget the names of their parents newly dead.

The poet turns argumentatively critical:
No documents are found in our houses.
No object we make will last two generations.
No skills are handed down
but how to live each day with the flies...
In these sheds between compulsive howl and silence,
between young and old, what knowledge falls?...
And the real fathers?
Those who in fact dropped sperm in broken cisterns...
There is no way to know them,
unless to presume that they were much like us.

Sailing from theme to theme, from image to image that transcends and envelops the readers, Moritz proposes "The Sphinx" (*The Tradition*, 1986). The poem begins as an enigmatic, challenging treatise on existence *(excerpts)*:

Who knows how to exist? I was
not given the power for this task.
To create what I would be in my own image.
To make a life by casting my body into time...,

Later, it reveals in turns as a talking creature, unfurls into a discourse of scriptural implications. Like the Sphinx (curiously, a winged creature with the body of a lion and the face of a woman in Greek mythology; in Egyptian lore, the face is a man's), the poem traverses various stages, sneaks into "*ancestors, images, stories…*," into the "*barbarous itching of desire at all seasons…*," "*into this crumbling form…*" and emerges "*left (…) forever / at the door of the desert and the tomb.*"

Beauty, an axiom in the search of higher poetry, accompanies the poem. Beauty is to be reckoned with as strife towards that beatitude the poet propounds. Let's read the stanza below *(excerpts)*:

If only I could remember falling from some beatitude.
If only some perfect form had once been mine,
and I could cast it before on the screen of night,
an image of a former self to stab me—
then, at least, like a wounded man, I would fall
in the direction of the pain
and thus move on.

Beauty is found too in shaking off nothingness, which starts with inconformity at being "*welded to this carcass.*" The poet seeks perfection, change, the symbolic reexamination of that beatitude he fell from, that exploration of the origins. In this respect, Moritz makes us remember William Faulkner, who said, "*If I were to choose between pain and nothing, I would choose pain.*" *(Taken from Love, by Leo Buscaglia, Fawcett Crest, 1972)* The poet accepts his condition, what is more, he embraces it: he will rise and "*thus move on.*"

"The Sphinx" is a poem where Moritz shows the broad tessiture of his elegant craft: "*Moritz brings together the near and far, the physical and metaphysical, through his deft use of image and metaphor.*" *(Taken from the Web)*

Splendor trails on in "April Song of Fear" (*Song of Fear*, 1992). Imagery becomes a mirror where the poet's pen draws away a dreamy scene. Let's read the first stanza:

It rained tonight. Now in the streetlight
the bells of one white hyacinth shine

in the midst of a lawn
from their tower a single evening built.

From this point, the poem enters an assortment of thoughts. Out of the rain motif come a series of stronger, prophetic lines in which the poet speaks loud and clear of his fears (fragility of life disclosed before him in a *"thing so soft"*) and his hopeful grasp for deliverance from being *"cut in two"* like the worm *(excerpts)*:

And a worm has drawn its full length out...
a thing
... so easily cut in two,
and cut, unaware of the horror of being so...
But I'm aware. Just as I saw the worm
I was striding swiftly,
proud of my fluid beauty
and my uncut male flower...
... give me power not to forget
you, whoever you are,
and repair your world before it comes to me.

When he was appointed Toronto's sixth poet laureate, Moritz gave a speech in which he spoke of the poet as someone who *"creates by means of humankind's most intimate, complex tool, the word, a tool that is one with the human body and soul." (Taken from the Web)*

An example of the body-soul connection with the word towards a spirit of hope, an earnest hortatory anthem, is "Song: It Does Not Matter" (*Song of Fear*, 1992). Moritz handles various expressive means in the language:

repetition (*"It does not matter"*), use of interjections (*"It does not matter!"*), which bestow upon the poem musicalness anticipated in the title. As a reader, I notice a subtle touch of irony, yet the poem is stimulating. Structurally, it steps from the structural poetry I had been reading so far. Let's have the last stanza:

It does not matter!
How foolish it is!
Now you need to repeat it!
Begin to live again!

If in the previous stanzas the phrase *"How foolish it is"* was a seemingly simple, stylistically unmarked element, by adding the exclamation mark in the last stanza it activates the ironical component and also a sheer affirmation of the foolishness the poet tries to drive the poem's addressee from.

Part III (1998-2000), with thirty-three pieces, gives us a closer poet in time. "Morning Again" (*A Houseboat on the Styx*, 1998) is a refreshing poem in which Moritz invites us, as usually, to the confidence of reflection. Fragments from the first stanza read,

Morning again. Ah, we've gone nowhere in the dark,
we are still here where we were: what a relief.
You get out your guitar...

As we proceed into the next stanza, we are met with the concept of *value* from a philosophical-sociological stance. What is actually valuable to humans resides between the poem's lines, especially in stanza two. Moritz commented, *"We'd better save the forests because otherwise we'll be out of lumber," but with venerating the forest as a beautiful existing thing... [It] is not useful, but it has things that you can use, and without it you have nothing you can use..." (Taken from a Web interview. The Sunday Edition's host Michael Enright)*, which allows to understand the notion of where humans see values around them.

Things acquire a value, viewed broadly as an object to benefit from, before the human eye as long as they are useful. Let's see what Moritz implies in these lines (an environmental, values-related angle is appreciated as well):

... a thousand shopfronts,
brick buildings all one height,

poles and wires dully glinting,
and among them the green-leaf clouds
of a few hopeful trees
memorious of forests—it all extends
out of sight, to the horizon…

The eternal non-conformist we had in "The Sphinx" returns to us in the last stanza:

At least in your music you are never satisfied.
In the depths
struggling, half asleep, to be content, you are
not satisfied. That much, sometimes, almost,
we're sure of.

A remarkable quotation from the Web states: *"Moritz is not an easily digested, standard-issue poet… Moritz is engaged in making something that is memorable and freshly meaningful rather than easy. Consistently through the years, he has built complicated patterns of diction that draw on sobriety and intimacy."*

I would add to it that what we need with Moritz is second and third readings. You cannot take his poems lightly; they deserve attention to the way tropes build themselves into the poetic construct and reify the poet's innermost concerns regarding everything within his vast poet's scope.

As I said at the beginning of my paper, any poem from Moritz would suffice to prove his prominence. Therefore, if we are after *"memorable and freshly meaningful"* poetry or target our interest on *"patterns of diction that draw on sobriety and intimacy,"* we may positively refer to "Science." Let's see the first stanza:

Knowing that girls once went naked under slender palms
didn't end my desire for these women
in mud-and-sweat-caked nylons.

At this early point, we might ask ourselves why "Science" as a title. The dictionary comes to our aid: *"The intellectual and practical activity encompassing the systematic study of the structure and behaviour of the physical and natural world through observation…"* or *"knowledge when it relates to the physical world and its phenomena…"* (Babylon, Digital Dictionary).

Besides, the word's etymology is *"to know."* So, in this poem the poet has acquired knowledge that comes from observing the behavior of the surrounding world. Moritz is linking, somberly, his personal experience to the sudden awareness of how it all works, what really happened to him. An allegiance to science, as voiced in the poem, presupposes a discovery too. Let's read the last stanza:

And the discovery I'm like all others, am nothing but others,
is what hardened the darkness close around me
and made me keep alone.

From *Conflicting Desire* (2000), I chose "Immediacy." Comfortably handling more expressive means, like onomatopoeia (both direct in *"chirr,"* and indirect in the repetition of the /r/ sound), Moritz writes an unusually short piece with sound as its prevailing element. One of the meanings of the title is "directness," which explains the excellent play with briefness and sensory stimulation. Let's enjoy it fully:

Cricket chirr, sounded quiet
that nobody can interpret or remember,
say this to the makers of noise: I ring where
the night colours are gathered, far under
the ringing in the ear.

In terms of the relevance of sound in poetry, I share with the readers what Moritz said to me in the survey: *"The other range of technical elements in a poem are the elements of sound. There, I have strong ideas about versification— mine is typically "free" but not entirely so: it's a "sprung rhythm" with a strong but free reference both to historical English versification and to the various traditions of twentieth-century free verse…"*

Also from *Conflicting Desire* is "Eternal." The poet sets the poem's tempo since the very first word, *"Slowly,"* to implicate us in the mood he has poured onto it. As many poets who address the topic of death, Moritz does it with delicacy, gentle gravitas swathing the lines that depict an atmosphere of loss-induced unawareness,

... image of one surrounded unaware
or half aware by decadence of city and night...

The mystique signaling the moments wafts surrealistically,
Somewhere: a brick
loosening from a wall. Time is stopped
and only she who has passed away seems to be passing away:
everything else, decadence, pain, knowledge
she is everything and is gone is eternal.

Part IV (2004-2008) with thirty-four poems features from *Night Street Repairs* (2004) — a book named one of forty-three "books of the decade" by the *Globe and Mail* in 2010 — a poem of tribute to a friend, "Memory of a Friend." This is a recurrent theme in all the poets included in this book. Shielded in his potent word, one which is, in his own opinion, *"one with the human body and soul,"* Moritz plays with surreal proposals *(excerpts)*:

unfinished walls...
the night watchman
still guarding the never-finished tower
against our shadow...
they still echo through our footsteps sounding
in empty alleys: steps that long ago
drowned, listening.

This dreamlike scenario flows on other expressive means, like personification:

... these streets don't stop
and don't change what they hold. They still lead through...
to water
and wasteland fervent in dream-masks of snow...

The Sentinel (2008) was Globe and Mail Top 100 Book of the Year. It was said to be "*An ancient voice, mournful like the wind, speaks to itself yet means to be overheard in A. F. Moritz's amazing poems.*" *(Taken from The New Measures, back cover comment on The Sentinel by John Ashbury)* About Moritz's work, Don McKay *(ibidem)* stated it "*… leaves me reassured about the potential efficacy of poetry, of mind engaged with world on all fronts – politically, mythically, philosophically.*"

I was attracted by another infrequently short piece, "Sound of Hungry Animals." In his interview, Moritz alluded to "*a little element of nature and a little element of beauty,*" when he was asked about the presence of the sparrow in his poetry. See the attraction of opposites in the line, "*… the self-hatred of their inseparable pack…*" In its own forthright way, this poem focuses on that nature-beauty symbiosis, told with directness:

There was a sound of hungry animals at night
or animals in the pain of their coitus
or the self-hatred of their inseparable pack…
and beneath my conscious prayer…
the one spirit spoke betraying my desire
for some good of which I could never be aware.

Finally, also from *The Sentinel*, I selected "Two Crickets," which is a poem on the same chord as the previous one.

Marvin Orbach's daughter, Ariella, introduced her father's *Redwing* (Hidden Brook Press, 2018) saying: "*… these poems speak of it. They speak of the destructive path that modern humanity is on, paving over everything that is alive. They speak of the power of observation, of sitting still and connecting with the life that flows around us. They speak of the joys of falling in love, and the desperation of the human condition. They speak of the simple beauty of insects, of a tree, and of course, of birds.*"

I quote Ariella because her statement is universal and coincides with Moritz's opinions: "People don't even appreciate them (reference to animals in the city) or say thank you. They hate them and find them lice-ridden and so forth. There's a poem in there that's just called "Love Song" in which the loved one is made equivalent to a sparrow which comes and lands on your table in a café and tries to get a crumb. It manages to survive and find its way, despite the fact that people are swatting at it and ignoring it. This seems to me an emblem of the way the sensitive person has to survive in modern society." (Taken from the afore-mentioned Web interview)

Moritz writes for these creatures too, both in the literal and the metaphorical senses. He is able to bring his theme to a crossroad where these senses mingle and coexist. This is evident in "Two Crickets." The poet's constant, skilled juxtaposition and transference from the natural to the social-personal plane renders a unique flavor to his writing, month allusions (a human creation) accommodated neatly into the poem's temporal skein.

Notice the epithet, *"stupid,"* added to *"we sing"* at the end, and the opposition between the cricket, that *"doesn't worry the song of longing he repeats"* and us, *"we sing stupidly free of doubt." (excerpts)*:

Outside, one cricket
singing with long still pauses–August is over.
And for the moment no one harries him
or pecks him up…
Listen and you seem to be in his peace
under the leaves of an impatiens flower…
August is over, for the moment no one harries
or eats us, we sing stupidly free of doubt.

From 2012 to 2015 (Part V in *The Sparrow*), Moritz selected twenty-two poems ("In the Dead of Night Only," analyzed in my introduction to Moritz, appears in this section). "Under Green Trees Far Away" (*Sequence*, 2015) gives us a sweet look at what surrounds the poet. The two first lines illustrate this well:

Under green trees far away
the splendor, the light over everything,
fills with shadows,

a voice, a gesture
answering another, excited hands and eyes
finding themselves
living.

Lummox Press published in 2018 an anthology of contemporary Canadian poetry, *Tamaracks: Canadian Poetry for the 21st Century*, edited by James Deahl. 113 fine poets were included. About the anthology, Terry Barker said it was among the most representative works of this type in the last hundred years. Bruce Meyer commented, "… *these are all tremendously readable, beautifully written, and entirely expansive poems that speak to the complexities and breadth of Canada. Deahl has presented us with a selection that shows the greatness of Canadian poetry from coast to coast…*"

Albert F. Moritz was invited and he sent three poems, "Baltimore May 2015," "Philosopher and Southern Ohio" and "Names of Birds," pieces which did not appear in *The Sparrow*. Needless to say his poetry contributed to the representativeness, readability, beauty and singularity that make a work universal and influential, as Barker and Meyer state.

In "Baltimore May 2015," Moritz spreads out the canvas of nature. Birds and flora are the divas in this pondering "roll-call" of nature the poet invites the reader to follow up with him *(excerpt)*:

Baltimore oriole singing from the tip
of a vast, spreading silver maple, and then
he goes quiet and flies, "swift as arrow", deep
into neighbor trees — his gold and blue
hardly visible up under the dazzling
dull sky.

Notice the transition from "*he goes quite*" to "*flies, 'swift as arrow', deep into…*" depicting the bird's fleetness and restlessness the way it actually happens, and the use of a simile ("*as arrow*") to liken his movement to a manufactured artifact. If we close our eyes for a second and retain these lines, the scene plays out in lively motion.

The ever-present sparrow accompanies the soothing description. Moritz
has talked about the sparrow recurrence (and his conceptual fauna theme)
in his work: "*I think that I've identified a lot with the sparrow. It seems to be a
denizen of the city that manages to survive as a little element of nature and a little
element of beauty in the little cracks and interstices that human beings leave — like
the remainders of nature which are almost all we have in most cities ... raccoons,
pigeons and so on...*" *(Taken from the Web interview) (excerpt)*:

The rose-colored crab apples are almost done
with snowing: they're clouds mostly green,
though over there a hungry sparrow can knock
a flurry of pink out of one. But the white crab tree
still is fresh, dropping nothing, dense,
and opening inward — indescribable thought-like
ways of passage among petals
for the air it freshens.

The nature-beauty aspect I have referred to in my analysis of other poems,
is retraced here by Moritz. As well, we realize how the thematic models he
outlines in his interviews, "*... a denizen of the city that manages to survive as
a little element of nature and a little element of beauty in the little cracks and
interstices that human beings leave*" (in reference to sparrows and other
creatures in the few city spaces they have been restricted to), unfailingly
appear in his poems *(ibidem) (excerpt)*:

Behind it: the closed,
quiet house front: a face of supreme
beauty pondering, with a look, all outward,
that doesn't know or care how it looks...

Moritz amalgamates a reality he describes and figments he dots onto the
unreeling setting *(excerpt)*:

the way
the wrinkled bark, the groins of limbs,
the passages to the interior of the tree,

all hide in the white petals. The way that the coming
race of humans, all female still in early embryo,
unthreatened, couples now,
beyond sight,
in a long lost scripture, not yet written,
in the orgy of imagination...

As I read and reread down the poem's second half to the end, I was trans-
ported to a French film (animated) I saw back in the 70s, *La Planète
Sauvage* (Laloux, 1973), for its allusions to little creatures, its sensuality
and fantasy contexts. The film is among my favorite ones, as is this poem
by Moritz.

His frankness trickles thickly in the second poem he sent for *Tamaracks*,
"Philosopher and Southern Ohio." Consider these lines *(excerpts)*:
only to die young
is a weakness, almost a sin — so fair
in a song it can make them cry...

Their God
is innocence — he doesn't exist as I
would require him to and still he makes
the truth of the world be the dandelion
that the eyes fall on as a breeze starts
freshening summer, and the man towels his forehead...

In the interview I have alluded in this paper, Moritz propounds: "... *I
experience all the stresses of modern society... these values of consumerism,
technology, increasing power and wealth are really a way to live. And of course,
they're a way to die... But it doesn't take a very sharp eye to look around and see
other, less obvious people who are clearly alone, sad and depressed...*" *(ibidem)* Read
these graphic lines from the poem's opening *(excerpts)*:

Praise those who finding themselves
alive on earth
pick up the work. Day after day

it never ends except that they call death
heavenly rest, and feel no guilt
in accepting it, as long as it comes late,
after a long or hard enough term of bearing
with the pain of the others.

Hear the poet's true-to-life voice *(excerpts)*:
the people all together
for the dead friend at a hilltop churchyard
with shadows of the circling hawks
sweeping their feet . . . the ugly people
all saints, the community in one place
around the body . . . But no more rest...

The poet is loyal to his stance as a poet, a human being, a citizen; solidly cohesive in his conceptions, which is perceived in his words: "*I have a great interest in society and a great desire to participate in society ... To participate in society you ought to be a full citizen, and you've got to go out and join a party and campaign or whatever you're interested in...*" *(ibidem)*

Moritz's social involvement and concern about nature prompts him to state, "*On the human side, poetry is exactly in the same position to mankind as the forest is on the natural side. The way we treat it is exactly the way we treat a waterfront or a river. We turn our back on it. We build ugly buildings that back right up to it. We throw garbage into it. We don't even remember that it is there anymore until it gets so stinking and poisonous that it now threatens us...*" *(ibidem)* And he pours his position onto these lines *(excerpt)*:

Praise them,
they hammer in a mine days and nights
and in the times remaining drive a mule
and an iron-prowed wood plough
on a steep slope for food. They help to poison
their own streams...

The third poem, "Names of Birds," is a piece filled with the warmth I have felt in the other four poets in this book when they speak of nature and family. Here, a Moritz who shelters in his memories without relinquishing his attention to nature: birds are at the center of this poem; but it is cobbled with the precious stones of family recollections epitomized in his father, intensely expressed. The poem is evocative, gentle *(excerpt)*:

Awake at dawn, recalling my father, crying,
unable to go to sleep again, and pretty soon
the first bird sings. Despair: when the first bird sings
and the first light comes and you haven't slept.
I curse myself: the many-noted melody
is its signature but I can't read its name.
my father knew the name of every bird,
every tree, bush and grass they played in,
every seed, bug and worm they ate. Their friend…

The child-poet calls out to his father. In his call, vehement melancholy ricochets from the call. The poet is aware in his flashback mediation, which leads him to a seminal blending with nature and family *(excerpt)*:

Father, where are you
so I can ask you and have you give me
the names? I always thought I'd take the time,
later, to learn them from you. my father knew
the name of every bird. And I see now: he knew
not just the name of every kind but every one.

The poet's interlocked association and personal-affective dialogue with nature, as he has frequently clarified, is evidenced in the end lines *(excerpt)*:

A scientist, he'd tell you birds have no names,
names are for people. But each bird does have a name,
a strange sort of word that exists only an instant
as it sings back to someone who greets it
and then it pauses, hoping to hear him again.

The last phrase, "*hoping to hear him again,*" tells us that for the poet the connection is secured in hope. This is valid for the two levels of textual interpretation: it is not only the bird that hopes; also the boy.

Moritz's *As far as you know* (House of Anansi, 2020) sparked the following comment: ..."*widely considered one of the defining and most beloved lyric poets of his generation." (Taken from the book's back cover)* To reach such a status, such a degree of perfection, or near-perfection, it requires talent, work, study, perseverance. Moritz has all of these. In his comments he said to me: "*I always try to achieve a perfection and satisfaction that I call provisional perfection, because I can't help knowing that, after I've perfected the poem, then in the future I will find things it I still want to change or add. I do believe it's possible to perfect a poem in the sense that you can let it go and know you won't be ashamed of it. It may come to seem much less successful than you now believe it to be, but at least you will recognize it as a worthy poem, and "good job". On the other hand, I've had the experience that I thought I reached this provisional perfection and I later find the poem to be faulty. So even provisional perfection can only be provisional.*"

"Terrorism" opens the book. It is a poem of epic proportion in length and significance. Moritz succeeds in transmitting the horror of his text by opposing disparate realities. Let's read the first lines:

Grackles and starlings
take the fountain:
           an October bath
           a ceaseless
while it lasts
      coming
going
   and coming
One terminus of their flurry: the wide bowl
and its twenty standing crystal
cords
    each one emerging as a stalk
rising
   the drops

separating
                now a necklace of diamonds
with no thread except direction...

In mid poem, a sudden ominous shift of tone,
Into the space between two trees
a jetliner
                emerges perfectly
                                        silent
faraway
                needle of light
                                        drawing no thread
So slow
                serene
                        univocal its flight
passing across the pure blue interval
Yet poor I expect
to see it fall from the sky
A globed flash
a star murdered in an instant
And I would find myself
thinking as if unconcerned
of the many
who died there
                        just now
                                in a blink of light
so far away
                engulfed
in the day's bright quiet
and the human bodies
ashes
        fragments
too distant to be distinguished
                                sifting down
through the air in the remote
catastrophe
                to me only a sudden

wink of change
like a glint off dew…

The lines below give us a solemn description of facts and after-facts. They
become the written witnesses of dark events:

       … Dread now
lives and pollutes
       in the birds' oblivious world
my dread
of the living emptiness like the sky
the days after Pearl Harbor…

In the earth's permanent facts the sky
is always empty
       of its airy navies
its commerce
       and is always silent
as on the first morning
       and that other first morning
the last the immediate
aftermath
of self
annihilation

       Always there
       is
       in the sky
the erasure of the human
and the sky's regathered
       silence
identical
with the silence before the human
the one same
       absence
now and always
       there in the sky…

The poem that titles the book, "As far as you know," gives us an every-day Moritz engaged in the codes of love, playing with memories, retrospectively carving his words. The first three lines dictate the poem's tenor,

When you last saw me I was waiting
and now that you will never see me again
for all you know I still am.

This is a poem depicting an experience anyone can have. It narrates a nostalgic afterglow of a relation. Moritz recalls,

… The time
it turned out was the last time I was sitting
staring across the top edge of the book
into something just above and past
the poem you couldn't see there on the page
between us. Or I was walking — many times
you saw me walking and I can't know
if once when you glimpsed me far away
in the park, too far away to hail,
and you thought you'd tell me later…

The last lines tremble gently, epigrammatically into a suspended, intriguing farewell:

… When you last saw me I was waiting
like you for us to meet. And now
I still am, as far as you know.

As I mentioned earlier, Moritz was invited to submit his poetry to *Tamaracks: Canadian Poetry for the 21st Century* (Lummox Press, 2018). The three poems he sent, "Baltimore May 2015," "Philosopher and Southern Ohio" and "Names of Birds," which I analyzed there. They are included in *As far as you know*, section **Childhood Friends**.

I made the mistake of wanting
the woman that I love
to be as you are always
naked, amorous, young,
and though shy to others, to me
always opening, always
desiring, demanding me.

The previous stanza is the beginning of "To the Soul." We are in the presence of the lyric poet, subjugated by the pleasure of love and sex, writing sensually charged phrases. Read the fragment below:

To save myself I try
withdrawing, but I have to see you,
abandoned Ariadne, self-stripped always
and crying on the beach. How beautiful
your breasts and eyes to the man
who would see you from the sea,
your naked back and open hips
to the man who approaches by
the grassy dunes. How weak,
how sporadic my powers to your
endless hunger, your pain.

This is a poem where mythology and biblical allusions live together. From Greek lore, Ariadne, the Cretan princess Moritz craves in the previous excerpt; from the Bible,

The first
words at the closing of the door
of paradise, when delight survived
but the omnipotence of the body
had been taken away, I know: Thank
God for the woman.

Whatever the perspective, the poet has managed to celebrate *the* woman. The man in the poet; a poet in the man.

With this volume I end my "initiation" study of Moritz's work and my long expedition with five Canadian poets. It takes deeper analysis of Moritz's (and the other five poets') motives and penmanship to further decode his poetics. Yet, the panoramic sketch I have attempted to outline here gives us a tentative clue of the precious gem we have portrayed, inlaid alongside four other stones, which I have appraised as exceptional.

Allow me to close with Moritz's definition of triumph, which aptly applies to his life and work. He aims at creating "… *an intensely paradoxical or dialectical vision in which the human being is, at least so far, never destroyed, but preserves innocence and possibility, and even triumphs — if we can understand triumph not as power, wealth, prestige, prominence, technical effectiveness, if we can understand it truly, that is to say, poetically." (Taken from the book As far as you know, Appendix 1. Author's Note on "Art Of Surgery")*

Writing

The sounds of silence
speak to poets
decoding webs of semantics
blending words and rhythms
showering stardust letters
over yearning paper sheets.

The sounds of silence visit:
The Muses of Poetry ride
above apparent muteness
deep-spurring the flanks of creation
weeping, giving birth
to the never-ending craft of writing.

Miguel Ángel Olivé Iglesias

Conclusions

In this book I have only been, as John B. Lee states, a mediator between poets and readers. I have only pointed at facts and meanings from my perspective so I may shed a modest shaft of light upon their reading act, which remains unsullied, ever selective and unique in each pair of eyes.

My study of these five Canadian poets allows me to safely put forth points of coincidence I list below:

Singular styles – universality latent and emergent in their distinct penmanship – that are recipient, repository and paradigm at the same time. Their poetry is heir of their ancestral forerunners, keeper of the accumulated legacy and inspiring pedestal for new generations, in a take-give cycle of creation and bequeathal that never ends.

Structural latitude. The poets shift to and from patterns, try different forms that comply with their intentions and let contents burst in a freed modality that suits their feelings. There is no voluntary or imposed or fixed constriction to the outflow of their emotions; only winged words pushing to take flight.

Later, editing, accommodation and completion. Besides, there is an indispensable, striking inclination in them as perfectionists. This will continuously take their poetic construct to a higher level of finish.

Sustained commitment to their land, to their geophysical and spiritual roots (their motivations, however, do not wane when they write about other places, the so-called traveling poems). It is evidenced when we read their poems and notice their earnest references to nature (an inherent national leitmotif), to geographies and seasons that humble and mesmerize them, to vast maps of wildlife (maritime, land, aerial – or imaginary) and wilderness.

Moreover, we see it in the native mysticism that rocked their cradle and forged dreams. It surrounds them and exudes from most of their pieces, a constituent that lies, in turn, in the very backgrounds at their fingertips (where they were born, where they grew up, where they settled), which ignite favorable impetus in the poets' drive and sensitivity.

Unavoidable, touching family-friend-wife themes. As much as I have seen this in world poetry, I believe that – in my personal experience – Canadian poets go the extra mile in wording, honoring and recalling facts, events, people, and names. Poems almost invariably state whom they dedicate poems or books to. Particularly moving are the ones written to their couples. Deahl (Gilda *(in memoriam)* and Norma), Lee (Cathy), Gutteridge (Anne), Sorestad (Sonia) and Moritz (Theresa), do not forget where or who they come from, they do not forget who they chose to share their lives with.

Adherence to hope. Even in the darkest texts the poets may have crafted, faith in a better tomorrow socially and personally speaking is felt. I do not see lost poets whirling in fatalistic maelstroms, presaging gloomy futures, crushing aspirations. Obviously, sadness is present in the cry of the bereaved man; criticism – sometimes hard, direct, poking social sores and human miseries – runs through the lines' swollen veins; urgent warnings abound. Yet, the poets find consolation in beauty and companion; they always see the light at the end of the tunnel of life.

The poets do not complain or lament forever: they seek healing in writing for themselves (to quench the urge), for others (advice, sharing, redemption), for posterity. They hold life, time, space and movement – existence – in the palm of their hands looking right at them, channeling them onto pages and pages of poetic heritage. It is praiseworthy.

Framed in the contexts I have exposed above, rich, sui generis imagery pulses and emanates. All five poets (and many more I have reviewed or read) handle language tools fruitfully, innovatively. They shape figurative means creatively exploring environment and innermost motifs, and pasting them on grateful paper. Disparate realities are fused, slid into the kiln, and out ceramics of ablaze, glistening, awesome, stunning originality.

An essential component of the poets' poetry is interconnectedness of rhythm and musicality. Both elements are unavoidable for them, and have a substantial influence on their composition structurally and stylistically speaking.

Sense of modesty and support. Despite the greatness and tight personal and professional agendas of the five poets presented in this book, none rejected, criticized or revealed an inkling of disapproval towards the ambitious – but worthy – project the publisher and I proposed them. Their involvement allowed me to compose faster than I had anticipated, even with the book's complex scope and the miles of material I had to read to integrate information into a voluminous corpus.

Their selfless, generous gestures of giving me their books, keeping a steady email exchange, assisting me in the detection of inaccuracies, correction of data, proofreading and suggesting, and allowing a modest Cuban professor to speak about their work, quote their poems and access their lives, is simply admirable. It has been my privilege to write about them and talk to them.

Cuban Apostle José Martí said that all of the world's glory fits in a grain of corn, and *"Juan Ramón Jiménez says in Time and Space, "Great is the small." (Taken from the book As far as you know, A. F. Moritz, Appendix 1. Author's Note on "Art Of Surgery")*. Glory and greatness reside in these five gems.

Despite the number of pages devoted in this book to each Canadian gem I have presented to the readers, it is impossible to include all the aspects of their lives and oeuvre. My purpose has been to outline them. It is a guiding glimpse at their enormous contribution as persons, writers, reviewers, teachers, editors, lecturers, etc. I am certain I have paved the way. As I stated in my Introduction, I have written this book looking at the poets *from my perspective, sifting them in my own terms* and *with my modest tools.*

It is impossible to model and compress within the frontiers of a single book, all of the significance and purport of their craft. The wisest approach is to take my book as an alternate source of departure towards further readings. Essentially, it must be clear that even with the quotations and illustrations that complement my personal analyses and "dissections," our most accurate, comprehensive approximation to their works ought to be reading, rereading and immersing constantly in their poetry.

One last comment: we do not need to fit these five distinctive poets into a Canadian style because they are, in fact, **the** *Canadian style*. They, as contemporary Canadian poets of such high standing, are the style that future poets will emulate, they are the model that others will imitate and follow. They are future Al Purdys, future Milton Acorns, future Dorothy Livesays. They are the best fountain to drink from in the inexhaustible Canadian spring. May this book be another *stone polisher* visiting the Canadian poetdom lode.

Thank you, James, John, Don, Glen, Al.

MSc Miguel Ángel Olivé Iglesias
Associate Professor. Holguín University, Cuba
CCLA Cuban President
Author, Poet, Writer, Reviser, Editor, Essayist

References

Babylon English. (Digital Dictionary).

BARKER, TERRY. *Beyond Bethune* (Synaxis Press, 2006).

Canada. Eyewitness Travel Guides. (Dorley Kindersley Limited, London Penguin Company, 2002).

Concise Oxford English Dictionary (Digital).

DEAHL, JAMES. *No Cold Ash* (Sono Nis Press, 1984).

DEAHL, JAMES. *Even This Land Was Born Of Light* (Moonstone Press, 1993).

DEAHL, JAMES. *Under the Watchful Eye* (Broken Jaw Press, 1995).

DEAHL, JAMES. *Blackbirds* (Unfinished Monument Press, 1999).

DEAHL, JAMES. *When Rivers Speak* (UnMon America, 2001).

DEAHL, JAMES. *No Star is Lost* (Lyricalmyrical, 2009).

DEAHL, JAMES. *Opening the Stone Heart* (Aeolus House, 2010).

DEAHL, JAMES and GROVE, RICHARD MARVIN. *North of Belleville* (Haiku and Photography)
        (Hidden Brook Press, 2011).

DEAHL, JAMES. *Rooms the Wind Makes* (Guernica Editions, 2012).

DEAHL, JAMES. *North Point* (Lyricalmyrical, 2012).

DEAHL, JAMES and WEST LINDER, NORMA. *Two Paths Through The Seasons.*
        (Cyclamens and Swords Publishing, 2014).

DEAHL, JAMES. *Unbroken Lines* (Lummox Press, 2015).

DEAHL, JAMES. *To Be With A Woman* (Lummox Press, 2016).

DEAHL, JAMES. *Red Haws to Light the Field* (Guernica Editions, Essential Poets, 2017).

DEAHL, JAMES and KATHERINE L. GORDON. *Landscapes* (Cyclamens and Swords, 2016).

DEAHL, JAMES. *Travelling The Lost Highway* (Guernica Editions, Essential Poets, 2019).

DEAHL, JAMES. *Earth's Signature* (Aeolus House, 2020).

DI NARDO, ANTONY. *Skylight* (Ronsdale Press, 2018).

DRAGLAND, STAN. "Al Purdy's Poetry: Openings." IN *Al Purdy. Essays on his Works*
        (Guernica Editions, 2002) (Edited by Linda Rogers).

GROVE, RICHARD MARVIN. *A Small Payback, Ode to Victoria Lake* (Hidden Brook Press, 2016).

GUTTERIDGE, DON. *Riel: A Poem for Voices.* Fiddlehead, 1968).

GUTTERIDGE, DON. *Coppermine* (Oberon Press, 1973).

GUTTERIDGE, DON. *Borderlands* (Oberon Press, 1975).

GUTTERIDGE, DON. *Tecumseh* (Oberon Press, 1976).

GUTTERIDGE, DON. *Lily's Story* (Bev Editions, 2014).

GUTTERIDGE, DON. *Home Ground* (Hidden Brook Press, 2018).

GUTTERIDGE, DON. *Village Dreaming* ((Hidden Brook Press, 2019).

GUTTERIDGE, DON. *Inking the World* ((Hidden Brook Press, 2019).

GUTTERIDGE, DON. *Out of the Blue* ((Hidden Brook Press, 2019).

GUTTERIDGE, DON. *The Star-Brushed Horizon* (Hidden Brook Press, 2019).

GUTTERIDGE, DON. *Invincible Ink* (Hidden Brook Press, 2020).

GUTTERIDGE, DON. *Lilacs in Lavender Light* (Hidden Brook Press, 2020).

GUTTERIDGE, DON. *Point Taken* (Hidden Brook Press, 2020).

GUTTERIDGE, DON. *Hearthbeat* (Hidden Brook Press, 2020) (Anthology).

Hearthbeat. (Hidden Brook Press, 2020) (Anthology) (Edited by Don Gutteridge).

Holy Bible. (Zondervan Publishing House, 1984) (Job 7:20).

https://en.wikiquote.org/wiki/Archimedes.

https://peacockjournal.com/glen-sorestad-two-poems.

https://www.britannica.com/biography/Antonin-Artaud.

https://www.amazon.com/-/es/Glen-Sorestad/dp/1894345975).

In a Springtime Instant. Selected Poems. (Mosaic Press, 2012). (Edited by James Deahl).

I.R. GALPERIN. *Stylistics* (Moscow Vyssaja Skola. 1981).

KENNEDY, CAROLINE. *She Walks In Beauty* (Hyperion, 2011).

LEE, DENIS. "The Poetry of Al Purdy." IN *Al Purdy. Essays on his Works.* Guernica Editions Inc.,
        2002. (Edited by Linda Rogers).

LEE, JOHN B. *Never hand me anything if I'm walking or standing* (Black Moss Press, 1997).

LEE, JOHN B. *An Almost Silent Drumming* (Cranberry Tree Press, 2001).

LEE, JOHN B. *Through Their Joined Hearts Drummed Like Larks.* (Passion Among the Cacti Press, 2004).

LEE, JOHN B. *Let Light Try All the Doors* (Rubicon Press, 2009).

LEE, JOHN B. "Even at the Worst of Times." IN *And Left a Place to Stand On*
        (Hidden Brook Press, 2009).

LEE, JOHN B. *You Can Always Eat the Dogs: the hockeyness of ordinary men* (Black Moss Press, 2012).

LEE, JOHN B. *Let Us Be Silent Here* (Sanbun Publishing, 2012).

LEE, JOHN B. *Burning My Father* (Black Moss Press, 2014).

LEE, JOHN B. *Secret Second Language of the Heart* (Sanbun Publishing, 2016).

LEE, JOHN B. *This is How We See the World* (Hidden Brook Press, 2017).

LEE, JOHN B. and RICHARD MARVIN GROVE. *Two Thousand Seventeen*
        (Sanbun Publishers. New Delhi. India, 2018).

LEE, JOHN B. *Beautiful Stupid* (Black Moss Press, 2018).

LEE, JOHN B. *Into a Land of Strangers* (Mosaic Press, 2019).

MORITZ, ALBERT F. *Song of Fear* (Brick Books, 1992).

MORITZ, ALBERT F. *Mahoning* (Brick Books, 1994).

MORITZ, ALBERT F. *Rest on the Flight into Egypt* (Brick Books, 1999. Third printing in 2000).

MORITZ, ALBERT F. *The Sentinel* (House of Anansi Press, 2008).

MORITZ, ALBERT F. *The New Measures* (House of Anansi Press, 2012).

MORITZ, ALBERT F. *The Sparrow* (House of Anansi Press, 2018).

MORITZ, ALBERT F. *As Far As You Know* (House of Anansi Press, 2020).

NERUDA, PABLO. *En el corazón de un poeta* (Instituto Cubano del Libro. Editorial de Ediciones
        Especiales, Biblioteca Familiar, 2006).

OLIVÉ IGLESIAS, MIGUEL ÁNGEL. Bridges Series Books IV, *Where the Heart Lies*
        (SandCrab Books, 2018) (Author, Translator).

OLIVÉ IGLESIAS, MIGUEL ÁNGEL. *In a Fragile Moment: A Landscape of Canadian Poetry*
        (Hidden Brook Press, 2020) (Author).

OLIVÉ IGLESIAS, MIGUEL ÁNGEL. "Ars Longa, Poetry Eternal. Comments on John Di
        Leonardo's *Conditions of Desire* (Poetry) (2018) Hidden Brook Press. Canada."
        IN *A Shower of Warm Light Upon this Land and Us. Reviews and Essays on Canadian Poetry*
        (work in progress).

OLIVÉ IGLESIAS, MIGUEL ÁNGEL. "A Shower of Warm Light Upon this Land and Us. A Review
        of James Deahl's *Even This Land Was Born Of Light* (Poetry) (1993) Moonstone Press. Canada."
        In *In a Fragile Moment: A Landscape of Canadian Poetry* (Hidden Brook Press, 2020).

OLIVÉ IGLESIAS, MIGUEL ÁNGEL. *A Shower of Warm Light Upon this Land and Us. Reviews and Essays on Canadian Poetry* (work in progress) (Author).

OLIVÉ IGLESIAS, MIGUEL ÁNGEL. *The Light Candling the Mind: Critic and Author in Harmony. Essays and Reviews on Canadian Literature* (Anthology) (work in progress) (Editor, Author).

OLIVÉ IGLESIAS, MIGUEL ÁNGEL. *Flying on the Wings of Poetry* (Hidden Brook Press, 2020) (Editor, Translator, Essayist).

OLIVÉ IGLESIAS, MIGUEL ÁNGEL, *The Divinity of Blue* (Hidden Brook Press, 2020) (Editor, Author, Translator).

OLIVÉ IGLESIAS, MIGUEL ÁNGEL. Bridges Series Books V, *The Heart Upon the Sleeve* (SandCrab Books, 2020) (Editor, Essayist, Translator).

OLIVÉ IGLESIAS, MIGUEL ÁNGEL. "Architects and Epitomes. A Word about Three Canadian Poets: Richard Marvin Grove (Tai), John B. Lee and James Deahl. Comments on poetry they have published in The Envoy, the CCLA newsletter (Poetry) (2019)." IN *A Shower of Warm Light Upon this Land and Us. Reviews and Essays on Canadian Poetry* (work in progress).

OLIVÉ IGLESIAS, MIGUEL ÁNGEL. "My College Canada; My Sentimental Canada. A Brief Reflection on Canada and its Influence on Canadians and Cubans." IN *A Shower of Warm Light Upon this Land and Us. Reviews and Essays on Canadian Poetry* (work in progress).

OLIVÉ IGLESIAS, MIGUEL ÁNGEL. "Lucky Seven: Monumental Architecture. A review of seven poems from John B. Lee's "Bread, Water, Love" (Poetry), in *These Are the Words*, by George Elliott Clarke and John B. Lee." IN *In a Fragile Moment: A Landscape of Canadian Poetry*. Hidden Brook Press, 2020.

OLIVÉ IGLESIAS, MIGUEL ÁNGEL. "The Canadian Titan of Land and Time. A review of some of Al Purdy's poems in Beyond Remembering: The Collected Poems of Al Purdy (Poetry) (2000) Harbour Publishing. Canada." IN *In a Fragile Moment: A Landscape of Canadian Poetry*. Hidden Brook Press, 2020.

ORBACH, MARVIN. *Redwing* (Hidden Brook Press, 2018).

PÉREZ LUENGO, ADONAY BÁRBARA; VELÁZQUEZ LEÓN, MANUEL DE JESÚS and GONZÁLEZ CUBA, ALISON "Cuba and Canada: Chosen Places in John B. Lee's Work." IN WEFLA-SECAN International Event, Cuba, 2015.

PURDY, AL. *Beyond Remembering. The Collected Poems of Al Purdy* (Harbour Publishing, 2000).

SHAKESPEARE, WILLIAM. *Complete Works of William Shakespeare* (Volume XVIII) (Philadelphia David McKay, Publisher, *no year*).

"Song of Songs" (The Holy Bible) www.biblegateway.com/passage/?search=Song...Songs).

SORESTAD, GLEN. *Leaving Holds Me Here: Selected Poems* (Thistledown Press, 2001).

SORESTAD, GLEN. *Blood & Bone, Ice & Stone* (Thistledown, 2006).

SORESTAD, GLEN. *Halo of Morning* (Leaf Press, 2006).

SORESTAD, GLEN. *Language of Horse* (Coracle Press, 2007).

SORESTAD, GLEN. *Road Apples* (Rubicon Press, 2009).

SORESTAD, GLEN. *What We Miss* (Thistledown, 2010).

SORESTAD, GLEN. *A Thief of Impeccable Taste* (SandCrab Books, 2011).

SORESTAD, GLEN. *Along Okema Road* (Rubicon Press, 2013).

SORESTAD, GLEN. *Hazards of Eden: Poems from the Southwest* (Lamar University Press, 2015).

SORESTAD, GLEN. *Water and Rock, with Jim Harris* (Lee Country Museum Press, 2017).

SORESTAD, GLEN. *Dancing Birches: Selected Poems* (Impremix Edizioni Visual Grafika, 2020).

Sweet Cuba. The Building of a Poetic Tradition: 1608-1958. (Hidden Brook Press, 2010). (Anthology)
(Edited by John B. Lee and Manuel De Jesús Velázquez León).

Tamaracks: Canadian Poetry for the 21st Century. (Lummox Press, 2018). (Edited by James Deahl).

The Ambassador. Canada Cuba Literary Alliance official magazine. (Volume 004, 2006).
www.CanadaCubaLiteraryAlliance.org.

The Ambassador. Canada Cuba Literary Alliance official magazine. (Volume 011, 2016).
www.CanadaCubaLiteraryAlliance.org.

The Ambassador. Canada Cuba Literary Alliance official magazine. (Volume 016, 2020).
www.CanadaCubaLiteraryAlliance.org.

The Beauty of Being Elsewhere. (Hidden Brook Press, 2021). (Edited by John B. Lee).

The Envoy. Canada Cuba Literary Alliance official newsletter (Issue 092, October 2019).
www.CanadaCubaLiteraryAlliance.org.

The Sunday Edition. (Moritz´s conversation with host Michael Enright).

Under the Mulberry Tree: Poems for & about Raymond Souster. Quattro Books Inc. 2014.
(Edited by James Deahl).

*Wikipedia: https://www.thestar.com/entertainment/books/2020/04/23/water-fountains-booksheart-surgery-the-un-
expected-feature-in-al-moritzs-new-poetry.html?rf).*

Poets' Bios and Publications

JAMES DEAHL

James Deahl was born in Pittsburgh in 1945, and grew up in that city as well as in and around the Laurel Highlands region of the Appalachian Mountains. He moved to Canada in 1970. He is the author (or, in the case of Tu Fu, translator) of twenty-nine literary titles. A cycle of his poems is the focus of a one-hour TV special, *Under the Watchful Eye* (Silver Falls Video Productions, 1993).

In addition to his writing, he has taught creative writing and Canadian literature at the high school, college, and university levels. He no longer teaches, and for the past fifteen years has mostly been a full-time writer/editor/translator. As a critic and literary historian, Deahl is the leading Acornic scholar.

As a scholar, Deahl has edited eight books by or for Milton Acorn:
– *Whiskey Jack* by Milton Acorn (HMS Press, 1986)
– *The Uncollected Acorn* by Milton Acorn (Deneau Publishers, 1987)
– *I Shout Love and Other Poems* by Milton Acorn (Aya Press, 1987)
– *The Northern Red Oak: Poems for and about Milton Acorn* (Unfinished Monument Press, 1987)
– *Hundred Proof Earth* by Milton Acorn (Aya Press, 1988)
– *Let the Earth Take Note* poems celebrating Milton Acorn (Milton Acorn Festival Publishing, 1994)
– *To Hear the Faint Bells* haiku by Milton Acorn (Hamilton Haiku Press, 1996)
– *In A Springtime Instant: The Selected Poems of Milton Acorn, 1950 – 1986* (Mosaic Press, 2012)

He has also edited:
– *Adder's-tongues: A Choice of Norma West Linder's Poems, 1969 – 2011* (Aeolus House, 2012)
– *Under the Mulberry Tree: Poems for & about Raymond Souster* (Quattro Books, 2013)
– *Tamaracks: Canadian Poetry for the 21st Century* (Lummox Press, 2018)

James Deahl lives in Sarnia, Ontario, with his wife, the writer Norma West Linder. He's the father of Sarah, Simone, and Shona, with whom he is translating the poetry of the 19th century Québécois poet Émile Nelligan.

A selection of his publications:

— *The Confederation Poets: The Founding of a Canadian Poetry, 1880 to the First World War* (Guernica Editions, forthcoming),

— *Earth's Signature: New & Selected Jackpine Sonnets* (Aeolus House, 2020)

— *Travelling The Lost Highway* (Guernica Editions, 2019)

— *Red Haws To Light The Field* (Guernica Editions, 2017)

— *To Be With A Woman* (Lummox Press, 2016)

— *Landscapes* (*with* Katherine L. Gordon) (Cyclamens and Swords, 2016)

— *Unbroken Lines* (Lummox Press, 2015)

— *Two Paths Through The Seasons* (*with* Norma West Linder) (Cyclamens and Swords, 2014)

— *North Point* (Lyricalmyrical, 2012)

— *Rooms The Wind Makes* (Guernica Editions, 2012)

— *North Of Belleville* (*with* Richard M. Grove) (Hidden Brook Press, 2012)

— *Opening The Stone Heart* (Aeolus House, 2010)

— *No Star Is Lost* (Lyricalmyrical, 2009)

— *Love Where Our Nights Are Long* (Laurel Reed Books, 2008)

— *If Ever Two Were One* (Aeolus House, 2008)

— *The River's Stone Roots: Two dozen poems by Tu Fu* (Serengeti Press, 2005)

— *When Rivers Speak* (Unfinished Monument Press, 2001)

— *Blackbirds* (Unfinished Monument Press, 1999)

— *Under The Watchful Eye* (Broken Jaw Press, 1995)

— *Tasting The Winter Grapes* (Envoi Poets Publications, 1995)

— *Even This Land Was Born Of Light* (Moonstone Press, 1993)

— *Heartland* (Envoi Poets Publications, 1993)

— *Geschriebene Bilder* (M+N Boesche Verlag, Berlin, 1990)

— *A Stand Of Jackpine* (*with* Milton Acorn) (Unfinished Monument Press, 1987)

— *Into This Dark Earth* (*with* Raymond Souster) (Unfinished Monument Press, 1985)

— *Blue Ridge* (Aureole Point Press, 1985)

— *No Cold Ash* (Sono Nis Press, 1984)

— *Steel Valley* (*with* Bruce Meyer & Gilda L. Mekler) (Aureole Point Press, 1984)

— *In The Lost Horn's Call* (Aureole Point Press, 1982)

— *Real Poetry* (Unfinished Monument Press, 1981)

JOHN B. LEE

In 2005 he was inducted as Poet Laureate of Brantford in perpetuity. The same year he received the distinction of being named Honourary Life Member of The Canadian Poetry Association and The Ontario Poetry Society. In 2007 he was made a member of the Chancellor's Circle of the President's Club of McMaster University and named first recipient of the Souwesto Award for his contribution to literature in his home region of southwestern Ontario, and was named winner of the inaugural Black Moss Press Souwesto Award for his contribution to the ethos of writing in Southwestern Ontario.

In 2011 he was appointed Poet Laureate of Norfolk County (2011-14) and in 2015 Honourary Poet Laureate of Norfolk County for life. A recipient of over eighty prestigious international awards for his writing, he is winner of the CBC Literary Award for Poetry, the only two time recipient of the People's Poetry Award, and 2006 winner of the inaugural Souwesto Orison Writing Award (University of Windsor).

In 2007 he was named winner of the Winston Collins Award for Best Canadian Poem, an award he won again in 2012. In 2016 he won Honourable Mention in the Cranberry Tree Press Chapbook Award and the Golden Grassroots Press Award, Honourable Mention in the Drummond Poetry Award, First Place in the Scugog Poetry Award, First Place in the Hour Glass Poetry Award, First Place in the Literary Encyclopedia Award, and Honourable Mention in the Peace Poetry Award.

He has well-over seventy books published to date and is the editor of seven anthologies including two best-selling works: That Sign of Perfection: poems and stories on the game of hockey; and Smaller Than God: words of spiritual longing. He co-edited a special issue of Windsor Review—Alice Munro: A Souwesto Celebration published in the fall of 2014.

His work has been published internationally in over 500 anthologies, journals, magazines, and has been translated into French, Spanish, Korean and Chinese. He has read his work in nations all over the world including South Africa, France, Korea, Cuba, Canada and the United States. He has received letters of praise from Nelson Mandela, Desmond Tutu, Australian poet Les Murray, and Senator Romeo Dallaire. Called "*the greatest living poet in English*" by poet George Whipple, he lives in Port Dover, Ontario, where he works as a full time author.

A selection of his publications:

– *The Heart Upon the Sleeve* (SandCrab Books, 2020) (anthology)
– *Flying on the Wings of Poetry* (Hidden Brook Press, 2020)
   (anthology)
– *This is How We See the World* (Hidden Brook Press, 2018)
– *Beautiful Stupid* (Black Moss Press, 2018)
– *MMXVII* (Sanbun Press, 2017)
– *These Are the Words* (Hidden Brook Press, 2017)
– *Secret Second Language of the Heart* (Sanbun Publishing, 2016)
– *Burning My Father* (Black Moss Press, 2014)
– *In This We Hear the Light* (Hidden Brook Press, 2013)
   (poetry with photographs by Richard M. Grove)
– *You Can Always Eat the Dogs: the hockeyness of ordinary men*
   (Black Moss Press, 2012) (prose memoir)
– *Let Us Be Silent Here* (Sanbun Publishing, 2012)

DONALD GEORGE GUTTERIDGE

Born in Sarnia General Hospital on September 30, 1937. Moved to Point Edward. In September of 1939 his father joined the air force and was soon stationed in Ottawa, where Gutteridge moved with both parents. In 1944 he contracted rheumatic fever and was hospitalized for a week, becoming a precocious reader.

In 1945 the family moved into the countryside, away from Gutteridge´s home village. In the Fall of 1951 he entered Chatham Collegiate Institute. In 1956 he entered The University of Western Ontario (UWO), registered in Honours English. he started to write longish homage poems. He had a job, teaching English to Grades 11, 12 and 13 at Elmira District High School in Elmira, Ontario, which made him fall in love with teaching.

He made a decision to go back to Western for a Master's degree so he went to Europe for a nine-week excursion with his wife, visiting England, Scotland, Ireland, France, Germany, Austria and Italy.

He taught English and acting as department head in Ingersoll Collegiate.

His first poem was published in a magazine: "This Maple in my Fallen Yard" in the Fiddlehead somewhere in 1961 or 1962. He started to write both short lyrics about Point Edward and several long poems about the Jesuits in Huronia, Champlain and LaSalle. In 1968 *Riel: A Poem of Voices* was published and received good reviews. Fiddlehead Poetry Books published his collection of Point Edward poems as *The Village Within: Poems Toward a Biography*.

In 1978 he wrote the first of his ten academic books and began teaching graduate courses in English pedagogy. Then came *All in Good Time* (Black Moss Press 1982). He joined The League of Canadian Poets, served on the executive, did public readings across the country. Sometime in 1984 or early 1985 the germ of a new novel arrived, *Lily's Story*.

After retirement, he started writing poems again. The principal focus in these numerous volumes (12 titles over 20 years and three more to come) was *Point Edward* with many occasional poems added, on family life, the process of writing itself and aspects of aging. His style also evolved. He began writing short poems that, as he has stated, gradually were subsumed by internal rhyme, assonance, consonance and alliteration, unlike the more free flowing lyrics of the earlier period with natural line breaks.

A selection of his publications:

– *Hearthbeat* (Hidden Brook Press, 2020) (anthology)

– *Point Taken* (Hidden Brook Press, 2020)

– *Lilacs in Lavender Light* (Hidden Brook Press, 2020)

– *Invincible Ink* (Hidden Brook Press, 2020)

– *The Star-Brushed Horizon* (Hidden Brook Press, 2019)

– *Out of the Blue* (Hidden Brook Press, 2019)

– *Inking the World* (Hidden Brook Press, 2019)

– *Village Dreaming* (Hidden Brook Press, 2019)

– *Home Ground* (Hidden Brook Press, 2018)

– *Lily´s Story* (Bev Editions, 2014)

GLEN SORESTAD

Born in Vancouver, but moved to the prairies when he was ten and grew up on a farm in east-central Saskatchewan, attending a one-roomed country school. He later became a schoolteacher and taught for over 20 years. He earned a Master's Degree in Education (with distinction) from the U of S. He began writing seriously in 1968, co-founded Thistledown Press in 1975 with his wife, Sonia, and quit teaching in 1981 to pursue his writing and publishing activities. He was President of Thistledown Press from 1975 to 2000.

Over the years, Sorestad's poetry and stories have been published across Canada, in the United States, in England, Scotland, Denmark, Finland, Norway, South Africa and Slovenia. He has authored or co-authored over twenty volumes of poems and his poetry has been frequently broadcast on CBC radio, on radio stations in the United States, and on state public radio in Norway and Slovenia. His poetry has been translated into several languages including French, Spanish, Norwegian, Finnish, Slovenian and Afrikaans.

He is the editor or co-editor of many anthologies of poetry and stories, including most recently an international anthology, *Something to Declare*, by Oxford University Press and a poetry anthology, *In The Clear*, from Thistledown Press. His poems have appeared in over 50 different anthologies and textbooks. One of his volumes of poetry has been the primary source for the play, A Place in the Shade by Rodney McLean. His short stories have also been anthologized; one of his stories was produced for television in Canada by Bravo TV.

Over the years, he has presented his poetry publicly in diverse venues – schools, colleges and universities, libraries, art galleries, bookstores, restaurants, coffee bistros, bars, community halls, churches, maritime museums, ski resorts, private clubs, a Medieval castle in Slovenia – even in the Cowboy Hall of Fame in Lea County, New Mexico. Most recently in March 2010, he read his poems in Norman, Oklahoma backed up by a jazz ensemble, The Dennis Borycki Trio.

In 1999, Sorestad was honoured with Life Member status in the League of Canadian Poets. In November of 2000, he was appointed the first Poet Laureate of Saskatchewan, becoming the first provincially or federally appointed Poet Laureate in Canada and serving until 2004. He was awarded the Saskatoon Book Award in November 2001 for *Leaving Holds Me Here*. In February 2003, Sorestad was a recipient of the Queen's Golden Jubilee Medal. He was granted Life Membership in the Saskatchewan Writers Guild in 2009. He was appointed a Member of the Order of Canada on June 30, 2010.

A selection of his publications:

– *Dancing Birches: Selected Poems* (Impremix Edizioni Visual Grafika, 2020)

– *Water and Rock, with Jim Harris* (Lee Country Museum Press, 2017)

– *Hazards of Eden: Poems from the Southwest* (Lamar University Press, 2015)

– *Along Okema Road* (Rubicon Press, 2013)

– *A Thief of Impeccable Taste* (SandCrab Books, 2011)

– *What We Miss* (Thistledown, 2010)

– *Road Apples* (Rubicon Press, 2009)

– *Language of Horse* (Coracle Press, 2007)

– *Halo of Morning* (Leaf Press, 2006)

– *Blood & Bone, Ice & Stone* (Thistledown, 2006)

– *Leaving Holds Me Here: Selected Poems 1975-2000* (Thistledown Press, 2001)

– *Today I Belong to Agnes* (Ekstasis Editions, 2000)

ALBERT FRANK MORITZ

Born April 15, 1947. Moritz was born in Niles, Ohio, and educated at Marquette University, Milwaukee, Wisconsin, from which he received a Ph.D. in eighteenth- and nineteenth-century British poetry. Since 1974, he has made his home in Toronto, where he has worked variously as an advertising copywriter and executive, editor, publisher, and university professor. He and his wife, Theresa, are Canadian citizens and also retain U.S. citizenship. He is presently the Blake C. Goldring Professor of the Arts and Society, University of Toronto, Victoria College. In 2019, he was named Poet Laureate of Toronto

He began writing poetry in early childhood. In Milwaukee, he was co-editor of a literary magazine, *The Shore Review*. Coming to Canada for reasons of his wife's doctoral studies, in 1974-75 he completed and published first book, *Here*, which was republished in revised form in 1990 and included with three other books of the 1970s and early 1980s in *Early Poems* (2002). He has published twenty books of poems, several books of translation (principally of poetry) from Spanish and French, and several nonfiction works, the translations and nonfiction often done in collaboration with Theresa Moritz.

His poetry has received the Guggenheim Fellowship; inclusion in the Princeton Series of Contemporary Poets; the Ingram Merrill Fellowship; the Award in Literature of the American Academy of Arts and Letters; the Beth Hokin Prize of *Poetry* magazine; the Elizabeth Matchett Stover Prize of the *Southwest Review*; the ReLit Award; the Griffin Poetry Prize; the Raymond Souster Award of the League of Canadian Poets, and other awards. He is a three-time finalist for the Governor General's Award for English language poetry, for his books *Rest on the Flight into Egypt* (1999), *The Sentinel* (2008) and *The New Measures* (2012).

A selection of his publications:

– *As Far As You Know* (House of Anansi Press, 2020)

– *Tamaracks: Canadian Poetry for the 21st Century* (Lummox Press, 2018)

– *The Sparrow* (House of Anansi Press, 2018)

– *The New Measures* (House of Anansi Press, 2012)

– *The Sentinel* (House of Anansi Press, 2008)

– *Rest on the Flight into Egypt* (Brick Books, 1999. Third printing in 2000)

– *Mahoning* (Brick Books, 1994)

– *Song of Fear* (Brick Books, 1992)

About the Author Miguel Ángel Olivé Iglesias

Miguel Ángel Olivé Iglesias is a professor, researcher and poetry, fiction and non-fiction author. He is a Canada Cuba Literary Alliance (CCLA) editor, *The Ambassador* Editor-in-chief, *The Envoy* Assistant Editor, and President in Cuba of the CCLA. He does translation, proofreading, reviewing and revision for the CCLA, along with compilation and anthologizing.

He is a member of the Mexican Association of Language and Literature Professors, VP of the William Shakespeare Studies Center and guest member of the Canadian Studies Department of the Holguín University in Cuba.

Born in 1965 in Bayamo, Cuba, he travelled to Holguín City in 1977 for his Junior, Senior High and College studies. Today he is an Associate Professor at the University of Holguín, with a Bachelor's Degree in Education, Major in English, and a Master's degree in Pedagogical Sciences. He has been teaching for thirty-three years and writing academic papers, lit reviews, poems and stories in Spanish and in English.

Miguel has written and published numerous academic papers in Cuba, Mexico, Spain and Canada. He publishes nationally and internationally on the issues of foreign language teaching, pedagogy, interdisciplinary approaches, axiology and the preservation of humankind's values, both material and non-material, from an educational perspective.

He publishes too his poetry, short stories and literary essays with Canadian publishing entities, like Hidden Brook Press and SandCrab Books, Canadian Stories Magazine, and Adelaide Group Lisbon-U.S.A., and translates, edits, reviews and proofreads newsletters, magazines, anthologies and books of Canadian and Cuban poetry and prose for the Canada Cuba Literary Alliance, project for which he is the President on the Cuban side. So far he has being the Editor of five CCLA books, published more than a hundred poems, six short stories and over forty critical reviews of poetry books and novels in different issues:

The Ambassador, official flagship of the CCLA; *The Envoy*, official newsletter of the CCLA; The Bridges Series Books, published by Hidden Brook Press and SandCrab Books; Adelaide Group in New York-Lisbon, and other anthologies by Hidden Brook Press and SandCrab Books and *Canadian Stories* magazine. He published a review book, *In a Fragile Moment: A Landscape of Canadian Poetry* (Hidden Brook Press, 2020) and his first full-length solo poetry book (bilingual), *Forge of Words* (Hidden Brook Press, 2020).

His poetic themes touch upon women, people, life, family, love, nature, and human values. The editor has been and is currently involved in many CCLA projects: his second review book, *A Shower of Warm Light Upon this Land and Us*; his second solo poetry book, *This Pulse of Life, The Words I Found*; editor and translator for the Bridges Series Book V, *The Heart Upon the Sleeve*, presenting two Canadian and two Cuban poets; editor and author in *The Divinity of Blue*, an anthology of seventeen Canadian and Cuban poets; and editor and translator for *Flying on the Wings of Poetry*, a compilation of four well-known Canadian poets.

SandCrab books recently published, 2020, the e-book he edited, *These Voices Beating in our Hearts: Poems from the Valley* (English-Spanish), where his poems and haiku appear together with the poetry of other ten Holguín poets.

He works in the Teacher Education English Department as a professor of English, English Stylistics and grad courses. He is also Head of the English Language Discipline. He uses his academic papers, essays, stories and poems in class for reading, debating and practicing the language, adding a didactic and formative element to his scientific and literary production. He also does poetry reading in co-curricular on-campus and community activities.

Title: Forge of Words

Author: Miguel Ángel Olivé Iglesias

ISBN:
Soft Cover – 978-1-927725-71-9 = 9781927725719
epub – 978-1-927725-81-8 = 9781927725818
Mobi – 978-1-927725-82-5 = 9781927725825

Title: In a Fragile Moment: A Landscape of Canadian Poetry

Author: M.Sc. Miguel Ángel Olivé Iglesias

ISBN:
Softcover – 978-1-927725-92-4 = 9781927725924
epub – 978-1-927725-93-1 = 9781927725931
mobi – 978-1-927725-94-8 = 9781927725948

This book is a collection of essays and reviews on Canadian Poetry by Master Scholar and Poet, M.Sc. Miguel Ángel Olivé Iglesias.

Check availability at your favorite eStore